Thorana S. Nelson
Editor

Education and Training in Solution-Focused Brief Therapy

Education and Training in Solution-Focused Brief Therapy has been co-published simultaneously as *Journal of Family Psychotherapy*, Volume 16, Numbers 1/2 2005.

Pre-publication REVIEWS, COMMENTARIES, EVALUATIONS . . .

The Haworth Press, Inc.

Education and Training
in Solution-Focused
Brief Therapy

Education and Training in Solution-Focused Brief Therapy has been co-published simultaneously as *Journal of Family Psychotherapy*, Volume 16, Numbers 1/2 2005.

The *Journal of Family Psychotherapy*™ is the successor title to the *Journal of Psychotherapy & the Family*™,* which changed title after Vol. 6, No. 3/4, 1990. The *Journal of Family Psychotherapy*™, under its new title, begins with Vol. 7, No. 1, 1996.

Circumplex Model: Systemic Assessment and Treatment of Families, edited by David H. Olson, PhD, Candyce S. Russell, PhD, and Douglas H. Sprenkle, PhD (Vol. 4, No. 1/2, 1989).* *"An excellent resource for the Circumplex Model." (The Family Psychologist)*

Women, Feminism, and Family Therapy, edited by Lois Braverman, ACSW (Vol. 3, No. 4, 1988).* *"Get the book, have it at your fingertips, and you will find it hard to put down." (Australian Journal of Marriage & Family Therapy)*

Chronic Disorders and the Family, edited by Froma Walsh, PhD, and Carol M. Anderson, PhD (Vol. 3, No. 3, 1988).* *"An excellent text, for it thoughtfully explores several of the critical issues confronting the field of family systems medicine. . . . It should have a long shelf life for both clinical and scholarly work." (Family Systems Medicine)*

The Family Life of Psychotherapists: Clinical Implications, edited by Florence W. Kaslow, PhD (Vol. 3, No. 2, 1987).* *"A first in the field, these innovative contributions by outstanding therapists/trainers will enable family therapists to understand and explore the reciprocal influences between the therapist's personal family system and professional life." (Jeannette R. Kramer, Assistant Professor of Clinical Psychiatry and Behavioral Science, Northwestern University Medical School)*

The Use of Self in Therapy, edited by Michele Baldwin, PhD, MSW, and Virginia Satir (Vol. 3, No.1, 1987).* *"Recognized masters share insights gathered over decades on how the person the therapist is the fulcrum around which therapy succeeds. Thirty-six masters, from Kierkegaard to Buber to Satir and Rogers . . . this collection of scholarly work imparts lasting information." (American Journal of Family Therapy)*

Depression in the Family, edited by Arthur Freeman, PhD, Norman Epstein, PhD, and Karen M. Simon, PhD (Vol. 2, No. 3/4, 1987).* *Here is the first book focused on treating depression through the family system.*

Treating Incest: A Multiple Systems Perspective, edited by Terry S. Trepper, PhD, and Mary Jo Barrett, MSW (Vol. 2, No. 2, 1987).* *"Both theoretical and clinical aspects of intrafamily sexual abuse are covered in this important book which stresses the need for a systemic approach in working with incestuous families." (Journal of Pediatric Psychology)*

Marriage and Family Enrichment, edited by Wallace Denton, EdD (Vol. 2, No.1, 1986).* *"A practical book. A good introduction to the history, philosophy, and practice of this group-based approach." (The British Journal of Psychiatry)*

Family Therapy Education and Supervision, edited by Fred P. Piercy, PhD (Vol. 1, No. 4, 1986).* *"Written by authors who are well-known and well-represented in the family therapy literature (Beavers, Duhl, Hovestadt, Kaslow, Keller, Liddle, Piercy, and Sprenkle) . . . individual chapters are well-presented and offer valuable, concrete guidelines." (Journal of Family Psychology)*

Divorce Therapy, edited by Douglas H. Sprenkle, PhD (Vol. 1, No. 3, 1985).* *"While focusing on the specific area of divorce, the book in fact adds richly to a more general knowledge of family dynamics." (The British Journal of Psychiatry)*

Computers and Family Therapy, edited by Charles R. Figley, PhD (Vol. 1, No. 1/2, 1985).* *"An ideal resource for clinicians who have a systemic orientation in their practice and who are intrigued with how recent developments in home computers might be applied as an adjunct to their clinical work." (Canada's Mental Health)*

Education and Training in Solution-Focused Brief Therapy

Thorana S. Nelson
Editor

Education and Training in Solution-Focused Brief Therapy has been co-published simultaneously as *Journal of Family Psychotherapy*, Volume 16, Numbers 1/2 2005.

The Haworth Press, Inc.

New York • London • Victoria (AU)
www.HaworthPress.com

Education and Training in Solution-Focused Brief Therapy has been co-published simultaneously as *Journal of Family Psychotherapy*, Volume 16, Numbers 1/2 2005.

The development, preparation, and publication of this work has been undertaken with great care. However, the publisher, employees, editors, and agents of The Haworth Press and all imprints of The Haworth Press, Inc., including The Haworth Medical Press® and Pharmaceutical Products Press®, are not responsible for any errors contained herein or for consequences that may ensue from use of materials or information contained in this work. Opinions expressed by the author(s) are not necessarily those of The Haworth Press, Inc. With regard to case studies, identities and circumstances of individuals discussed herein have been changed to protect confidentiality. Any resemblance to actual persons, living or dead, is entirely coincidental.

Cover design by Marylouise E. Doyle.

Library of Congress Cataloging-in-Publication Data

Education and training in solution-focused brief therapy / Thorana S. Nelson, editor.
     p. cm.
    "Has been co-published simultaneously as Journal of Family Psychotherapy, volume 16, numbers 1/2 2005."
    Includes bibliographical references and index.
    ISBN-13: 978-0-7890-2927-0 (hard cover : alk. paper)
    ISBN-10: 0-7890-2927-8 (hard cover : alk. paper)
    ISBN-13: 978-0-7890-2928-7 (soft cover : alk. paper)
    ISBN-10: 0-7890-2928-6 (soft cover : alk. paper)
    1. Solution-focused brief therapy–Study and teaching. I. Nelson, Thorana Strever.
 RC489.S65E36 2005
 616.89′14–dc22

                                        2005011234

Indexing, Abstracting & Website/Internet Coverage

This section provides you with a list of major indexing & abstracting services and other tools for bibliographic access. That is to say, each service began covering this periodical during the year noted in the right column. Most Websites which are listed below have indicated that they will either post, disseminate, compile, archive, cite or alert their own Website users with research-based content from this work. (This list is as current as the copyright date of this publication.)

Abstracting, Website/Indexing Coverage . . . . Year When Coverage Began

- *Biology Digest (in print and online)*
  <http://www.infotoday.com> **1992**

- *Biosciences Information Service of Biological Abstracts (BIOSIS)*
  a centralized source of life science information
  <http://www.biosis.org> . . . . *

- *Business Source Corporate: coverage of nearly 3,350 quality*
  magazines and journals; designed to meet the diverse
  information needs of corporations; EBSCO Publishing
  <http://www.epnet.com/corporate/bsourcecorp.asp> **2003**

- *Criminal Justice Abstracts* . . . . *

- *EBSCOhost Electronic Journals Service (EJS)*
  <http://ejournals.ebsco.com> **2001**

- *Educational Research Abstracts (ERA) (online database)*
  <http://www.tandf.co.uk/era> **2002**

- *EMBASE.com (The Power of EMBASE + MEDLINE*
  Combined) <http://www.embase.com> **1990**

- *EMBASE/Excerpta Medica Secondary Publishing Division.*
  Included in newsletters, review journals, major reference
  works, magazines & abstract journals
  <http://www.elsevier.nl> **1990**

(continued)

(continued)

*Exact start date to come.

*Special Bibliographic Notes related to special journal issues
(separates) and indexing/abstracting:*

- indexing/abstracting services in this list will also cover material in any "separate" that is co-published simultaneously with Haworth's special thematic journal issue or DocuSerial. Indexing/abstracting usually covers material at the article/chapter level.
- monographic co-editions are intended for either non-subscribers or libraries which intend to purchase a second copy for their circulating collections.
- monographic co-editions are reported to all jobbers/wholesalers/approval plans. The source journal is listed as the "series" to assist the prevention of duplicate purchasing in the same manner utilized for books-in-series.
- to facilitate user/access services all indexing/abstracting services are encouraged to utilize the co-indexing entry note indicated at the bottom of the first page of each article/chapter/contribution.
- this is intended to assist a library user of any reference tool (whether print, electronic, online, or CD-ROM) to locate the monographic version if the library has purchased this version but not a subscription to the source journal.
- individual articles/chapters in any Haworth publication are also available through the Haworth Document Delivery Service (HDDS).

ABOUT THE EDITOR

Thorana S. Nelson, PhD, is Professor of Marriage and Family Therapy at Utah State University in Logan, Utah. Her co-edited books include (with Frank Thomas) *Tales from Family Therapy* and (with Terry Trepper) *101 Interventions in Family Therapy* and *101 More Interventions in Family Therapy*, which have been translated into Chinese. She also is co-editor with John Frykman of *Making the Impossible Difficult: Tools for GettingUnstuck.* Dr. Nelson is the Intervention Interchange section editor of the *Journal of Family Psychotherapy* and is a Clinical Member and Approved Supervisor with the American Association for Marriage and Family Therapy.

Education and Training in Solution-Focused Brief Therapy

CONTENTS

SOLUTION-FOCUSED TRAINING AND SUPERVISION

Introduction:
The Birth of the Solution-Focused
Brief Therapy Association

The culmination of this project is truly exciting for me. In March of 2002, about 30 or 35 people interested in sharing ideas about teaching and training solution-focused brief therapy (SFBT) met together in Hammond, Indiana. We had been invited by Steve de Shazer, Insoo Kim Berg, Yvonne Dolan, and Terry Trepper, who had discussed together their desire for such a meeting–a meeting that would not be about doing SFBT, but about how we teach others about the philosophy and the approach.

We started in true SFBT workshop fashion: solution-focused warm-ups. Several people shared their favorite warm-ups (e.g., see the Name Game in this volume) and we had an hilarious time trying to come up with more than five positive "J" adjectives. We talked about our favorite exercises and hand-outs and moved into philosophy and ideas for future meetings.

The group met again in June and in October. We watched a student work with a client who had been in therapy in the university clinic for a long time with several rotating therapists and then we acted as several teams, sending in compliments and comments and a suggestion: come back when you know what you want. We found out later that the client decided quickly what he wanted: to move on with his life and to get out of northern Indiana!

We wanted to talk about what is and what is not solution-focused in terms of practices of therapy. From this we generated ideas about what is good therapy but not unique to SFBT, what is unique to SFBT, and what is not good therapy from a SFBT perspective.

[Haworth co-indexing entry note]: "Introduction: The Birth of the Solution-Focused Brief Therapy Association." Nelson, Thorana S. Co-published simultaneously in *Journal of Family Psychotherapy* (The Haworth Press, Inc.) Vol. 16, No. 1/2, 2005, pp. 1-2; and: *Education and Training in Solution-Focused Brief Therapy* (ed: Thorana S. Nelson) The Haworth Press, Inc., 2005, pp. 1-2. Single or multiple copies of this article are available for a fee from The Haworth Document Delivery Service [1-800-HAWORTH, 9:00 a.m. - 5:00 p.m. (EST). E-mail address: docdelivery@haworthpress.com].

Available online at http://www.haworthpress.com/web/JFP
Digital Object Identifier: 10.1300/J085v16n01_01

We decided to form an association and did so in October. We have a Website (*www.sfbta.org*) and a listserv (see the Website for subscription instructions). The sole purpose of the association is to host an annual conference dedicated to SFBT and we have had our first one: Solutions 2003 was held in Loma Linda, California, in November and was a great success. A second conference was held in November of 2004 in Park City, Utah, and more are planned.

Finally, our "Founders'" group decided to put our teaching and training ideas together, solicit others' ideas, and publish them, resulting in this double volume of the *Journal of Family Psychotherapy* as well as the simultaneously published book. That book or double issue of the journal is what you are now reading. It is full of great articles, snippets, and handouts on philosophy toward teaching SFBT, descriptions of workshops both short and long, and exercises from people who actually do this stuff. These people have been very generous with us and I hope that you appreciate their efforts.

Some of the pieces have been around for a long time and the contributors not only don't claim to be the authors, but also may or may not even remember from whom they were borrowed. These are attributed to "contributors" rather than authors. The publication has been divided into sections so that readers may more easily find what they are looking for: articles, essays, or exercises. No attempt has been made to edit the pieces beyond basic forms of punctuation, grammar, and clarity. We leave it to you, the readers, to make sense of the pieces and to modify for them for your own particular use. If you have pieces of your own that you think others might enjoy, please feel free to e-mail me (*Thorana.Nelson@usu.edu*) so that we might consider them for publication in future issues of *JFP*.

Now, sit back, relax, and get ready to enjoy the submissions and to get excited about your next teaching workshop on SFBT!

Thorana S. Nelson

FOUNDERS' MEETINGS

This series of articles describes the founding of the Solution-Focused Brief Therapy Association and two students' reactions to the initial workshops.

The Founders' Meetings

Thorana S. Nelson

KEYWORDS. SFBT training, student experiences

The "Founder's Group" of the Solution-Focused Brief Therapy Association started out as a training seminar with Steve de Shazer. We weren't very organized and the group evolved over time. We wanted to share training ideas and exercises and we wanted to work with each other as colleagues. The meetings were held at Purdue University in Calumet, which has an accredited Marriage and Family Therapy program. To help us out, several students were invited to participate as "volunteers." However, it became clear very quickly that our group was not going to have anything to do with a hierarchy that placed students in a "don't-know-anything-so-keep-quiet" position. Students were invited to participate and were asked direct questions about their ideas and experience.

For one of our meetings, we observed a live session, conducted by Sara Smock. Shelley Clymer was our camera person. Sara was a very courageous therapist to show her work to 30 or so experienced solution-focused brief therapy trainers! She and Shelley were calm debriefers and seemed to enjoy the experience once they figured out that we weren't going to let them fade into corners. A third student, Ellie Cunanan from Virginia, joined us as well and her voice joined the others'.

Thorana S. Nelson is affiliated with Utah State University, 2700 Old Main Hill, Logan, UT 84322-2700.

[Haworth co-indexing entry note]: "The Founders' Meetings." Nelson, Thorana S. Co-published simultaneously in *Journal of Family Psychotherapy* (The Haworth Press, Inc.) Vol. 16, No. 1/2, 2005, pp. 5-6; and: *Education and Training in Solution-Focused Brief Therapy* (ed: Thorana S. Nelson) The Haworth Press, Inc., 2005, pp. 5-6. Single or multiple copies of this article are available for a fee from The Haworth Document Delivery Service [1-800-HAWORTH, 9:00 a.m. - 5:00 p.m. (EST). E-mail address: docdelivery@haworthpress.com].

Available online at http://www.haworthpress.com/web/JFP
Digital Object Identifier: 10.1300/J085v16n01_02

Our experience would not have been as rich without the students. Although they were a bit intimidated at first, that didn't last long. I believe that their experience, and ours, exemplifies what solution-focused brief therapy is about: therapists learn from clients, trainers learn from trainees. What follows are accounts from Shelley and Sara of their experiences as participants in our group.

Reflection on SFBTA Involvement

Shelley R. Clymer

KEYWORDS. SFBTA, non-judgmental environment, student perspective

The first "workshop" meeting with Steve de Shazer was in the spring of 2002. I was a second-year student in my Masters program for Marriage and Family Therapy at Purdue University Calumet, and was invited by a fellow student to help out at the workshop. I was only one of two students that were allowed to volunteer at the first workshop, due to the exclusivity of the group and intense focus on one theory–solution-focused therapy. My expectation was that I would contribute to the workshop like I always had contributed as a grad student volunteering at workshops or conferences: organizing chairs and materials, making sure the lights were dimmed at precisely the correct time and reduced to the hue preferred by the presenter, and other similarly small but necessary tasks. Little did I know at that time that my involvement would far exceed any volunteer work I had ever done for a meeting of this nature.

The workshop began and Steve de Shazer began speaking, while the other student, Sara, and I sat in the back, expecting to listen from a distance and observe the master at work. Soon it became clear that this "workshop" would not only be attendee-involved, but that Steve actually wanted our opinions, our input, and our thoughts as students. What an odd and amazing request from a

---

Shelley R. Clymer is a graduate student from Highland, IN.

[Haworth co-indexing entry note]: "Reflection on SFBTA Involvement." Clymer, Shelley R. Co-published simultaneously in *Journal of Family Psychotherapy* (The Haworth Press, Inc.) Vol. 16, No. 1/2, 2005, pp. 7-9; and: *Education and Training in Solution-Focused Brief Therapy* (ed: Thorana S. Nelson) The Haworth Press, Inc., 2005, pp. 7-9. Single or multiple copies of this article are available for a fee from The Haworth Document Delivery Service [1-800-HAWORTH, 9:00 a.m. - 5:00 p.m. (EST). E-mail address: docdelivery@haworthpress.com].

Digital Object Identifier: 10.1300/J085v16n01_03

presenter at a workshop, I thought–actually encouraging students to express their ideas! From that point forward, Sara and I were members of the workshop, part of the process, and attendees with contributions that actually meant something.

This was quite a change from my expectations and previous experience in large workshops such as this. I had mixed feelings: how exciting, yet how scary–I am just a student, and all of these attendees are all professionals who will hear my thoughts on the content and process of the meeting. This was, needless to say, a bit intimidating; however, there was such a non-judgmental feeling from everyone, such a welcoming of ideas and a genuine interest in the student perspective that my intimidation eventually turned to acceptance, which allowed me to speak more freely and honestly. When I look back on that, I realize now that this was really a meta-process happening that mirrored that of solution-focused therapy: In order to allow people to free up the clutter and blockage in their mind and be more clear to themselves, we must allow them to feel welcomed and relaxed. This is only one of the small yet significant pieces that I took from this experience. The small pieces are often the most important.

Following the workshop that weekend, it was decided to continue with the workshop several months later, to extend the solution-focused knowledge and contributions that individuals have made. The next meeting was set, and Sara, my fellow student, was to do a live-supervision case with one of her clients during the meeting. This was yet another opportunity awarded to a student that would commonly be unavailable. The opportunity to get live supervision from a twenty-person team of solution-focused professional therapists doesn't come along very often. Sara did a wonderful job and we learned much from the process. Due to my interest in becoming a future supervisor myself, this was a valuable experience to learn from those who have been doing it for many years; the level and amount of expertise in the room was exhilarating. Following this meeting, it was decided to create an "association" from the meetings, and another meeting weekend was scheduled to iron out more details of this idea.

The next meeting resumed where the last had left off, with a determination to make an annual meeting of solution-focused professionals a regular occurrence in order to continue and further the solution-focused approach. It was ultimately decided that an annual conference would uphold this tradition we had started in Hammond, Indiana, at that first workshop. The Solution-Focused Brief Therapy Association (SFBTA) was born, and the first conference was held in November of 2003 at Loma Linda University.

A conference committee was decided at this meeting, with about six professionals and two student representatives. I was fortunate to be recommended for the committee as a student consultant, and have since been a part of the process of creating an initial SFBTA conference as well as a second conference held in November of 2004 in Park City, Utah. My contributions have been minimal–an opinion or recommendation here or there, but my involvement has always been encouraged and my ideas respected. This is the continuing legacy of this association and its founding members, I believe: the encouragement and belief in the next generation of solution-focused therapists–the students. The first conference was a culmination of the ideas and hopes for the future of solution-focused therapy, with support of student involvement that is held with similar respect as the practicing professionals. I think this speaks highly of the open nature of our practicing solution-focused professionals in the field, and gives me a promising outlook for the future, as a student and as a therapist.

A Student's Response
to the SFBT Training Meetings:
The Future Looks Bright

Sara A. Smock

KEYWORDS. SFBT, training, self of the therapist

First of all, I must say that it has been a wonderful opportunity to be a part of the SFBT training meetings. I have considered it a privilege to experience the collaboration of seasoned brief therapists. I would like to thank everyone for allowing me to sit in on and participate in these training meetings.

Initially, the thought of meeting with distinguished brief therapists was somewhat intimidating. I expected to be a fly on the wall listening to Steve de Shazer discuss the topic of training individuals in SFBT. Of course, as a student who is interested in SFBT, I was thrilled to be an eavesdropper on such an important topic. Much to my surprise, Steve did very little talking and the group led the path through discussion.

During our first meeting, I was asked by different group members to share my perspective as a student. Although terrified, I was honored that this select group of therapists wanted to hear my perspective. It became evident from the first meeting that collaboration, even between master therapists and students, was encouraged and welcomed. I was excited that trainers were actually asking trainees what they thought about the process of learning SFBT. I thought

Sara A. Smock is a doctoral candidate from Roanoke, VA.

[Haworth co-indexing entry note]: "A Student's Response to the SFBT Training Meetings: The Future Looks Bright." Smock, Sara A. Co-published simultaneously in *Journal of Family Psychotherapy* (The Haworth Press, Inc.) Vol. 16, No. 1/2, 2005, pp. 11-13; and: *Education and Training in Solution-Focused Brief Therapy* (ed: Thorana S. Nelson) The Haworth Press, Inc., 2005, pp. 11-13. Single or multiple copies of this article are available for a fee from The Haworth Document Delivery Service [1-800-HAWORTH, 9:00 a.m. - 5:00 p.m. (EST). E-mail address: docdelivery@haworthpress.com].

Digital Object Identifier: 10.1300/J085v16n01_04

to myself, "This is the way it should be!" Just as SFBT sees the client as the expert, the trainee became a valuable source of the process of training. As a student, I had never thought about my own personal course of learning SFBT. I knew that this particular theory really "clicked" with me but couldn't describe the process. Being allowed to share my perspective of learning SFBT was very helpful as a developing therapist.

After the first meeting, I reflected on the entire experience and looked forward to our next meeting just months away. I was excited about the possibilities that could stem from these meetings. I became aware of an opportunity for a student to do a live case consultation in front of the group during the next meeting. Although this task would be extremely anxiety-provoking, I decided to volunteer. The collaborative environment of the group allowed me to become brave enough to bring in a case.

During the second training meeting, I presented a long-term client for the case consultation. The group decided to split into three smaller groups in order to examine training from various perspectives. I remember feeling support from each of the three groups during the different stages of the consultation. The feedback that I received from the various groups was very helpful. What I found remarkable about the entire process was that the principles of SFBT held true in the supervision. Being supervised by a purely SFBT group not only made an impact on me but also immensely aided my client.

The plans for the third meeting included possibly forming an association. I could not believe that I had the opportunity to collaborate with the group on forming an association. When it was decided by the group that the association would host an annual conference, I became very excited. The group stressed that the conference should give students a chance to present their research and collaborate with professionals. From a student's perspective it was exciting to know that the conference would promote an environment where seasoned professionals and students could co-present. In order to ensure that the future of SFBT continues and expands, it is important to include students. If students like me are invited to be trained by and collaborate with prominent solution-focused therapists, the future of SFBT looks bright.

As I reflect upon the entire experience, I am amazed at the impact it has made on others and me. Being a part of these meetings has allowed me to explore my own process of learning SFBT. By understanding my own theoretical journey, I can help trainers and other trainees. Finding effective means to communicate SFBT is essential for training future therapists. Another student, who was present at the meetings, used the energy and ideas from the group to do research on how individuals learn SFBT. This project is another important product of the meetings.

Personally, I walked away with hope for my generation of Solution-Focused Brief Therapists. We talk about creating options for our clients, so why not do the same for current and future therapists? Creating opportunities for Solution-Focused Brief Therapists to connect and support one another will definitely make things easier for my generation and generations to come to positively affect our world.

USING SOLUTION-FOCUSED BRIEF THERAPY

Solution-Focused Brief Therapy was founded by Insoo Kim Berg and Steve de Shazer. This series of articles demonstrates several different ways the ideas of SFBT can be used.

Solution-Focused Group Therapy

Ron Banks

KEYWORDS. Group therapy, solution-focused, training

GENERAL

Rather like an orchestra, the group members are all equal, with a 'conductor' who is 'first among equals.' The 'orchestra conductor' faces a group of experts in their own instruments, just as the therapist or conductor faces a group who are experts in their own lives. This process focuses participants' attention on the 'conductor's' respect for them and helps them to respect others.

The 'conductor' is there to keep the process on track. A flip chart is necessary.

The mix of the group can be of any kind–a therapist as 'conductor' with (a) a group of clients, (b) a mix of clients and trainees, (c) other therapists, wishing to know more about SFT, with their clients, or (d) any mix at all, as long as the 'conductor' is trained to keep the process on track. It is basically individual therapy conducted in a group setting.

Confidentiality is agreed to.

Depending on the mix, one person volunteers to be the client or a visiting therapist introduces a client.

Ron Banks is affiliated with Littlebrook House, The Brownings, Box, Corsham, Wiltshire, SN13 8HP, England.

From the practice at his SFT Group Clinics. With gracious acknowledgement to "Solution Talk" by Ben Furman and Tapani Ahola.

[Haworth co-indexing entry note]: "Solution-Focused Group Therapy." Banks, Ron. Co-published simultaneously in *Journal of Family Psychotherapy* (The Haworth Press, Inc.) Vol. 16, No. 1/2, 2005, pp. 17-21; and: *Education and Training in Solution-Focused Brief Therapy* (ed: Thorana S. Nelson) The Haworth Press, Inc., 2005, pp. 17-21. Single or multiple copies of this article are available for a fee from The Haworth Document Delivery Service [1-800-HAWORTH, 9:00 a.m. - 5:00 p.m. (EST). E-mail address: docdelivery@haworthpress.com].

Digital Object Identifier: 10.1300/J085v16n01_05

Throughout the process, the 'conductor' needs to be vigilant to ensure that

1. The language does not degenerate into pathology. The language should be imaginative, positive, and creative. This can be achieved by gentle reframing, by asking a question that gets the process back on track, or by asking for clarification in terms that focus on the positive.
2. Although SFT is future oriented, there is often a perceived need for giving an explanation for the problem. Any explanations that are given should be productive and imaginative. Explanations and actions taken to solve problems are interconnected. If a client is determined, though, then let the client keep his/her explanation. Explanations should not be examined in terms of whether they are correct or not, but in terms of what action is needed to be taken. The 'conductor' might ask, "Suppose the problem is caused by so-and-so, what would you do in that case?"
3. Connections between problems, especially where one is perceived to be the cause of another, need to be challenged. Treat each problem independently and go for just one. Sometimes, resolving one resolves all. It is impossible to know for sure whether one problem does cause another. Reversing the presumed cause and effect and seeing what happens can set the challenge. In the final analysis, the client, of course, decides, but at least, the challenge is there.
4. In general, throughout the process, any problem should be reframed so that it becomes a friend. This can be achieved by asking questions that help the client see the problem in a different light. The 'conductor' might ask, "Has this hardship made you stronger or weaker?" Or, "Did you learn a lot from that ordeal?" Or, "How on earth did you survive that?" Or, "Perhaps the others here have some ideas about how this problem can be seen as a resource?"

There are 6 steps in the process:

1. Introduction–Outline of problem
2. Clarification–Participants get things clear
3. Acknowledgement–Acceptance and pacing of the problem and positive feedback
4. The miracle scenario–Positive visions of the future
5. Building on progress and sharing credit
6. Closure–Next steps for the client

As an additional step, the treating of 'problems as friends' can be run, as in Paragraph 4 above, as a subpart to Step 3.

STEP 1: INTRODUCTION

The client outlines the problem, as briefly or as fully as s/he decides. If the client has been brought by a visiting therapist, that therapist may wish to add to the description of the problem, as long as the client has previously agreed.

STEP 2: CLARIFICATION

Any group member, in any order, asks questions of the client to clarify aspects of the problem, the process continues until clarification is complete. The questions are for clarification only and are not meant to delve into pathology. The 'conductor' needs to be vigilant during this stage.

STEP 3:
ACKNOWLEDGEMENT, ACCEPTANCE,
PACING AND POSITIVE FEEDBACK

Each member is invited to comment:

1. First, to acknowledge and accept the client's story with empathy, appropriately pacing the client's state. Group members may wish, at this stage, to draw upon their own experiences of a similar problem or difficulty briefly and state how they overcame it or made progress. The 'conductor' might say, "That seems very painful. (Amplify as necessary.) I imagine that there are others here who might want to sympathize or who have had similar experiences and tackled them successfully. Who would like to comment?"
2. Second, specifically to highlight the client's strengths, resources, qualities and coping skills, the 'conductor' might say, "What is it that impresses you about the way this client has tackled the problem so far? What do you see as his/her strengths?" *Use flip chart! Have someone write down these resources and give them to the client afterwards.*

STEP 4:
THE MIRACLE SCENARIO
AND POSITIVE VISIONS OF THE FUTURE

Since no one knows what the future will bring, it is a wonderful place for constructive conversations. Positive visions of the future enable people to see their current difficulties as phases in a continuing narrative, where hardships are steps to a better tomorrow. From this viewpoint, problems can be seen as valuable learning experiences.

The conductor might say, "The people here seem to think you have a lot going for you. What do you think the people here would see, in the future, that would let them know that your problem has gone for good or that you have made significant progress?" Or, "Imagine that a year has passed and you decide to write a letter to all of us with good news. What would the good news be?" Or, "If you were to imagine that your life is like a novel and the next chapter is a happy one, what will happen in it?" Or, "What will your life be like when this pain is all over? What would we all notice?" Or, "If a good friend of yours had a dream in which you were happy and doing fine, what kind of a dream would it be?" The thing to keep in mind at this stage is to accept any negative statement and ask what the client might notice as well, or instead, or what would happen next.

If the client finds it difficult to fantasize a positive future, the 'conductor' might come up with his/her own fantasies of the client's future, invite those present to do the same, and then let the client comment on those fantasies. Hearing other peoples' fantasies on his/her future compels the client to become involved. It is sometimes necessary to fantasize a dark future, which, when completed, paves the way for the possibility of a positive vision.

Even a client who has contemplated suicide can be led towards the future by asking, "Suppose that after you die, you find yourself at the pearly gates. You are greeted courteously by an angel who informs you that you have been granted a second chance. When you return to earth, you find that your problems are gone and that your life is very satisfactory. How would life be for you then?"

It is also possible to leave the door open for the creation of alternative future visions, even if it only means writing a question mark on the flip chart.

STEP 5:
BUILDING ON PROGRESS AND SHARING CREDIT

Just talking about improvement, whether small or substantial, temporary or enduring, has an encouraging effect on people. "What might you see as any improvement at all when compared with the worst you have been?" And, "How did you do that?" And, "What was helpful?" And, "Who was helpful at that time?" "What did you do to make that happen? " "Did you figure that out all by yourself, or did someone else help you?" "Was that new for you?" "Where did you get that idea?"

Others can be brought in to add their own comments and draw upon their own experiences to amplify whatever progress has been mentioned. It might need others before this stage if there are difficulties for the client in identifying progress to tease out of the client any signs of improvement.

Whatever the improvement, it is important at this stage to give compliments to the client covering the whole process, not just the improvements made. The 'conductor' can start it off, and compliment others who have been mentioned during the session. The participants are then invited to give their own compliments. They should range far and wide–family, partner or spouse, previous therapist, etc.

After the compliments, the client is invited to thank everyone who has contributed to progress so far. Many may not be present, but any credit should be shared, even among those who have passed away. The group may wish to suggest others that the client has forgotten. Sharing credit gets everyone on your side to make further improvements, even the psychiatrist who 'failed' to help the client! One just never knows!

STEP 6:
CLOSURE–NEXT STEPS FOR THE CLIENT

The client is asked, "What has been most helpful to you during this session?" It is the client's turn to do the talking. "And anything else?" is a question that should be repeated often to tease out every single bit of help.

Finally, the client is asked, "What next small step will you take to ensure continued progress?" Again, some time and trouble needs to be taken, maybe helped by the other participants, to ensure that the 'next step' (or 'steps') is described in as specific behavioral terms as possible–the more detail the better.

At the end, the client should be thanked for the cooperation shown and the participants should also be thanked for their contributions.

BIBLIOGRAPHY

Furman, B., & Ahola, T. (1992). *Solution talk: Hosting therapeutic conversations.* New York: Norton.

Working with Multiple Stakeholders

Rayya Ghul

KEYWORDS. Solution-focused brief therapy, multiple stakeholders, model of practice

This is an interactive method that was developed for a short workshop (45 minutes) with a group of 20 occupational therapists working in child and adolescent services who were attending a national conference (National Association of Paediatric Occupational Therapists). When working with children, parents, teachers, and other people may have a shared interest in the changes that are desired.

I wanted to emphasize the systemic aspects of working in a solution-focused way and highlight how meanings are negotiated to enhance outcomes. The success of the workshop relies on drawing out the pre-existing expertise of the participants. It was deliberately designed this way because I did not have detailed knowledge of the work of occupational therapists in this field. Using this type of method requires a lot of thinking on your feet but is great fun and casting the audience as 'experts' means they immediately feel that SFBT can be integrated into what they already do.

This method should work with any group of professionals who host meetings that involve more than one stakeholder interest.

Rayya Ghul is a member of the Institute of Learning and Teaching, Lyminge, Kent, England.

Address correspondence to: Rayya Ghul, Allied Health Department, Canterbury Christ Church University College, Canterbury CT1 1QU, England.

[Haworth co-indexing entry note]: "Working with Multiple Stakeholders." Ghul, Rayya. Co-published simultaneously in *Journal of Family Psychotherapy* (The Haworth Press, Inc.) Vol. 16, No. 1/2, 2005, pp. 23-26; and: *Education and Training in Solution-Focused Brief Therapy* (ed: Thorana S. Nelson) The Haworth Press, Inc., 2005, pp. 23-26. Single or multiple copies of this article are available for a fee from The Haworth Document Delivery Service [1-800-HAWORTH, 9:00 a.m. - 5:00 p.m. (EST). E-mail address: docdelivery@haworthpress.com].

METHOD

I introduced the idea that within all systems there is esoteric and shared knowledge. I defined esoteric as 'understood/intelligible by only a small number of people with special knowledge or initiation.' I explained that this is important because children and adolescents think differently from adults or have different meanings and interpretations of words or behaviours. This type of introduction could be adapted to suit different stakeholder groups.

I drew a Venn diagram on a whiteboard (you could use a flip chart or prepared Overhead Transparency [OHT] plus OH pens) (Figure 1).

I defined the intersecting space as 'shared knowledge' and the other spaces as the child's and the parents' esoteric knowledge. I then asked the audience to tell me what might be in each of the spaces.

Examples of responses:

Child's esoteric knowledge: How to wind up mum
I have a gun/bag of dope hidden in my room
If I whine I will get what I want
Who I'm friends with at school

Parents' esoteric knowledge: How much money we have and what it needs to be spent on
Things that might be happening in the future, e.g., house move
Things going on in the parents' relationship

Shared knowledge: Rules of the house
What food family members like
Birthdays

FIGURE 1

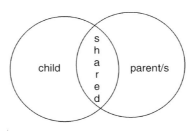

I explained that when one is working in a solution-focused way, the esoteric knowledge you are trying to bring into the open is rather special–it is the strengths, resources, activities, behaviours and so on that exist and contribute to a desired change or times when things work.

I asked the group to give me a typical problem that they might be expected to deal with. A member of the group said 'messy eating.' I asked what the desired change would be and it was defined as 'eating tidily.' I then worked with the group to draw out possible esoteric knowledge from the child and parents in response to some solution-focused questions. If you are working with a group you can put the desired behavior or change they identify after the highlighted part of the questions:

- *How will each party know* the child is eating tidily?
- *What difference will it make* when the child is eating tidily?
- *What is already happening towards* the child eating tidily?
- *What do you know that gives you hope* the child will be able to eat tidily?
- *What would be the first small step* to getting the child to eat tidily?

Using the Venn diagram, I wrote the responses up and then included the contribution from the occupational therapists' esoteric knowledge. Using arrows, I highlighted how the conversation moved all this hidden knowledge into the shared domain where it could be heard by everyone (Figure 2).

I stressed how, sometimes, the therapist might have to negotiate meanings to make sure that everyone understands the same thing by the words in

FIGURE 2

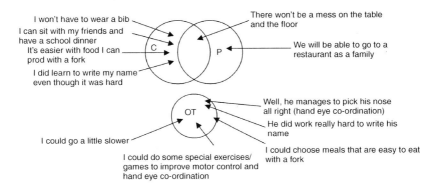

the shared domain. As an example, I said that when I asked my children to tidy their room, I had to make sure they didn't secretly invoke the 'small print' and put up the 'subject to the following terms and conditions' OHT:

Subject to the following terms and conditions,

I can shove all my dirty and clean clothes into one drawer with no attempt to sort them out or fold them although single socks and underpants may be hidden in inaccessible corners of my room and never found until we move house. Small pieces of Barbie accessories can be put in the same drawer as beads, game counters and pieces of jigsaw puzzles that I'm not sure which box they belong in any more. Books can be put on shelves higgdlepiggledy and anything that I still can't think of what to do with will be pushed as far as possible under the bed which includes sweet wrappers, apple cores and leaking drinks cartons that I shouldn't have had up there in the first place.

A Thumbnail Map
for Solution-Focused Brief Therapy

Lance Taylor

KEYWORDS. Solution-focused therapy

INTRODUCTION

At a certain stage of learning the solution-focused model, students say that they know about most of the questions and how to use them. Now they want to become more "smooth" in their interviewing. No doubt part of what helps therapists become more proficient and natural is simply a matter of time and practice. Another factor is that of developing a sense of direction and flow in solution-building conversations. At any point in a therapy session, the therapist has a number of choices for different ways to structure the conversation. Where should we begin? Are there identifiable stages or aspects in building solutions? In what order should we address the different stages? How do we know when to explore one stage more, or when to move on to the next? This thumbnail map has proven helpful to both trainees and supervisors because it gives a fairly straightforward and comprehensive overview for structuring the conversation. It is small enough to be packaged in practical and portable formats.

Lance Taylor has a private practice in Cochrane, Alberta, Canada.

Address correspondence to: Lance Taylor, Box 619, Cochrane, AB, Canada, T4C 1A7.

[Haworth co-indexing entry note]: "A Thumbnail Map for Solution-Focused Brief Therapy." Taylor, Lance. Co-published simultaneously in *Journal of Family Psychotherapy* (The Haworth Press, Inc.) Vol. 16, No. 1/2, 2005, pp. 27-33; and: *Education and Training in Solution-Focused Brief Therapy* (ed: Thorana S. Nelson) The Haworth Press, Inc., 2005, pp. 27-33. Single or multiple copies of this article are available for a fee from The Haworth Document Delivery Service [1-800-HAWORTH, 9:00 a.m. - 5:00 p.m. (EST). E-mail address: docdelivery@haworthpress.com].

Available online at http://www.haworthpress.com/web/JFP
Digital Object Identifier: 10.1300/J085v16n01_07

THE LANGUAGE OF PROBLEMS

This thumbnail map orients toward the terrain of the actual therapy session and landmarks of progress based on client language. Clients typically begin conversations with therapists by describing their troubles. Following are five patterns of language that are commonly observed in the course of clients' communicating the complaint.

> What I *don't* want.
> When things go *wrong*.
> Forces *beyond* my control.
> I'm *stuck*.
> I expect *more troubles* to come.

THE LANGUAGE OF SOLUTIONS

As clients begin to make the shift from problem talk to solution talk, five corresponding alternatives in language are observable.

> What I *do* want.
> When things go *right*.
> Forces *within* my control.
> I'm *progressing*.
> I see some *positive possibilities*.

SOLUTION-FOCUSED THERAPY: HELPING CLIENTS SHIFT THEIR THINKING, TALKING, AND ACTION

An effective solution-focused interview eases clients into a focus on solutions. For training purposes, it is helpful to present the map in the following format as an overhead, as a handout, or as a fridge magnet, entitled Five Key Shifts in Language.

What I *don't* want	→	What I *do* want
When things go *wrong*	→	When things go *right*
Forces *beyond* my control	→	Forces *within* my control
I'm *stuck*	→	I'm *progressing*
More troubles to come	→	*Positive possibilities*

A highly effective solution-focused interview would be one that assists the client to proceed from the language of 'what I don't want' to some 'positive possibilities.' This remark should be qualified with the comment that solution-focused interviewing carefully avoids pressuring or hurrying clients and therefore, a good session goes as far along this path as is comfortable for the client at the time.

LINES OF ENQUIRY

These five shifts in language are facilitated by five lines of enquiry. Another view of the map is presented to trainees this way, entitled Five Key Lines of Enquiry.

What is the goal?
When do little pieces of that happen?
How do you do that?
What good things result from that?
What's next?

LINES OF ENQUIRY AND SPECIFIC
SOLUTION-FOCUSED QUESTIONS

In the hands of advanced practitioners, many of the typical solution-focused questions can be used in several different lines of enquiry. Having said that, it is possible and useful to sort the questions roughly into categories. This helps trainees become purposeful in their interviewing. Some training groups have developed the idea of a questions toolbox that can begin with the following stock items. The therapist's own customized questions can be added as time goes on or for special populations.

What is the goal:

- (Miracle question) Suppose that one night while you are sleeping, a miracle happens, and the problem that brought you here today is solved. How would you find out in the morning that the miracle had happened?
- (Pre-session change question) Our clients often tell us that between the time they call to make an appointment and the time they actually meet with us, some things are already different. What have you noticed about your situation?

- What will have to happen as a result of our talk to today for you to say it was helpful?
- How will you know that coming to therapy is doing some good?
- How will you know that you don't need to come to therapy any more?
- (Coping question) With things being as difficult as they have been, how on earth have you coped so far?

When do little pieces of that happen:

- The day after a miracle, what is one of the first things you would do? Then what?
- When was a time that a little bit of that miracle actually happened?
- Who else noticed that things were a bit better? What tipped them off?
- What tells you that you will be able to achieve some of that goal?
- What is an example of a time in the future when you might do things differently in that way?

How do they do that:

- How did you do that!?
- So when your husband stops being abusive toward you, starts to respect you, what is it that you will be doing differently?
- When your kids start to listen a little better, how will you and your wife be parenting differently to keep that going?
- How have you been cooperating with the medication to get these good results?

What good things result from that:

- How was that helpful?
- What good things happened as a result of that?
- How did people react differently to you then?
- What would your children say is different about you when you do more of that?
- If that were to happen more and more over the next six months, what difference would that make in your life?
- (Scaling question) On a scale of 1 to 10, where 1 is the problem at its worst, and 10 is the day after a miracle, where would you say things are right now?

What's next:

- On the same scale from 1 to 10, how would you know when you are one step up? What would it take for that to happen? On a scale from 1 to 10, how confident are you about doing that? What would it take for your confidence to be higher?

- What is one small thing you could imagine doing (without worrying about whether it is possible to do, without promising to do it) that would lead to you being a half step or one step higher on this scale?

A MEMORY DEVICE: TEAM

The earliest questions used in a solution-focused interview often bring out the goal in the form of a *title* (*T*), a name that is quite general or perhaps a little vague. Subsequent questions help the client move the conversation into the detail of *events* (*E*), actual occurrences. Further progressions inquire into personal *agency* (*A*), holding people responsible for their successes, and then *movement* (*M*) or progress. Finally, questions about possible next steps usually elicit another *title* (*T*), which can then be further explored in this somewhat circular fashion (see Figure 1).

GUIDING CONVERSATION USING THE MAP

The benchmark line of enquiry is the first one: what is the goal, what does the client want. When sessions are in trouble it is most often the case that they need to get back to this central question. As soon as the client is able to generate a title for the goal, it is time to move into the events level of questioning. It is good to stay here for a good long time, bringing out all kinds of tiny details. Then it is productive to move into agency questioning. Once the person has spoken of their role in the success, it is useful to shift into movement questions. Once they acknowledge some real benefit of their efforts, it is useful to pursue ideas for next steps, beginning with a title.

FIGURE 1

Language shift	Line of enquiry	Acronym
What I *don't* want → What I *do* want	What is the goal?	**T**–for title
When things go *wrong* → When things go *right*	When do little pieces of that happen?	**E**–for events
Forces *beyond* my control → Forces *within* my control	How do they do that?	**A**–for agency
I'm *stuck* → I'm *progressing*	What good things result from that?	**M**–for movement
More troubles to come → *Positive possibilities*	What's next?	**T**–for title

A CASE EXAMPLE

The map's distinctions in language and lines of enquiry are not always immediately obvious to trainees. Details from actual case examples, such as the one below, help bring the map to life.

A man is referred because he is "depressed." [*A title for a problem that he doesn't want.*] After awhile, he is asked the miracle question and he says he would "be happier, he would look forward to the day." [*Titles for some things he does want.*]

When was a time that you were a little bit happier? Well, "one day last week I woke up in the morning, actually got out of bed, had a shower first thing, put on real clothes." [*Descriptions of actual events, a time when things went right.*]

How did you do that? He "rolled out of bed right when the alarm went off instead of laying there thinking about troubles." [*A specific behavioral choice that is within his control, agency.*]

How was that helpful? Well, he "was able to get up and get going, get some things starting to happen, once he got some things started, it was easier to keep going, he was more productive and the day was more satisfying." [*Some good results, some movement or progress.*] Where would you put things these days on a scale from 1 to 10? How would you rate that better day last week?

What would indicate you had moved up to the next notch on the scale? Well, "if I started exercising again." [*The title or name of a next step.*]

So, when you exercise, what things specifically, do you do? I "used to swim at Lindsay Park in the mornings, walk the stairs at work deliberately." [*Descriptions of actual events.*] And so on . . .

APPLICATIONS FOR THE MAP

This map originally emerged 'behind the mirror.' Observing many sessions with therapists at literally every level of skill development was informative: watching how they organized the interview, how the observing team tracked the process, and what ideas they picked to phone in. In training and supervision, it proved useful to have a frame of reference posted on the wall in the observation room. The team assisting the session can quickly reflect on the five lines of enquiry to determine where the interview has gone so far, which areas require more focus and detail, and what might be the next direction to take.

Once therapists become familiar with this format, they use it to actually guide their own sessions. It also is quite productive for therapist self-evaluation. After a session ends, the therapist can quickly review the five lines of enquiry, recalling what was done in each area and the content that was elicited. If areas were missed, it is useful to reflect on why that happened. Sometimes it will be because that was as far as the client could be gently taken. Sometimes it will be because the therapist forgot that line of enquiry, got distracted, or gave up too soon.

Participants in workshops find the summary of shifts in language straightforward and easy to understand. It gives a fairly specific, functional definition of solution talk, which makes it easier to comprehend the intent of solution-focused interviewing and to identify changes that the clients are making. The map has been used to structure role-play interviews in workshops. One member of a group of three to five plays the client. One of the group plays interviewer. Others in the group track the interview according to the map, take notes on details in each line of enquiry, use the map to generate suggestions to support the interviewer, and then review the interview afterwards.

One agency that recently contracted to have their staff trained in the model wanted to make their recording format consistent with their interviewing format. Their new framework for a session note incorporates the five lines of enquiry.

Another emerging application for this map is in the area of self-help. Individuals who have experience with making this shift from problem talk to solution talk find it helpful to walk themselves through the five lines of enquiry when they are troubled about something. The primary contribution of previous experience is to know what qualifies as a good answer and to know how to persist through to a result. In a brief time, people can help themselves make a dramatic shift from a problem-focused state to a solution-focused state.

PACKAGING THE MAP

Some therapists divide their in-session notepad into four quadrants (Titles, Events, Agency, Movement) and then keep notes in the quadrants according to the questions they are asking and the comments that clients are making. A natural benefit of this practice is that blank areas on the notepad stand out and prompt the therapist to attend to that area.

BIBLIOGRAPHY

DeJong, P., & Berg, I. K. (1998). *Interviewing for solutions.* Pacific Grove, CA: Brooks/Cole.

de Shazer, S. (1985). *Keys to solutions in brief therapy.* New York: Norton.

Miller, S. D., Duncan, B. L., & Hubble, M. A. (1997). *Escape from Babel.* New York: Norton.

Walter, J. L., & Peller, J. E. (1992). *Becoming solution-focused in brief therapy.* New York: Brunner/Mazel.

NGP Triangle Exercise

Tomasz Switek

KEYWORDS. Solution-focused training

This exercise is aimed at developing the professional's ability to conduct solution-focused talk about clients' needs, goals, and possibilities while taking into consideration clients' readiness to talk about particular topics or to do something with her/his life. At the beginning of the exercise, we divide the group into four smaller teams. Each team works on one of the topics listed below by putting a short list on the flip chart:

1. In what way can we ask and talk about clients' needs?
2. In what way can we ask and talk about clients' goals?
3. In what way can we ask and talk about clients' possibilities (resources)?
4. What observable factors can tell you during the talk that the client is ready to talk with you as a therapist about particular topics, and what are the signs from the client's side that she/he is not ready to do so?

During this work, participants should use all of their experiences connected with professional activity as well as with their private lives.

Tomasz Switek is a therapist and trainer, Polish Solutions Focused Team, Solutions Focused Therapy Institute, Inowroclaw, Poland.

Address correspondence to: Tomasz Switek, Szarych Szeregow 7a/6, 88-100 Inowroclaw, Poland.

[Haworth co-indexing entry note]: "NGP Triangle Exercise." Switek, Tomasz. Co-published simultaneously in *Journal of Family Psychotherapy* (The Haworth Press, Inc.) Vol. 16, No. 1/2, 2005, pp. 35-37; and: *Education and Training in Solution-Focused Brief Therapy* (ed: Thorana S. Nelson) The Haworth Press, Inc., 2005, pp. 35-37. Single or multiple copies of this article are available for a fee from The Haworth Document Delivery Service [1-800-HAWORTH, 9:00 a.m. - 5:00 p.m. (EST). E-mail address: docdelivery@haworthpress.com].

Digital Object Identifier: 10.1300/J085v16n01_08

After making the lists of questions, ways of talk, and observable factors, each team reads its list to the rest of the whole group. On that basis we work on developing more and more useful items.

We then invite people to divide into teams of three (client, therapist, observer). We present to them NGP triangle (Needs, Goals, Possibilities) schema and its idea (see Figure 1). NGP Triangle is a play area for having a conversation about the clients' needs, goals, and possibilities and, at the same time, take into consideration the clients' readiness to talk with us about particular topics. We suggest that the "theoretical" way to have conversation is to:

> *start from NEEDS, go to GOALS, and then go to POSSIBILITIES.*

In this exercise, however, we are not going to follow "theory" but to follow practice, so in every team, participants will decide where they are going to start their conversation:

> *from NEEDS or from GOALS or from POSSIBILITIES* and to where they will go with this conversation:

> *start from NEEDS go to GOALS go to POSSIBILITIES*
> *start from NEEDS go to go POSSIBILITIES to GOALS*
> *start from GOALS go to NEEDS go to POSSIBILITIES*
> *start from GOALS go to POSSIBILITIES go to NEEDS*
> *start from POSSIBILITIES go to GOALS go to NEEDS*
> *start from POSSIBILITIES go to NEEDS go to GOALS*

We also stress that during this conversation, participants can change areas of their conversation as many times as they find useful and helpful. One condition is to stay with the focus of the conversation on these three areas only: NEEDS > GOALS > POSSIBILITIES.

The aim of this conversation is to help clients to find out their NEEDS, to state some GOALS that are rooted in these NEEDS, and to explore POSSIBILITIES in satisfying those NEEDS by achieving the GOALS. During this conversation, the therapist should respect the client's readiness to talk about proposed topics.

The therapist moves on the schema of the NGP triangle during the conversation. She/he can use a pawn like in the parlor game. After 15 minutes of conversation, the observer and the therapist change roles. So, the observer becomes the therapist and the therapist becomes the observer. The task of the observer is to write down all useful actions from the side of the therapist.

At the end of the conversation we take a short break. During the break, the observer and therapist prepare a short message to the client about his or her needs, goals, and possibilities.

FIGURE 1

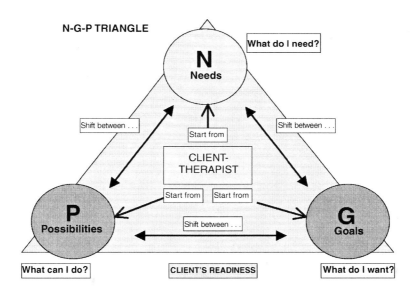

N-G-P TRIANGLE

The client prepares a short message about which things were useful for her/him during that conversation. After that, the observers present their reflections on what was useful from the side of therapist. If required, we can talk about that experience with the whole group.

'Voices':
An Exercise in Developing Solution-Focused Conversations with the Mentally Ill

Alasdair J. Macdonald

KEYWORDS. Solution focus, mental illness, voices, training

INTRODUCTION

As a consultant psychiatrist in the United Kingdom I have been using solution-focused brief therapy within mental hospitals since 1988. We have trained many staff who work in mental illness settings. However, we also have many trainees from other settings who have no experience in work with the mentally ill. These staff often encounter behavior that they regard as equivalent to mental illness, especially if they work with young people or in the field of substance misuse (see Bertolino & Thompson, 1999).

Staff, without specific experience of work with the mentally ill, often find it difficult to initiate solution-focused conversations with such clients. This may arise from the long tradition that mentally ill persons are 'different' in their

Alasdair J. Macdonald is a Honorary Consultant Psychiatrist, Carleton Clinic, Scotby, Carlisle, England.

Address correspondence to: Alasdair J. Macdonald, 8 Wellgate Close, Scotby, Carlisle CA4 8BA, England.

[Haworth co-indexing entry note]: "'Voices': An Exercise in Developing Solution-Focused Conversations with the Mentally Ill." Macdonald, Alasdair J. Co-published simultaneously in *Journal of Family Psychotherapy* (The Haworth Press, Inc.) Vol. 16, No. 1/2, 2005, pp. 39-42; and: *Education and Training in Solution-Focused Brief Therapy* (ed: Thorana S. Nelson) The Haworth Press, Inc., 2005, pp. 39-42. Single or multiple copies of this article are available for a fee from The Haworth Document Delivery Service [1-800-HAWORTH, 9:00 a.m. - 5:00 p.m. (EST). E-mail address: docdelivery@haworthpress.com].

ways of communicating. This tradition has come about partly through the stigmatizing and labeling of mental illness by the general population. It has also come about through the professionalization of mental illness care and the consequent jargon and air of mystery around responses to mental illness. In everyday practice, Vaughn and coworkers (1995, 1996) have shown the enormous benefits of using solution-focused brief therapy within mental illness units and services.

The following exercise was devised in order to introduce staff to the use of solution-focused brief therapy when there are concerns about mental illness. The class need not be familiar with solution-focused brief therapy nor with mental health practice.

PURPOSES OF THE EXERCISE

- Reduce anxiety related to conversation about 'mental illness' symptoms.
- Demonstrate that tracking the client's language is helpful and that it can be improved by practice.
- Demonstrate the effect of using solution-focused brief therapy style questions.
- Highlight the value of compliments.

EXERCISE

The topic is introduced through the class sharing their experiences of talking with unusual clients. The class are asked to divide into groups of four or five. One person from each group is asked to volunteer to act as a client. The 'client' is given a sheet of instructions with which to begin developing their presentation. Some trainees have fears of becoming 'contaminated' by mental illness in playing such a role. The instructions make it easier for them to see the role as separate from their 'real' self.

SAMPLE HANDOUT

- YOU HEAR VOICES FOR TWO MONTHS FROM OUTSIDE; SOMETIMES FROM RADIO OR TV.
- CANNABIS MAKES THE VOICES WORSE.
- YOU LIVE WITH YOUR PARENTS.
- PARENTS' ATTITUDE TO THE VOICES:

- FATHER SAYS, 'STUPID; IGNORE THEM'; MOTHER CRITICIZES FATHER FOR SAYING THIS.
- MUSIC HELPS
- MEDICINE HELPS BUT YOU OFTEN DO NOT TAKE THEM

The others in the group are asked to act as a composite interviewer, each asking one question and then allowing the person on their left to ask the next question. Each question must include a word or phrase used by the client in their last response. The client can elaborate their role as they wish. The interviewers may elect to conduct a solution-focused interview or may ask questions based on other styles of conversation. Either is acceptable for the purposes of this exercise.

The trainer circulates from group to group, reminding each to ask questions in turn. It is important that everyone contributes to the process of question and answer. The groups also need to be reminded to use something from the client's language in every question.

After a suitable length of time (15-20 minutes), the groups are told to finish the exercise. Each group member is asked to give a compliment to the client. In practice, they may choose to do this in role or out of role.

In seeking feedback from the class it can be helpful to ask about any use of solution-focused brief therapy questions and about the views of the trainees about using and attending to the client's language in this way. Seeking feedback from the 'clients' is often helpful to the whole group. Contrary to the group's expectations, the 'clients' have usually enjoyed the conversation and the compliments. This builds confidence in the group about their ability to talk to the mentally ill.

Debriefing of 'clients.' In closing the discussion, the teacher asks if all the 'clients' in the class are confident that they are back to themselves. If not, they are asked to perform a simple de-roling exercise such as standing up, turning round, and sitting down again. This also serves to remind the other class members that their colleagues were playing a role for their benefit.

Experiential level of the exercise. 7-8.

Time for the exercise. The exercise and feedback can be completed within 40 minutes for a class of 20. Larger classes or more detailed discussions will extend the time.

The exercise can be repeated with different members taking the role of 'clients' or with other sets of instructions designed to bring in desired topics. The exercise can be extended to other topics such as a history of substance misuse or specific aspects of solution-focused brief therapy.

NOTE

An informative discussion on the social definition and management of 'mental illness' can be found in Bittner, E. (1967). Police discretion in emergency apprehension of mentally ill persons, *Social Problems, 14*, 278-292.

REFERENCES

Bertolino, B., & Thompson, K. (1999). *The residential youth care worker in action: A collaborative, competency-based approach.* New York: Haworth.

Vaughn, K., Webster, D.C., Orahood, S., & Young, B.C. (1995). Brief inpatient psychiatric treatment: Finding solutions, *Issues in Mental Health Nursing, 16*, 519-531.

Vaughn, K., Young, B.C., Webster, D.C., & Thomas, M.R. (1996). A continuum-of-care model for inpatient psychiatric treatment. In: S.D. Miller, M.A. Hubble, & B.L. Duncan (Eds.) *Handbook of solution-focused brief therapy* (pp. 99-127). San Francisco: Jossey-Bass.

Negotiating Goals in Conjoint Therapy: From Virtual to Actual Practice

Roger Lowe

KEYWORDS. Negotiating goals, conjoint therapy, issues and exercises

When teaching solution-oriented therapies to trainees I have found that one of the most easily grasped ideas is that of 'well-formed' goals (De Jong & Berg, 2002). Practitioners may differ in the precise way they use this term, but in general it refers to the process of gently but persistently shifting the conversation towards preferred, future-oriented actions. Typical characteristics of well-formed goals include a focus on observable actions, the presence of desirable behaviors rather than the absence of problems, a description in interactional terms, an emphasis on process (small steps or signs of change) rather than a final outcome, and a focus on actions that are within the client's control. Negotiating well-formed goals is an ongoing process of elaboration and clarification rather than a specific phase or task (as in 'goal *setting*'). Therapists have developed terms such as 'goaling,' 'preferencing' (Walter & Peller, 2000), and 'goal clarification' (Lipchik, 2002) to highlight this sense of unfolding process. Trainees tend to respond to these concepts and can learn quite quickly to use this group of skills in individual therapy.

Roger Lowe is affiliated with the Queensland University of Technology, School of Psychology and Counseling, Carseldine, Australia.

Address correspondence to: Roger Lowe, Queensland University of Technology, Beams Road, Carseldine, Q4034, Australia.

[Haworth co-indexing entry note]: "Negotiating Goals in Conjoint Therapy: From Virtual to Actual Practice." Lowe, Roger. Co-published simultaneously in *Journal of Family Psychotherapy* (The Haworth Press, Inc.) Vol. 16, No. 1/2, 2005, pp. 43-49; and: *Education and Training in Solution-Focused Brief Therapy* (ed: Thorana S. Nelson) The Haworth Press, Inc., 2005, pp. 43-49. Single or multiple copies of this article are available for a fee from The Haworth Document Delivery Service [1-800-HAWORTH, 9:00 a.m. - 5:00 p.m. (EST). E-mail address: docdelivery@haworthpress.com].

43

However, they often experience much more difficulty in negotiating well-formed goals when practicing conjointly with couples or families. Most trainees learn individual therapy first and can find the shift to conjoint therapy to be challenging and confusing. A number of typical difficulties arise. When asked about their hopes or goals, clients often use this opportunity to attack others and to set off a negative chain reaction (e.g., blaming others and demanding that they should change first); clients often state very different or even mutually exclusive goals that seem to offer no chance of connection (e.g., one member of a couple wants to end the relationship and the other wants to maintain it); there may be many different goals that keep changing throughout the session; or clients may tend to argue in the session and the idea of well-formed goals gets lost in the heat. Faced with these kinds of situations, trainees are often thrown out of stride and become confused. They may lose track of the different goals that emerge, and may be unsure about the most appropriate pattern of interaction to use. For example, in what circumstances is it better to talk with individuals at length or move the conversation rapidly around the room, or address the group collectively? When is it helpful to invite family members to respond to what others have said and when is it not? How do you avoid the perception of taking sides?

With trainees who are new to the dynamics of conjoint work, I suggest the following rule of thumb: Where an emotional climate of negativity and complaints is evident (typically at the beginning of the first session), it is usually more productive to develop an *individual conversation* with each person, rather than to address the whole group or invite clients to respond to what others have said. Later, when a more collaborative atmosphere has been established, and the conversation has turned to exceptions and resources, it can be more useful to invite clients to respond to each other and build on successes. In other words, when the going is tough, it is important to focus on developing a collaborative relationship *between the therapist and each individual*. Later, when the emotional climate changes, we can invite people to interact with each other. While all rules of thumb are somewhat crude, I have found this guideline to be useful in assisting trainees to stay focused and avoid confusion. It is important to emphasize that we are still doing relationship therapy even though we are talking to one person at a time. Why? Because we are talking to the speakers about their relationship concerns and hopes, and we are simultaneously attempting to influence this conversation for the benefit of the listeners. As always, we assume that the process of goal negotiation is not an academic exercise in assessment but is change-inducing in itself. One difference between individual and conjoint therapy is that in the latter, it is potentially change-inducing for both speakers *and* listeners.

In order to assist trainees to make the transition to negotiating goals in conjoint work, I have found the following two exercises to be helpful. The first helps trainees to develop a relationship perspective while working with one client. This experience of 'virtual' relationship therapy acts as a bridge to actual conjoint work. The second exercise involves negotiating goals in actual conjoint work. In both exercises, trainees are asked to frame their questions with both speakers and listeners in mind, and to be mindful of their own use of language. They are also asked to introduce relationship questions where appropriate and to listen for the possibilities of shared goals. As Lipchik (2002) suggests, a cardinal rule in family therapy is to avoid too much talk about differences and to focus where possible on what family members share.

TRAINING EXERCISE 1

Purpose: To assist the development of a relational perspective when negotiating goals with one client.

Participants: "Therapist," one "client," and one observer.

Experience level: Participants should be familiar with the principle of 'well-formed' goals and have experience negotiating these in individual contexts.

Process: The role-play situation involves a complainant-type relationship in which the client (Person A) complains about the behavior of a family member or partner (Person B) who is not present in the session. As is typical in this kind of scenario, Person A agrees that a problem exists in the relationship but insists that Person B needs to change!

Instructions to therapist: The therapist is to talk with Person A for 10-15 minutes and attempt to negotiate well-formed goals. The therapist begins with a general statement such as, 'I'd like to ask what brings you in and how you are hoping our talk will be helpful.'

However, in order to develop a relationship perspective, the therapist is also asked to *imagine that Person B is also in the room* and can hear everything that is said by Person A and the therapist. The therapist is to consider *both* Person A and Person B as clients and to craft questions for Person A that might allow the imaginary Person B to hear something different. The therapist must also be mindful of their own language in order to avoid inadvertently siding with one client against the other.

In addition, the therapist is instructed to bring Person B into the conversation where appropriate, using various kinds of relationship questions, and to listen for the possibility of shared goals. Some sample relationship questions (posed to Person A) might include:

- If John were sitting here with us and had been listening to everything you have said so far, what would have surprised him the most?
- What would he say is different about the way you have been talking to me, compared to the way in which the two of you typically talk? What difference do you think this might make for him?
- If your relationship were going more the way you would like it to be, what would be different between you? What would you both be doing differently?
- If I were to ask John if he also was distressed about your relationship and would like things to be different, what do you think he might say? What specifically would he like to be different between you?
- Having heard you talk about your hopes for the relationship in the way you have today, do you think he might share some of these hopes?
- If John began to make some of the changes you are hoping for, how would he notice you respond? What would he say might encourage him to persevere?

Debriefing: At the end of the conversation:

(a)   Observer asks Person A:

- What did the therapist do to help you shift your perspective?
- To what extent did you feel that the therapist was supportive of you?
- At various points did you feel that the therapist was taking either your side or Person B's side? What effect did this have?

(b)   Observer asks the Therapist:

- How did the experience of imagining the presence of Person B make a difference? In what ways was it helpful or unhelpful?
- Were there moments when either Person A or Person B might have felt you were siding with the other? If this occurred what did you do to redress the balance?
- If you had a choice would you prefer to keep working only with Person A, or would you prefer the actual presence of Person B? What factors might influence your preference?

(c)   All participants may offer additional feedback and reflections, exploring implications for future sessions in this scenario.

The participants can then switch roles and begin another cycle. Allowing a maximum of 15 minutes for the interview and 10 minutes for debriefing, the exercise totals about 25 minutes for each cycle.

For trainees who are unused to conjoint therapy, this exercise provides a useful stepping stone by encouraging a relationship perspective while working with one client. It assists therapists to be mindful of language and to maintain a sense of connection and commitment to both of the parties involved. After experiencing the exercise, trainees can take the next step as demonstrated in Exercise 2.

TRAINING EXERCISE 2

Purpose: To practice negotiation of goals in conjoint therapy.

Participants: Therapist, two or more clients (i.e., a couple or family members), and at least one observer.

Experience level: Participants should be familiar with the principle of 'well-formed' goals and have some experience negotiating these in individual contexts. They also should have completed Training Exercise 1.

Process: The role-play situation again involves a complainant-type relationship in which the clients each want others in the session to change. The therapist develops an individual conversation with each person at a time, while the others listen.

Instructions to Therapist

(a) The therapist begins with a general statement such as: 'I'd like to talk to each of you in turn about why you are here and how you are hoping our talk will be helpful. Who'd like to go first?'

You may also wish to specifically emphasize the pattern of conversation you will be using:

> Couples and families often have a lot of different issues to discuss and often have different points of view, so to help me avoid getting confused I usually like to start by talking for a while with each person in turn to discuss out how you are hoping that coming here will be helpful. While I'm talking to each person, the others have an opportunity to listen. Sometimes, talking and listening like this can be helpful in itself . . .

(b) The therapist talks to each client for 5 minutes or so, attempting to acknowledge the client's viewpoint and experience but to gradually effect a shift of focus from complaints to requests. The observer can act as a timekeeper. Again the therapist attempts to craft questions that allow both the speaker and listeners to hear something different, and is asked to use appropriate relationship questions and listen for common goals.

The aim is to arrive at a point where each client has clarified his/her hopes for the future and has had the opportunity to hear all other participants do the same. No attempt will be made to encourage the conversation further. The interview ends with the therapist's summarizing each person's goals, and reflecting on any commonalities that might have emerged.

(c) At the end of this process, the observer interviews each client, using questions such as:

- When you were in the *speaking* position, what questions or comments helped you to experience your situation differently?
- To what extend did you feel heard and understood?
- What did the therapist ask or say that helped you shift from a complaining to a requesting stance?
- What would have helped this process further?
- To what extent did your experience in the speaking position affect your subsequent experience as a listener?
- When you were in the *listening* position what did you hear the speakers (client and therapist) say that helped you to experience the situation differently?
- What did the speakers say that encouraged you to shift from a complaining to a requesting stance?
- What did the therapist say that interested you as a listener?
- What would have helped this process further?
- To what extent did your experience in the listening position affect your subsequent experience as a speaker?

The observer then interviews the therapist:

- To what extent do the comments of the clients reflect your own experience of the exercise?
- What would you like to add to their comments?
- What client comments were surprising?
- As you reflect on the client comments, what can you appreciate about your use of goal development skills?
- What have you learned from the exercise that will help you to build on your skills in goal development with couples/families?

(d) All participants may then discuss likely scenarios for future sessions:

- Based on what has been learned, what would be the likely focus of the next session?
- Which goals would take precedence?

- How could goals be prioritized (e.g., short and long term)?
- To what extent have mutual goals been elicited?
- If goals appear incompatible, what is the next step (for example, should clients be seen separately?)

The total time for this exercise is 30-45 minutes, depending on the number of clients and the specific scenario. Participants can then switch roles and begin another cycle.

CONCLUSION

As therapists become more experienced, they are able to respond more intuitively to opportunities as they occur and develop the ability to keep track of several conversations simultaneously. Experienced therapists, therefore, may find the suggested structure of talking to clients individually somewhat constraining. However, I have found that the skills and guidelines I have discussed can be very helpful for trainees who are relatively new to conjoint therapy. They provide a systematic way to reduce confusion and maintain a focus on negotiating well-formed goals in a 'culture of complaint.' The two sequential exercises I have described provide a way for trainees to make a gradual transition from individual to conjoint work, and to feel more comfortable with the virtual and then the actual presence of multiple clients.

REFERENCES

De Jong, P., & Berg, I. (2002). *Interviewing for solutions* (2nd Ed.). Pacific Grove, CA: Brooks/Cole.

Lipchik, E. (2002). *Beyond technique in solution-focused therapy: Working with emotions and the therapeutic relationship.* New York: Guilford Press.

Walter, J., & Peller, J. (2000). *Recreating brief therapy: Preferences and possibilities.* New York: Norton.

Engagement Through Complimenting

Insoo Kim Berg
Peter DeJong

KEYWORDS. Changing agency atmosphere, observing for competence, promoting client change, types of compliments

Solution-focused (SF) therapists and consultants are often called into a milieu that is saturated with problem-focused thinking and discouragement and asked to change the situation to something more positive and hopeful by applying SF thinking and techniques. While there are several ways to begin the SF process, complimenting is among the simplest, easiest, and most useful. It can quickly lead to noticeable transformations that can be amplified using other SF techniques. There at least three types: direct, indirect, and self-compliments. Direct compliments involve observing for what seems to be useful or successful in clients and then, thinking these observations may be helpful to bring to clients' awareness, doing so with direct statements. For example, "I can see from the way you talk to your child that you are a thoughtful mother." Such statements are sincere observations and interpretations of which clients may not have been aware and sometimes have difficulty accepting no matter how genuinely given.

Insoo Kim Berg is affiliated with the Brief Family Therapy Center, Milwaukee, WI. Peter DeJong is affiliated with Calvin College, Grand Rapids, MI.
Address correspondence to: Insoo Kim Berg, 1907 Wauwatosa Avenue, Milwaukee, WI 53213 or Peter DeJong, Sociology and Social Work, Calvin College, 3201 Burton SE, Grand Rapids, MI 49546.

[Haworth co-indexing entry note]: "Engagement Through Complimenting." Berg, Insoo Kim, and Peter DeJong. Co-published simultaneously in *Journal of Family Psychotherapy* (The Haworth Press, Inc.) Vol. 16, No. 1/2, 2005, pp. 51-56; and: *Education and Training in Solution-Focused Brief Therapy* (ed: Thorana S. Nelson) The Haworth Press, Inc., 2005, pp. 51-56. Single or multiple copies of this article are available for a fee from The Haworth Document Delivery Service [1-800-HAWORTH, 9:00 a.m. - 5:00 p.m. (EST). E-mail address: docdelivery@haworthpress.com].

Available online at http://www.haworthpress.com/web/JFP
Digital Object Identifier: 10.1300/J085v16n01_11

Indirect compliments are elicited from clients by asking them questions from the points of view of those familiar to clients. By formulating questions this way, we are asking clients to view situations through the lenses of those who know them better than we do and those often more credible. For example, one might ask, "What do you suppose your teacher would say you are best in at school?" Or, another example: "What would your best friend say you are like when you are calmer and gentler?" By introducing the teacher's or best friend's perspectives into the conversation, we can begin to hint at the probable, positive reputations of clients among those who know them best. Because most clients do not reflect on themselves and their situations in this manner, it is always a good idea to allow them plenty of time to collect their thoughts and formulate their responses.

Self-complimenting involves phrasing questions in such a way that clients are placed in the position of describing their successes and hidden abilities, often for the first time. For example, one might ask a woman who has just left her physically abusive partner any number of questions that could lead to self-compliments: "Whose idea was it to leave him?" "How did you know this was the time for you to do it?" "Was it difficult for you to decide to do this?" "Did it surprise you that you did it?" "What is it about you that you were able to take this step?" Self-complimenting can seem more natural and credible to clients than direct complimenting because clients are the ones who are providing the observations and interpretations.

In what follows, we offer two examples of how complimenting was used to engage persons in situations where collaterals wanted to see the persons change but the persons themselves did not seem initially to be customers for change.

Recently, I (IKB) was doing a round of workshops in Florida and got to stay with a colleague (Lee Shilts) and his wife (Margaret Shilts), who is a teacher in an alternative classroom for difficult and troubled children, each of whom has a long list of failures and behavioral problems. One young boy in particular (Calvin) was especially challenging and provocative to this gifted teacher with 27 years of experience teaching special problem children in the 6th grade. Calvin has had a long history of heavy-duty behavior problems that includes climbing high into a tree and threatening to jump in front of his classmates in school. On that particular occasion, his mother and the fire department were called. Almost daily, Calvin would push the limits. Despite many efforts by many school staff, nothing so far had proved to put Calvin on the road to positive change in his classroom. After an evening of discussion about children like Calvin and, more generally, what schools might do differently to be more helpful to these children, Lee and I decided to visit and observe some community schools and make a visit to Calvin's classroom. Of course, upon entering the classroom, Margaret introduced us to the children. I was introduced as "a lady who travels all over the world and talks to people about how to help other people with their problems." Calvin, who sat in the farthest corner from me and Lee, came up to us and asked me several questions about where I had been: "Have you been to New York?" I answered, "Yes." "Have you been to Chicago?" Calvin went on asking about an impressive list of cities, all of which I had visited. His eyes got larger and larger. Finally, he came up with his most important question: "Have you ever been to Boston?" I said, "Yes." He asked, "Wow, how many times?" I answered, "Four or five times." His eyes got very large, he became silent and thoughtful, and he returned to his seat and began concentrating and *working quietly.* Of course, the other children also wanted to talk to the visitors and we turned our attention to them, forgetting for the moment about Calvin.

That evening, Margaret was rather sheepish, saying she had wanted to show me how bad Calvin's behavior could be, but somehow Calvin had decided not to cooperate. Lee and I decided to send Calvin a letter complimenting how he was able to sit still and concentrate on his work, even though there were other children making lots of noise and commotion. We wrote we were very impressed with each of these things. Margaret delivered the letter to Calvin the following morning. A week later I received a note from Calvin. It was written in pencil in a half-torn notebook, and read,

> Hi Mrs. that goes all around the world. Thank you for the letter by the way. When I was in class doing my work I was not paying attention to the class. I was just paying attention to my work and that's all I try to do. Thanks for the letter and can you draw if you can a picture for me and I will draw a picture for you just give it to Mrs. Shilts. She will give it to me. Thanks for the letter again. Calvin.

Margaret informed me that Calvin had carried the letter from Lee and me in his back pocket for an entire week. She also said he achieved a B in reading and completed all his work that week. He was the best behaved she has ever seen him. Calvin's mother called and asked, "What is this about a letter?" This was the first time she had called the school.

A second example of engagement through complimenting comes from the work that both of us have been conducting with Children's Protective Services (CPS) of the Family Independence Agency (FIA) in Michigan. Part of this project has involved shadowing workers on CPS investigations. FIA leadership wanted CPS workers to learn SF ways of engaging families and use these at the same time they were investigating allegations of abuse and neglect. The reasoning was that if the allegations were substantiated, the workers would have to develop a cooperative relationship with the family in order to reduce risk and enhance family functioning. Upon beginning this process, we found that most CPS workers were uneasy with being shadowed and many thought SF procedures constituted a therapy that, even if they did learn its techniques, they would not have enough time to employ in their role. Rather than view these workers as resistant, we decided to view them as competent and, when invited to shadow, we would pay attention for and compliment what the worker was doing that was useful for the family. With encouragement from supervisors, a few workers began inviting each of us to shadow. On the way to a visit we would ask about the purpose of the visit (investigation or follow-up), what the worker hoped to accomplish, and what would have to happen in the visit for the worker to feel it had been useful for the family. When workers expressed concern for the safety of the children and the needs of the family, we complimented those commitments along with the seriousness and thoughtfulness with which the worker approached the visit. During the visit we observed for those things the worker did that were useful and any apparent immediate positive outcomes such as the caretaker's willingness to talk to the worker and share important information about the children and the family's situation. We complimented the worker on these early positive outcomes during the drive back to the office.

It was not long before we started having other workers come up to us when we visited county offices and ask us if we would care to shadow them that day. More and more they also asked us to participate in the interviews, thus opening up opportunities to model SF practices. Of course, we said yes to all these invitations. Supervisors also approached us and told us that our visits were improving morale and changing the atmosphere around the office. Realizing what an important impact complimenting was having in engaging workers and, in the process, starting to appreciate how difficult and demanding effective CPS practice is and how isolated and unappreciated many CPS workers feel, we hit upon a way to reinforce and amplify our complimenting. The day after one of us had made a visit to a county office, that person would write an e-mail to each of the workers shadowed. In addition to sending it to the worker, we also copied it to the worker's supervisor and the program manager. Here are two examples of the e-mails:

Kim,

I appreciated your willingness to let me shadow yesterday. It was enjoyable to bring such good news to a client. Congratulations on winning the exception for a monetary grant for your customer,[1] all the more so because that does not happen often. I can imagine you have to have all the key information organized and at your finger tips to make something like that happen. I was also impressed by your networking with the FINANCIAL AID

Worker. Interestingly, I happened to update Andrew[2] before leaving yesterday about our project (as I do every 6 to 8 weeks) and we ended up talking about the importance of such communication among workers in different programs within FIA. I thought your work was a good example of what he thinks is helpful to families and we talked about ways to encourage more of it. I imagine that you have ideas about how to do that too. He appreciates your work on this case.

Thanks, too, for all the insight about needed areas of service for teens and adult foster care homes where customers can have their children with them, and your thoughts about how to ask about customers' informal resources and what they have done about their situations before deciding on additional services. I was going over my notes this morning and can see that next time I'll have to ask to tape our conversation so I can transcribe it–because it was so full of good ideas! Your heart for the families and finding creative ways to handle situations without removing children if at all possible really came through. I learned a lot! See you next week. Peter

Jennifer,

I appreciate your taking me out on the case Monday. Your opener about "what do you want to do with this situation" to the grandmother really gave her the space to give her point of view and thinking about how to do what was best for her grandchildren and her daughter who she thinks is so heavily into drugs. The grandmother calling you "dear" by the end of our visit and telling her grandchildren to give you a hug should be on tape and made public because it runs so counter to the bias you hear sometimes about CPS workers. I'm sorry I was unable to go with you on the follow-up visit to Alice; I got caught up in trying to repair my recording equipment. I wonder if you found her. Anyway, thanks again. I learn something every time I go out with a worker and going out with you and seeing how you relate to people increases my appreciation for your skill and respect for families. Hope we can do it again! Peter

Complimenting begets gratitude and reciprocal complimenting. We often receive messages from workers like this one: "Thank you for your kind words. Looking forward to seeing you next week." Or, as a supervisor commented about one of our e-mails to a worker: "Bravissimo!!!! Is this another example of a kinder, gentler CPS?" These responses, of course, only led us to expand our complimenting to other participants in the organization. For example, after supervisors conducted case conferences with workers that we attended, we sent them e-mails. We did the same with the program manager and director after we observed staff meetings that each led. Our attempt was always to do reality-based complimenting of any strengths-based, solution-focused practice we observed. Just as with young Calvin, the process engaged most everyone and contributed to a milieu of confidence, hopefulness about positive client outcomes, and, generally, increased expectations for the work day's possibilities.

NOTES

1. Clients are called customers by FIA.
2. The county's FIA director.

TEACHING EXERCISES

For the first time, a series of articles on exercises and ideas for training in solution-focused brief therapy is presented. Included are openers, concept training, training on questions, crowd pleasers, and complimenting.

Openers

Lance Taylor

KEYWORDS. Solution-focused, training

Credit–This exercise is swiped from Insoo Kim Berg. In a workshop in Calgary some time ago, she asked people to get together with 4 or 5 of their neighbors and say something about question #1 below. It was a lovely icebreaker. Not much processing initiated by Insoo afterwards, as I remember, but I'm not sure about that.

Since I saw Insoo do this, I've cloned the other versions. The list is constantly growing because I entertain myself on the way to training sessions by trying to invent a new one to use that day. These also are quite nice for those ongoing training situations where we get to return to a group a few times. Then, they're not really icebreakers anymore but I find them to be powerful tone-setters. I recently got some feedback thanking me for my 'question of the month.'

1. What is something that has happened to you already today that is the kind of thing that makes life worth living?
2. When was a recent time you felt a lightness of spirit?
3. What is some small but precious accomplishment you have had lately?

Lance Taylor has a private practice in Cochrane, Alberta, Canada.
Address correspondence to: Lance Taylor, Box 619, Cochrane, AB Canada, T4C 1A7.

[Haworth co-indexing entry note]: "Openers." Taylor, Lance. Co-published simultaneously in *Journal of Family Psychotherapy* (The Haworth Press. Inc.) Vol. 16, No. 1/2, 2005, pp. 59-60; and: *Education and Training in Solution-Focused Brief Therapy* (ed: Thorana S. Nelson) The Haworth Press, Inc., 2005, pp. 59-60. Single or multiple copies of this article are available for a fee from The Haworth Document Delivery Service [1-800-HAWORTH, 9:00 a.m. - 5:00 p.m. (EST). E-mail address: docdelivery@haworthpress.com].

Available online at http://www.haworthpress.com/web/JFP
Digital Object Identifier: 10.1300/J085v16n01_12

4. What is something you have learned or enjoyed in the past hour (day/week/month/year)? What is something you do differently as a result of that learning?
5. When have you appreciated your connection with another person?
6. When have you done a piece of work that you were proud of? How did you do that?
7. What is something better about your work lately?
8. When has something touched your heart recently?
9. When have you felt effective recently? What personal strengths or resources did you call upon to do that?
10. In what way have you been feeling more effective in your work lately?
11. What is something that has restored your faith in people recently?
12. What is something that is going better in your life lately?
13. What is some positive development in your health lately?

The Name Game

Heather Fiske
Brenda Zalter

KEYWORDS. Brief therapy, solution-focused, training

Type of Audience: Students, workshop participants at any level, supervisees; groups

Group Size: This exercise can be done effectively with any number. In groups larger than 20, time constraints usually mean that participants must be divided into smaller groups.

Experience Level: Introductory to advanced

PURPOSE OF THE EXERCISE

- As a warm-up
- To introduce participants to one another
- To establish a positive, fun learning environment
- To begin working with compliments
- To set the stage for a solution-focused group message

Heather Fiske is a psychologist and has a private practice in Toronto, Ontario, Canada.

Brenda Zalter is affiliated with the Credit Valley Hospital, Mississauga, Ontario, Canada.

Address correspondence to: Heather Fiske, 35 Scarborough Road, Toronto, ON, Canada M4E 3M4 or Brenda Zalter, 35 Pirie Drive, Dundas, ON, Canada L9H 6X5.

[Haworth co-indexing entry note]: "The Name Game." Fiske, Heather, and Brenda Zalter. Co-published simultaneously in *Journal of Family Psychotherapy* (The Haworth Press, Inc.) Vol. 16, No. 1/2, 2005, pp. 61-62; and: *Education and Training in Solution-Focused Brief Therapy* (ed: Thorana S. Nelson) The Haworth Press, Inc., 2005, pp. 61-62. Single or multiple copies of this article are available for a fee from The Haworth Document Delivery Service [1-800-HAWORTH, 9:00 a.m. - 5:00 p.m. (EST). E-mail address: docdelivery@haworthpress.com].

Experiential Level of the Exercise (1-10): (Instructions aside) this exercise is a 10.

Time Frame for the Exercise, Debriefing: 5-15 minutes depending on the size of the group(s)

Instructions: Participants are asked to introduce themselves with:

- Their first names
- A positive adjective beginning with the first letter of their first names, e.g., "I'm Brenda, I'm bodacious." Often we suggest that the adjective should be something that makes them good at what they do, or helpful in working with a particular population, or that says something important about their personal style.

The instructor typically demonstrates by going first. One of us has set a personal challenge of coming up with a different adjective each time (please send lists of words beginning with "h"). When people are stuck for an appropriate adjective, the other participants are encouraged to come up with possibilities. A thesaurus or *The Book of Positive Qualities* may be consulted if available.

As a variation, participants may be asked to identify a symbol or object beginning with the first letter of their names.

RESOURCES

- Any thesaurus
- Downs, Jim (1996). *The book of positive qualities.* New York: Warner.

CLOSING COMMENTS

This exercise is extremely brief and a great way to begin a workshop or course. The instructor is encouraged to write down the names and adjectives. This "resource list" can then be utilized in a number of ways:

- As a memory tool for middle-aged instructors such as ourselves
- As a basis for encouraging participants to notice instances of these positive qualities in action throughout the course
- As a list of compliments to be used for the construction of a solution-focused group message

Moan, Moan, Moan

Rayya Ghul

KEYWORDS. Solution-focused, solution-focused thinking, training, workshop

EXERCISE IN PAIRS

Choose which partner will be the supervisor and which the supervisee. The supervisee should complain about something about work at length and in great detail for 5 minutes. The supervisor should not interrupt or say anything. Head nods, etc., are acceptable.

When the supervisee has finished complaining, the supervisor should take a short break and formulate a set of compliments for the supervisee based on what they have just heard and then deliver them to the supervisee.

Swap roles and do the exercise again the other way.

Rayya Ghul is a member of the Institute of Learning and Teaching, Lyminge, Kent, England.

Address correspondence to: Rayya Ghul, Allied Health Department, Canterbury Christ Church University College, Canterbury CT1 1QU, England.

[Haworth co-indexing entry note]: "Moan, Moan, Moan." Ghul, Rayya. Co-published simultaneously in *Journal of Family Psychotherapy* (The Haworth Press, Inc.) Vol. 16, No. 1/2, 2005, p. 63; and: *Education and Training in Solution-Focused Brief Therapy* (ed: Thorana S. Nelson) The Haworth Press, Inc., 2005, p. 63. Single or multiple copies of this article are available for a fee from The Haworth Document Delivery Service [1-800-HAWORTH, 9:00 a.m. - 5:00 p.m. (EST). E-mail address: docdelivery@haworthpress.com].

Digital Object Identifier: 10.1300/J085v16n01_14

Complaining Exercise

Josée Lamarre

KEYWORDS. Therapy skills, solution-focused, training

This is a good exercise for developing listening skills. I found it on the SFT-List a couple of years ago and since then, I have been using it very often with a lot of success. People love to complain and realize that if they settle their mind to listen to the positive in the complaints, they can discover them.

This exercise is done in pairs, one playing the therapist and the other, the client. The client complains to the therapist for about five minutes and the therapist does nothing but listen attentively and watch non-verbal gestures. The clients may use the opportunity to complain about some personal issue. Then the therapist takes a few minutes to construct a set of compliments for the client based on what they have just heard and delivers it to the client. The compliment must be sincere and pertinent. Examples include, "Wow, you are really a persistent person!" "What dedication to your son!"

After the exercise, each person is asked to tell the group about the highlights of the exercise for them in one or two sentences.

Josée Lamarre is affiliated with the *Centre de psychothérapie stratégique*, Montréal, Quebec, Canada.

Address correspondence to: Josée Lamarre, 2160 Boul Perrot, Notre-Dame De L'ile, Perrot, Quebec J7V 8P4, Canada.

[Haworth co-indexing entry note]: "Complaining Exercise." Lamarre, Josée. Co-published simultaneously in *Journal of Family Psychotherapy* (The Haworth Press, Inc.) Vol. 16, No. 1/2, 2005, pp. 65-66; and: *Education and Training in Solution-Focused Brief Therapy* (ed: Thorana S. Nelson) The Haworth Press, Inc., 2005, pp. 65-66. Single or multiple copies of this article are available for a fee from The Haworth Document Service [1-800-HAWORTH, 9:00 a.m. - 5:00 p.m. (EST). E-mail address: docdelivery@haworthpress.com].

Digital Object Identifier: 10.1300/J085v16n01_15

The Clients:

> It was amazing. I felt completely understood because of the compliments.

> I was amazed how much of my personality the other person got just from me complaining.

The Therapists:

> Listening to the complaining in order to make compliments really forced me to listen attentively so as to have an experience of being properly listened to.

> It is amazing how much we must miss because we usually turn off when people complain.

> The compliments sort of forced me to have new ideas about what I could do.

Eat Just One Raisin

Eric E. McCollum

KEYWORDS. Solution-focused brief therapy, mindfulness

According to Steve de Shazer, one of the lessons therapists can learn from the philosopher Ludwig Wittgenstein is: "Don't think, but observe." Steve's remark brought me up short the first time I heard it. After years of learning more and more elaborate and compelling theories about why people did what they did, and how therapy could help them not do it anymore, I was being invited, it seemed, into a desolate land of flat and colorless description. Fragments of old hospital admission notes sprang to mind: "Patient was oriented X3, with evidence of slowed thinking and depressive affect." What help, I wondered, could come from observations such as these?

Then I remembered an exercise I first did at a workshop led by Jon Kabat-Zinn and Saki Santorelli–developers of Mindfulness-Based Stress Reduction (Kabat-Zinn, 1990). At the beginning of the workshop, Jon and Saki passed around raisins and then invited us to suspend our preconceptions of "raisin" and instead use our 5 senses to gather as much information as possible about the small, wrinkled objects in our hands. My raisin felt stiff and gritty. It smelled slightly sweet and, although I would have said a raisin was "brown"

Eric E. McCollum is affiliated with Virginia Tech University, Falls Church, VA.

Address correspondence to: Eric E. McCollum, Marriage and Family Therapy Program, Virginia Tech University, 7054 Haycock Road, Falls Church, VA 22043.

[Haworth co-indexing entry note]: "Eat Just One Raisin." McCollum, Eric E. Co-published simultaneously in *Journal of Family Psychotherapy* (The Haworth Press, Inc.) Vol. 16, No. 1/2, 2005, pp. 67-69; and: *Education and Training in Solution-Focused Brief Therapy* (ed: Thorana S. Nelson) The Haworth Press, Inc., 2005, pp. 67-69. Single or multiple copies of this article are available for a fee from The Haworth Document Service [1-800-HAWORTH, 9:00 a.m. - 5:00 p.m. (EST). E-mail address: docdelivery@haworthpress.com].

Available online at http://www.haworthpress.com/web/JFP
Digital Object Identifier: 10.1300/J085v16n01_16

before doing this exercise, careful observation revealed a rainbow of color—from dark mahogany shadows to shiny white highlights.

After a few moments of observation, we put a single raisin in our mouths, feeling the texture change as the warmth of our tongues softened the raisin's skin. Then one bite, and an explosion of flavor. A second bite. More flavor. Chewing slowly, and feeling the intricate dance of tongue, teeth and jaws, we watched the initial burst of flavor fade until the raisin, reduced to pulp, was finally swallowed. By putting aside the concept of "raisin," and simply observing the thing itself, a previously unnoticed world emerged.

I use this exercise to illustrate the power of observation when training therapists in solution-focused approaches. We have been taught that observation is a merely passive activity, the prelude to the "real work" of therapy. But observation is an intervention and it is more powerful than we might ever guess. If we bring the same level of mindful attention to clients' visions of the future without the problem to their recollections of times the problem didn't occur, to their musings about what would tell them a miracle had happened, that we bring to eating just one raisin, new worlds will open for them. And for us.

HOW TO DO THE RAISIN EXERCISE

I start with individual-serving-sized boxes of raisins and give a box to each participant. I ask them not to open the box until I tell them to. I try to use neutral words (e.g., "object" instead of "box" or "raisin") to help participants step away from their reactions to a verbal label and the associations to that label and instead just encounter the object itself. Following is an example of the instructions I typically give, based generally on Kabat-Zinn, 1990. Allow plenty of time between each instruction for the participants to deepen their experience. I usually ask for feedback throughout the exercise but it is also possible to wait until the end for people to describe their experience. The instructions:

> Begin by just using your 5 senses to explore the object in your hand [the box]. What does it feel like in your hand? What does it sound like? What colors are on it? What does it smell like? Taste it if you want. What does it taste like? What does it feel like when you taste it? Using just your 5 senses, what else do you notice about this object?

> Inside the square object you are holding are several other small objects [raisins]. Take one out. Using all your senses except taste, what can you discover about this object? What color is it? Is it just one color? How does it feel? How does it smell? Does it make a sound? What else do you notice?

Now put the object in your mouth. Don't bite or chew, just experience what it feels like in your mouth. What taste does it have? What texture? Do the texture and taste change the longer it is in your mouth? Does it feel different in different parts of your mouth?

Now take just one bite. What do you notice now? Keep paying attention to the taste and texture. Take another bite. Now another. What do you notice? Chew the object.

Now, while paying attention to your tongue, teeth and mouth, swallow the object. What do you notice about chewing and swallowing? What tastes and textures are left in your mouth after you swallow?

REFERENCE

Kabat-Zinn, J. (1990). *Full-catastrophe living: Using the wisdom of your body and mind to face stress, pain and illness.* New York: Dell Publishing.

Inside and Outside

Steve de Shazer

KEYWORDS. Solution-focused brief therapy, training exercise

Groups of six are set up with one person role-playing a client and one person serving as an observer. The other four are to role-play being one therapist. They do this by taking turns asking one question each after the first question. Each subsequent question must be related, in some way, to the previous response/answer. The observer's task is to keep track of how the therapist's questions are related to the previous response/answer. Furthermore, they are to watch for differences between Part One and Part Two. (Part Two can either be explained now or at the end of Part One.)

Part One: The first question, which is the traditional SFBT first question to the client is, "What needs to happen here–in our work together–so that you know that coming here has been worth it to you?" Each of the 4 questioners gets two or three turns to ask questions, depending on how much time is available.

Part Two: "Now all of you, except for the observer, need to pretend that round one did not happen. With the same observer and client, try this substitute first question: 'What needs to happen here–in our work together–so that your best friend knows that your coming here has been worth it to you, not a

Steve de Shazer is affiliated with the Brief Family Therapy Center, Milwaukee, WI.
Address correspondence to: Steve de Shazer, 1907 Wauwatosa Avenue, Milwaukee, WI 53213.

[Haworth co-indexing entry note]: "Inside and Outside." de Shazer, Steve. Co-published simultaneously in *Journal of Family Psychotherapy* (The Haworth Press, Inc.) Vol. 16, No. 1/2, 2005, pp. 71-72; and: *Education and Training in Solution-Focused Brief Therapy* (ed: Thorana S. Nelson) The Haworth Press, Inc., 2005, pp. 71-72. Single or multiple copies of this article are available for a fee from The Haworth Document Delivery Service [1-800-HAWORTH, 9:00 a.m. - 5:00 p.m. (EST). E-mail address: docdelivery@haworthpress.com].

waste of time for you?'" Again, each of the four questioners gets two or three turns to ask questions.

DISCUSSION

Taking each group in turn:

1. Begin by asking the observer from one of the groups to compare round one with round two, beginning with anything he/she observed and then to talk about how the therapist's questions were related to the client's responses/answers.
2. Next, ask the client to make comparisons between round one and two. Focus on how they helped the therapist to ask useful questions.
3. Ask the people playing the therapist what they learned from the exercise. Then ask for a comparison (if it does not happen spontaneously). Focus on how the client helped them ask useful questions.
4. Then the next group, then the next, and the next, etc.

Parts One and Two can be reversed.

Pathologies to Descriptions: Moving from Problem to Solution DSM (Diagnostic Solution Method)

Thorana S. Nelson

KEYWORDS. Solution-focused training, diagnoses, problem talk

Audience: Beginners, often master's level students. Useful as an exercise in an assessment class where the DSM is taught or with groups where the DSM is used. Can be used with experienced clinicians in helping them move from pathologizing to solution descriptions. The exercise assumes that some basic foundational ideas of SFBT have been introduced to the participants.

Purpose: To help those who typically think in terms of diagnoses, deficits, dysfunction, and pathology to begin to think in solution-building terms related to "difficult" issues and diagnoses. People begin to experience how solutions do not need to be related to problems.

Instructions: Divide the participants into groups of four or five. They will be taking turns as the "client," the "therapist" or "interviewer," and observers. Each person will take on the "role" of a diagnosis in the current DSM, including the "V" codes–so-called "relational" diagnoses. The group should be told that they may each choose their own diagnoses, but that it will be most useful if a variety of

---

Thorana S. Nelson is affiliated with Utah State University, Logan, UT.

Address correspondence to: Thorana S. Nelson, 2700 Old Main Hill, Utah State University, Logan, UT 84325.

[Haworth co-indexing entry note]: "Pathologies to Descriptions: Moving from Problem to Solution DSM (Diagnostic Solution Method)." Nelson, Thorana S. Co-published simultaneously in *Journal of Family Psychotherapy* (The Haworth Press, Inc.) Vol. 16, No. 1/2, 2005, pp. 73-74; and: *Education and Training in Solution-Focused Brief Therapy* (ed: Thorana S. Nelson) The Haworth Press, Inc., 2005, pp. 73-74. Single or multiple copies of this article are available for a fee from The Haworth Document Delivery Service [1-800-HAWORTH, 9:00 a.m. - 5:00 p.m. (EST). E-mail address: docdelivery@haworthpress.com].

73

Axis I and Axis II codes are used. Facilitators can decide how long each part should take.

Part I: The "clients" choose a diagnosis and read through the descriptors for that disorder (several copies of the DSM are needed for this exercise). The "therapists" interview the clients about why they are in therapy and the client responds with descriptions from the DSM, effects of the diagnosis or disorder in the family, and complaints about the difficulties they face with this disorder or diagnosis, including relationships with family, friends, coworkers, and professional helpers. The therapists ask questions related to the problem and its details. This will be somewhat familiar to most of the participants.

Part II: After the clients are interviewed, the "role" is passed to another person and yet another in each group takes on the task as interviewer. During this round, the therapists ask the clients about other aspects of their life that might not be related to the problem, but that often are assessed: employment, school, relationships, etc.

Part III: The roles are passed once again and, this time, the therapists ask about how those aspects that are not related to the problem serve as strengths and supports for the client. In this round, the tone of the interviewing should move from general strengths and supports to specific strengths and supports that affect the problem or that are present when the problem is not present or is not as problematic.

Part IV: The roles are passed once again. In this part, the interviewers help the clients develop goals using the Miracle Question or other solution-building practices. It may help to post the basic formats of the MQ, scaling, and exception questions on a chart for those who are not familiar with it.

Part V: In this part, after passing the roles to the next people, the interviewers may choose to ask the Miracle Question, exception questions, or scaling questions to help the client describe ways and times and supports that move from the problem descriptions of the DSM to non-problem, exceptions, coping-times, small movements, and other descriptions related to their goals. All questions must be built on the clients' previous answers and must be related to the goals.

Debriefing: Participants are invited to debrief in their small groups to discuss their experiences as therapists, clients, and observers. Groups are then invited to report to the larger group for general discussion. As questions are raised about concerns of having the conversation move to non-problem and solution-building talk, group members are invited to respond from their own experiences.

Variations: This exercise also can be conducted with several "clients" as family members, coworkers, or other natural systems that may be seen in therapy. It can be particularly useful when participants work in agencies where SFBT is not familiar and the participants wish to learn about how to work with others in those agencies using solution-building ideas. In those cases, the "clients" include coworkers, consultants, administrators, etc.

The Disease Concept and SFT: Difference in Action

Kathryn C. Shafer

KEYWORDS. Solution-focused, training, alcohol, addictions, substance abuse, disease model

TYPE OF AUDIENCE

- Students, workshop participants at any level, supervisees
- Clients in individual, group, family, or couple treatment

Group Size: Minimum 5 participants.

Experience Level: Introductory to advanced; no experience with solution-focused ideas or applications is necessary. Some experience with substance abuse treatment and the disease concept preferred.

PURPOSE OF THE EXERCISE

- As a warm-up
- To begin recognizing the difference between problem-focused and solution-focused methods in practice

---

Kathryn C. Shafer is affiliated with the University of South Florida, Tampa, FL.

Address correspondence to: Kathryn C. Shafer, 116 Ocean Pines Terrace, Jupiter, FL 33477.

[Haworth co-indexing entry note]: "The Disease Concept and SFT: Difference in Action." Shafer, Kathryn C. Co-published simultaneously in *Journal of Family Psychotherapy* (The Haworth Press, Inc.) Vol. 16, No. 1/2, 2005, pp. 75-78; and: *Education and Training in Solution-Focused Brief Therapy* (ed: Thorana S. Nelson) The Haworth Press, Inc., 2005, pp. 75-78. Single or multiple copies of this article are available for a fee from The Haworth Document Delivery Service [1-800-HAWORTH, 9:00 a.m. - 5:00 p.m. (EST). E-mail address: docdelivery@haworthpress.com].

Available online at http://www.haworthpress.com/web/JFP
Digital Object Identifier: 10.1300/J085v16n01_19

- To recognize SFT methods in a group learning environment
- To obtain a range of group interactions and input
- To introduce solution building based on clients' responses
- To practice solution building in a variety of age groups
- To practice developing a picture of a more positive future
- To enhance "getting out of the box" (this exercise is literally a "warm-up"; it gets people moving, thinking, talking, often laughing and connecting as well. The learning process increases when thinking is challenged, and flows more easily. Participants are more engaged when they move their bodies and interact with each other.)
- As learning tool, to evaluate progress and change in clients' responses
- To involve all training participants
- To demonstrate how solution-focused methods can be adapted and immediately applied to a variety of practice settings.

Experiential Level of the Exercise (1-10): Instructions aside, this exercise is a 10.

Time Frame for the Exercise, Debriefing: Time depends on the size and experience level of the group; knowledge, attitudes, and beliefs about the disease concept of addiction; what they've heard about SFT; the number of questions asked; and how much furniture has to be moved. As an introductory exercise, it can be completed in as little as 15 minutes; 20-30 minutes is more typical.

INSTRUCTIONS

Ask participants to break into groups (or number people off). Once the groups are established, have someone volunteer to be "the client." When this person is identified, have the client leave the room. When the client leaves the room, tell the remaining participants that when the client comes back in, they are the therapists. As such, they will take turns asking questions or making statements based on the disease model of addiction. Such questions may include, "how many meetings have you gone to," "you need to go to ninety meetings in ninety days," "you are in denial of your disease," "are you ready to make a commitment to abstinence," etc., and to act like they know all the answers, not the client.

You (the trainer) go out and greet the clients and give them a case to role play with the group of therapists they are returning to. Then bring the clients back into the room and the interaction begins. Once this has gone on for about 5 minutes (you can usually feel the tension in the room), ask the clients to share with the larger group how they feel about the therapists they are talking to. This brings up lively discussion and the reactions from the client include, "Why bother?" "I'm not in denial" even to the point where some say "I'm leaving."

After the discussion, the therapists are then asked how they feel about the interaction. This is usually quite difficult for them, but then a discussion takes place on how a therapist with this mindset, based on the *clients' responses*, would document what took place. The language used to describe this type of interaction often includes: the client is "in denial," "resistant," "unable to accept the disease concept," "hasn't reached bottom yet," "is defiant," etc. More discussion then takes place about how this often can reflect the attitudes of the therapist, not accurate descriptions of the mindsets of clients. A discussion then ensues on how this problem-focused approach labels the client for failing to agree or accept the lead of the therapist. Discussion then can take place of the culture of the treatment center: the therapist, treatment center, etc., is the authority. The client will not succeed or may fail (not surrender to the disease) unless they do what the authority states (complete abstinence, 90 meetings in 90 days, etc.).

At this point, the trainees may need to let out a long, relaxing exhale because a lively discussion about many things has just taken place. Then you ask the clients to stand up and go out of the room for the second half of the exercise. You (the trainer) then go back into the room and tell the therapists that this time they are to give the clients their undivided attention. Then, one by one, each therapist takes a turn asking SFT questions, based on the *client's responses*.

The first question they will ask is: *What do you want?*–and stay there. This part of the exercise can be challenging, especially for the seasoned therapist who already has in her/his head what the next question will be–*before the client answers the question.* Pacing is discussed and how a theme they might use to integrate SFT might be: before you make up your mind, open it–getting out of the box and into many possible solutions the client has depending on what they want.

You, the trainer, in both phases of the experiential exercise can walk around and assist the therapists and clients by offering questions and answers they might give. This will help generate the activity in the role plays. Discussions then take place on how the client feels with this interaction and how it would be written up using SFT language:

- Client wants the wife/husband/family to stop focusing on the drinking/substance abuse.
- Client is considering attending AA meetings to learn more about how his or her drinking is affecting their life.
- Client is willing to cut down on drinking this week (state how much).

- Client states he/she will try different ways to respond to the family when they focus on his/or her drinking, such as _____.
- The very first small step the client is willing to try to cut down the drinking is _____.

Once the exercise is over, thank everyone and have them return to their seats. During the rest of this exercise, time is spent exploring what was helpful and useful. Some time also is spent on how this exercise might make a difference with the next substance abuse client the participants have in terms of the language they will use, and how they may document the interaction.

Handouts: None specific to the exercise; a handout would include samples of SFT questions.

CLOSING COMMENTS

Used early in the training process, this exercise sets a tone for participants' learning to challenge their knowledge, attitudes, and beliefs about substance abusers and treatment philosophy–instantly. The exercise elicits the skeptic, the judge, is active, and is participatory–it opens their minds and views about addiction treatment in an open supportive forum. This exercise promotes group interaction and encourages exchange of concepts and ideas.

For the trainer, this experience of hearing and seeing how mindsets of therapists are challenged and put into action is exciting. It opens the door to influencing change in the practice of addiction treatment–offering many solutions and possibilities for the client.

Listening and Constructing with Timeouts

Peter DeJong

KEYWORDS. Co-constructing meaning, learner participation, solution-focused connecting, solution-focused listening, teaching exercise

When observing therapy sessions, experienced solution-focused practitioners believe they can pick out practitioners who are being solution-focused. Often they will speak about whether those being observed are "doing it" or not. In my opinion, the core, non-negotiable "it" of solution-focused therapy (SFT) is the ability of practitioners to listen for hints of possibility and then formulate responses–especially questions–that connect to these hints, regularly incorporating clients' words into their responses. The hints that practitioners listen for and connect to are client meanings about what clients might want along with related exceptions, personal strengths, and outside resources. Formulating questions about these hints invites clients into conversations that co-construct new meanings about more satisfying futures and ways to make these happen that are grounded in clients' capacities and resources.

Learning how to listen and co-construct in SF ways is very challenging! Students and practitioners new to SFT often will see an opportunity to ask the miracle question, give a compliment, or ask an exception question, but they

Peter DeJong is affiliated with Calvin College, Grand Rapids, MI.

Address correspondence to: Peter DeJong, Sociology and Social Work, Calvin College, 3201 Burton SE, Grand Rapids, MI 49546.

[Haworth co-indexing entry note]: "Listening and Constructing with Timeouts." DeJong, Peter. Co-published simultaneously in *Journal of Family Psychotherapy* (The Haworth Press, Inc.) Vol. 16, No. 1/2, 2005, pp. 79-82; and: *Education and Training in Solution-Focused Brief Therapy* (ed: Thorana S. Nelson) The Haworth Press, Inc., 2005, pp. 79-82. Single or multiple copies of this article are available for a fee from The Haworth Document Delivery Service [1-800-HAWORTH, 9:00 a.m. - 5:00 p.m. (EST). E-mail address: docdelivery@haworthpress.com].

Available online at http://www.haworthpress.com/web/JFP
Digital Object Identifier: 10.1300/J085v16n01_20

79

struggle with how to continue the co-construction process around a given hint of possibility. Their tendency is to ask one or two questions, "get stuck," and then either move to another area of SF conversation or revert to old, non-SF ways of conversing. When asked what would be useful to them, these new learners say they need more ideas about how to sustain the conversation. One way to get more ideas is to observe an experienced practitioner on tape or in person and then discuss what the practitioner is doing and how. This is useful but it does not actively involve the instructor's audience. The exercise described below goes one step further by inviting new learners into the process of formulating the next SF response. It calls for an instructor or workshop leader experienced in SFT to do a live interview, periodically taking "time outs" to ask new learners about evolving client meanings, what to ask next, and how to word subsequent questions.

Type of audience: University classes or workshop audiences.

Group size: 0 through 50 learners.

Experience level: From advanced beginners (those who have at least read about and seen a videotape of SFT) to more experienced SF practitioners who want to improve their skills.

Purpose: To demonstrate SF listening and responding while drawing on learners' ideas for sustaining SF co-construction.

Experiential level: 50% instructor talk and demonstration; 50% audience participation.

Time frame: 30-75 minutes; 10-15 minutes debriefing.

INSTRUCTIONS

1. Focus on a particular area of SF conversation such as getting started with an involuntary client, conducting a miracle-question conversation, asking "what's better," or co-constructing a sense of client competence.
2. Before conducting the exercise with beginning learners, make sure they have had a basic introduction to the area of conversation you will address. This can be done in a university setting by assigning reading and viewing a demonstration video before class. In a workshop setting, the leader can provide the introduction before conducting the exercise.
3. Arrange for a guest or audience participant to be a client and play her- or himself or a client with whom she or he is familiar. Brief that person as necessary about the area of SF conversation to be addressed.
4. Brief the audience about the client's situation and indicate the area of SF conversation you will demonstrate.
5. Before beginning the interview, instruct learners that they are going to assist you in conducting the conversation with the client. You will begin

the interview and their task is to write down the client's emerging meanings in the client's words. Repeat what you are inviting the client to co-construct with you; for example, a miracle picture, and what they should be listening for. They should write down key words and phrases that the client uses to express elements of their miracle. Explain that every 2 to 4 minutes you will take a time out from the interview to consult with the audience about the emerging client meanings and how to connect to them in solution-focused ways.

6. Before beginning the interview, also ask for 2 or 3 volunteers to notice and write down the ways in which you (with the audience's input) make SF connections and to star those that seem most useful. Tell everyone you will return to the observers' findings after the interview is completed.

7. Begin the interview. Take the first timeout and ask the audience for the client meanings that have emerged so far. Be sure to get the client's words for the meanings and have a volunteer record them on a flip chart or overhead so everyone can see them. Then ask for ideas for how you can connect to the meanings, amplify them, and continue the co-construction process. Expect that most of the ideas expressed will be solution-focused, but if they happen to be problem-focused or otherwise not useful, point that out and ask what might be done instead. As ideas emerge, shape them by asking how the useful idea could be formed into a question or a response that incorporates the client's words. Continue interviewing, taking timeouts, recording client meanings, and getting the audience's input for the time available.

8. In the debriefing, ask the observers for the "SF connectors" they noticed and which seemed most useful. After the observers have had a chance, ask the audience for additional SF connectors they might have noticed. Have a volunteer record these on a flip chart or overhead.

Lists of questions: Retain the list of SF connectors generated. If you wish, after completing the exercise, you can go to a similar exercise where you break the audience into pairs with one person as an interviewer and the other a client. Each pair can conduct a SF conversation similar to the one just demonstrated using the connectors generated earlier and still up on the overhead. Remind interviewers to listen for and write down the words for emerging client meanings as they interview and then draw on their list of SF connectors to formulate the next question.

Handouts and resources for follow-up: Have the list of SF connectors copied and distributed to participants for later use.

Closing remarks: I have conducted this exercise in classroom and workshop settings. Learners tell me they prefer a live to a videotape demonstration and that they find a demonstration with timeouts more useful than one without. They appreciate the timeouts because they allow the participants to incorporate their input into the interview and to hear what others are thinking as the interview unfolds. I think the exercise also models what experienced SF practitioners listen for and the critical thinking processes they employ in order to formulate the next SF question or response. The exercise can take pressure off less experienced or less confident presenters because the timeouts allow the presenter to draw on useful ideas from the audience participants. This exercise has become my preferred way of introducing the different areas of SF conversation and demonstrating the usefulness of SF co-construction in different interviewing situations. Once an audience has participated in this exercise and developed a clearer sense of what to listen for and has generated its own list of SF connectors, they are more able and willing to practice on their own in small groups or pairs.

Ever Appreciating Circles

Paul Hackett

KEYWORDS. Appreciation, the ripple effect, learning by doing, training

Group size: This exercise is designed to be used with any group size.

Experience level: All levels from the novice to the experienced can be included in this exercise.

Purpose of exercise: The purpose of the exercise is simply to allow people to consider the competencies in their lives and others' that are 'hiding in the light'–those things that are right under our noses that we take for granted and possibly under value.

Experiential level of exercise: The exercise is designed to allow people to notice outside of training situations the minutiae of competencies within their daily lives. The presenter needs to be clear as to the instructions given (see below) and the way of noticing that is expected.

Time frame: The optimum time to undertake this exercise is at the end of the day's training–in effect a homework assignment. Dependent on the trainer, the exercise can either be shared verbally or written instructions given. If the training is over several days/weeks it may be useful to allow the participants a chance to appreciate the circles more and ask in subsequent training what they have noticed.

Paul Hackett is a social worker in Loughborough, Leics, England.
Address correspondence to: Paul Hackett, c/o 88 Tuckers Road, Loughborough, Leics, LE11 2PJ, England.

[Haworth co-indexing entry note]: "Ever Appreciating Circles." Hackett, Paul. Co-published simultaneously in *Journal of Family Psychotherapy* (The Haworth Press, Inc.) Vol. 16, No. 1/2, 2005, pp. 83-84; and: *Education and Training in Solution-Focused Brief Therapy* (ed: Thorana S. Nelson) The Haworth Press, Inc., 2005, pp. 83-84. Single or multiple copies of this article are available for a fee from The Haworth Document Delivery Service [1-800-HAWORTH, 9:00 a.m. - 5:00 p.m. (EST). E-mail address: docdelivery@ haworthpress.com].

Digital Object Identifier: 10.1300/J085v16n01_21

Instructions: We all need confirmation that our lives and actions are worthwhile. Without confirmation, behaviors either ossify or become stagnated. Why should you go the extra mile if no one sees you in your running shoes? Indeed those people who succeed simply for themselves usually require others to hear and confirm this message. Chris Iveson of the Brief Therapy Practice (London, UK) told a story once about being in traffic where each good deed–letting someone in, courtesy, allowing space for learner drivers–ripples through the city.

What we suggest is that at the end of training today, tomorrow or whenever it makes most sense, begin the day with an appreciative eye. Look for the things people do that you appreciate, particularly those hidden right in front of you. When you see them, acknowledge them verbally or nonverbally. Then pay attention over the next day/couple of days to any evidence of the appreciative circle rippling back to you. Keep going!

SUGGESTED QUESTIONS

1. What do you notice at home that you appreciate?
2. What do you notice about the way your colleagues/friends that you most appreciate?
3. Without people saying anything, in what ways do they make your day?
4. What effect does it have on you?
5. When you tell them what you appreciate about them, what difference do you notice to them physically, verbally? Do they smile more?
6. When you notice the appreciative circle rippling back, what difference does it make to you?

Success and Failure

Sue Young

KEYWORDS. Solution-focused, training, success, strengths

Type of audience: I have used this exercise with teachers, career advisers, school mentors, peer mentors, and teaching assistants. It's become a favorite of mine!

Group size: From 10 to 70 so far!

Experience level: Raising awareness, initial training

Purpose of the exercise: To get the point across that change is more likely to happen when you are enabling the client to focus on success and strengths rather than on failings and weaknesses.

Experiential level of the exercise: 8–mainly experiential (I can't help ramming the point home!)

Time frame for the exercise: 20 to 30 minutes, including debriefing

Instructions (pre and post): Ask the question (slowly!):

> I want you to think of a time you succeeded. Pick something like when you passed your driving test, did well in an exam, got a job you particularly wanted, etc. . . . First of all, think of the immediate feelings that accompanied the success, and secondly, what sort of self talk did those feelings provoke.

Sue Young is affiliated with the General Teaching Council for England, North Ferriby, East Yorkshire, England.

Address correspondence to: Sue Young, The Little House, 22 Humber Road, North Ferriby, East Yorkshire, HU14 3DW, England.

[Haworth co-indexing entry note]: "Success and Failure." Young, Sue. Co-published simultaneously in *Journal of Family Psychotherapy* (The Haworth Press, Inc.) Vol. 16, No. 1/2, 2005, pp. 85-86; and: *Education and Training in Solution-Focused Brief Therapy* (ed: Thorana S. Nelson) The Haworth Press, Inc., 2005, pp. 85-86. Single or multiple copies of this article are available for a fee from The Haworth Document Delivery Service [1-800-HAWORTH, 9:00 a.m. - 5:00 p.m. (EST). E-mail address: docdelivery@ haworthpress.com].

Digital Object Identifier: 10.1300/J085v16n01_22

> In twos, tell each other, and find out these things from each other, two
> minutes each way–I'll call out when it is time to swap over.

Then, get them to feed back either from what they said themselves or what
they heard from their partners, to a flip chart. You will get feelings of happy,
excited, exhilarated, proud, greater self-esteem, etc., and (maybe) nervous.
For self-talk you will get things like, "I knew I could do it," "I've really done
well," "I'm clever," "What's next? I can do anything now!" "Hard work pays
off," etc. No comments are necessary.

Then ask them to

> Think of a time you failed–pick something small and contained like
> when you didn't pass your driving test, didn't get that job you wanted, or
> didn't pass that exam–Think of the immediate feelings and the self-talk
> that accompanied them–immediate is important–anyone can be philo-
> sophical in the long run! In twos, one minute each way.

Feedback to flip chart–feelings you will get are bitter, unhappy, frustrated,
embarrassed, etc., and self-talk like, "I wonder who will know about this,"
"I'm rubbish at this," "I'm not doing that again, I didn't want it anyway," etc.
You may also get things like, "I will work harder next time."

Ask them to compare the two flip chart sheets. The lesson is that, in essence, when we succeed, we are more optimistic and confident of our own
competence. We reinforce a mindset that is open to the future and to continuing change, whereas failure makes us defensive and less open to the future and
to change. This is pretty obvious from the feedback sheets.

So, for example, if a parent wants help with a child who is 'out of control,' it
is more helpful to them to call to mind times when the child has behaved well
and how they managed that, rather than when they failed to control the child's
behavior.

Closing comments: Therefore, to promote change, we need to put clients
into the mindset that goes with success rather than failure. That way, we make
them more open to change and optimism about the future. Usually I add something like, "Everyone in this room is relatively successful, but many of our clients (in my case pupils, parents) are faced with failure everyday. One of the
ways we can help is by finding and recognizing their successes, however
small, so that they can envisage succeeding and resolving their problems in the
future, using their existing skills."

This exercise has always gone well for me and introduces solution-focused
ideas perfectly. It counteracts the initial feelings that some participants in the
workshops may have that we must find out and point out to clients what they
are doing wrong before they can be helped to succeed.

Curious Questioning

Lance Taylor

KEYWORDS. Solution-focused, training, questions, interviewing

Credits: I learned the basic version of this exercise from Lisa Berndt.

Participants talk in pairs. The interviewee thinks of a trivial, boring subject from daily living. The interviewer asks curious questions about that subject for 5 minutes. Switch roles and go for another 5 minutes.

The first version can take the form of 'idle' curiosity. It is good training in stepping out of the expert position, listening, and amplifying a small experience by simply eliciting detail. Subsequent repetitions can be more 'guided' curiosity, starting with being selective about *what* to be curious about, e.g., positive events, goals, or exceptions. Then, curiosity can be guided by *how* to be curious following some themes such as agency, difference, and next steps that amplify solutions. To use the second and third levels of the exercise, have people pick subjects such as 'something that is better about my therapy (my life, my relationship, etc.) lately.'

Follow-up discussion can focus on what participants notice about how this posture of interviewing affects the interviewer, the interviewee, and the subject of the discussion.

Lance Taylor has a private practice in Cochrane, Alberta, Canada.

Address correspondence to: Lance Taylor, Box 619, Cochrane, AB, Canada T4C 1A7.

[Haworth co-indexing entry note]: "Curious Questioning." Taylor, Lance. Co-published simultaneously in *Journal of Family Psychotherapy* (The Haworth Press, Inc.) Vol. 16, No. 1/2, 2005, p. 87; and: *Education and Training in Solution-Focused Brief Therapy* (ed: Thorana S. Nelson) The Haworth Press, Inc., 2005, p. 87. Single or multiple copies of this article are available for a fee from The Haworth Document Delivery Service [1-800-HAWORTH, 9:00 a.m. - 5:00 p.m. (EST). E-mail address: docdelivery@haworthpress.com].

Available online at http://www.haworthpress.com/web/JFP
Digital Object Identifier: 10.1300/J085v16n01_23

Harry's Magic Square

Harry Korman

KEYWORDS. Solution-focused brief therapy, miracle question

Take a piece of A4 [letter] paper and fold it into quarters and then unfold it. Write on each box consecutively, 'problem,' 'miracle,' 'scale,' and 're-sources.'

In the 'problem' box, write down the descriptions of the problem in the client's (or family's) own words.

In the 'miracle' box, write down the answers to the miracle question or other 'preferred future' questions in their own words.

In the 'scale' box, write down the answers to the scaling question/s and mark where they are now.

In the 'resources' box, write down any qualities, strengths, internal and external resources that the client/s have mentioned in answers to the other questions. Add a couple of your own that you can back up.

When the paper is full (assuming you don't have larger than normal handwriting!), take the break. If you need more than one paper you probably have too much information. If there is nothing in any of the boxes (other than 'problem') you have too little.

Harry Korman is affiliated with SIKT, Malmö, Sweden.

Address correspondence to: Harry Korman, Shabersjoby, 23392 Ivedala, Sweden.

Harry gratefully acknowledges help for this exercise to his friend, Rayya Ghul.

[Haworth co-indexing entry note]: "Harry's Magic Square." Korman, Harry. Co-published simulta-neously in *Journal of Family Psychotherapy* (The Haworth Press, Inc.) Vol. 16, No. 1/2, 2005, pp. 89-90; and: *Education and Training in Solution-Focused Brief Therapy* (ed: Thorana S. Nelson) The Haworth Press, Inc., 2005, pp. 89-90. Single or multiple copies of this article are available for a fee from The Haworth Document Delivery Service [1-800-HAWORTH, 9:00 a.m. - 5:00 p.m. (EST). E-mail address: docdelivery@ haworthpress.com].

Digital Object Identifier: 10.1300/J085v16n01_24

During the break, collect your information. You need a statement you can feed back saying:

- Their problem in their own words ('problem' box) and expressing sympathy for this difficult and serious problem and the hard work that lies ahead in order to solve it.
- You then express some admiration for the good things they want to have happen in their life ('miracle' box) and their good sense and realism for wanting exactly these things.
- Tell them how impressed you are by their having already started with (things between 0 and their point on scale) and at their resources.

Then bridge with something like: "So because of all this I/we have this idea that might/could be useful."

- *If they know how they did it*, tell them to do more of it.
- *If you know they don't know how they did it,* tell them they must be doing something right and ask them to try and figure out what that is till you see them the next time ("pay attention to whenever good things happen and you make them happen/what makes them happen").
- *If you are very confused,* tell them you are very confused and then give them all the compliments you can think of and ask them to pay attention to whatever happens that they want to continue to have happen.
- *If they have a clear picture of what the miracle will look like* (you will intuit this), ask them to pretend the miracle (or part of it) is happening on certain days. If they are uncertain about whether they can do that, add a random element like a coin toss or a secret practice time.

"Deck of Trumps"–
One of the Ways for Being Helpful
to Clients and Professionals in Becoming
as They Want to Be!

Tomasz Switek

KEYWORDS. Solution-focused training

In this article, I will present a procedure for working with clients and professionals called "Deck of Trumps." This procedure is based on the experiences of many therapists whose work has been my inspiration and refers to the principles of Solution-Focused Brief Therapy developed at the Brief Therapy Family Center in Milwaukee (USA). "Deck of Trumps" is available in Polish, English, Dutch, Spanish, French language versions, and soon should be in other language versions.

PROCEDURE'S STRUCTURE

"Deck of Trumps" is divided into two stages: The first focuses mainly on redescribing the client's reality and the second focuses on planning, continu-

Tomasz Switek is a therapist and trainer, Polish Solutions Focused Team, Solutions Focused Therapy Institute, Inowroclaw, Poland.

Address correspondence to: Tomasz Switek, Szarych Szeregow 7a/6, 88-100 Inowroclaw, Poland.

[Haworth co-indexing entry note]: " 'Deck of Trumps'–One of the Ways for Being Helpful to Clients and Professionals in Becoming as They Want to Be!" Switek, Tomasz. Co-published simultaneously in *Journal of Family Psychotherapy* (The Haworth Press, Inc.) Vol. 16, No. 1/2, 2005, pp. 91-101; and: *Education and Training in Solution-Focused Brief Therapy* (ed: Thorana S. Nelson) The Haworth Press, Inc., 2005, pp. 91-101. Single or multiple copies of this article are available for a fee from The Haworth Document Delivery Service [1-800-HAWORTH, 9:00 a.m. - 5:00 p.m. (EST). E-mail address: docdelivery@haworthpress.com].

Digital Object Identifier: 10.1300/J085v16n01_25

ing, and introducing strategies and noticing how these influence the client's present life.

A dozen or so formulas can be used by the therapist and client in these two stages.

The first stage. The first step is to choose with the client one of the formulas from parts 1-13 based on his needs and preferences.

part 1–Me as a parent
part 2–Me as a spouse or life partner
part 3–Me as a worker
part 4–Me believing in God
part 5–Me using my own free time constructively
part 6–Me behaving in accordance with my own values
part 7–Me coping with life's difficulties
part 8–Me achieving successes
part 9–Me as a woman/man
part 10–Me showing a strong will, resisting temptations
part 11–Me taking care of my health and body
part 12–Me controlling my own behaviors and impulses
part 13–Universal, for use according to the needs of client

In trainings for professionals you can use also two other parts called:

Me . . . . . . doing effective solution-focused brief therapy
Me . . . . . . working effectively in solution-focused way

These two parts are presented in this paper. Parts 1-13 and the two focused on solution-focused ways of working and doing therapy can be used during trainings as a scenario for conducting solution-focused talk during role play exercises or as a way for professionals to examine their own work.

The choices of the leading titles for the thematic parts of the Deck of Trumps (parts 1-12) were based on my experiences working with people. I observed what was important to them and in what degree, what was needed, and what had received a high subjective value. Of course, the list is not a complete one; part 13, which is open, can accommodate your client's specific needs. As you can easily notice, particular parts of Deck of Trumps are focused on the client's person in the perspective of social roles or in the perspective of having some abilities.

The aim of the first stage is to help clients to notice that, besides having deficits and faults, they also are the owners of some resources and possibilities, and to redefine in a more useful way description of the client's self-reality *(eusémie).*[1]

After choosing one of the formulas, the client answers the questions included in the chosen formula. The client may do this alone or together with some helpful person, perhaps with you as a therapist. The questions help the client to analyze particular aspects of life and functioning in each area, which lead to redescriptions of the client's reality. Particular questions in the formulas lead the client to use his or her imagination and to think about: (1) good and desired functioning in the specified area of life by creating the picture of the "preferred future" in the chosen area of life; (2) when and how he/she was able to behave in such a manner–"exceptions"; (3) internal and external resources and other factors that are helpful in functioning in the desired way. Bringing these resources and possibilities to the light of day is made possible by analyzing personal experiences from the client's life in a constructive way. This makes it easier for the client to see and internalize resources and to make more effective use of them in the preferred future. Eliciting, amplifying, and reinforcing the person's resources is one very effective strategy in providing psychological help; and (4) defining his/her present situation in the chosen area by using homogenous numeric scales from 1 to 10.

After answering the questions, the client can decide whether to continue to work toward introducing some solutions in the specified area of life. If yes, together you go on to the second stage. If not, you may stay in the first stage and choose another formula if the client expresses a need for continuing to work together or you may put the formulas aside. In many cases, helping clients in changing their way of perceiving one's reality, to realize what one wants, what one can and is able to do, what is strong in oneself, and what was and can be helpful is sufficient therapist input and clients continue introducing other desired changes on their own.

The second stage. Parts "Deck of Trumps–Formula for Change–1" and "Deck of Trumps–Formula for Change–2" are adjusted for use with the chosen formula from thematic parts 1 to 13.

At this stage, the client prepares to introduce some changes in her/his life and to check out how those changes are suitable for her or him. What works? What is good to continue? Which strategies need to be changed? The aims of these two formulas are:

1. to help the client to plan the direction and the way of continuing and introducing changes on the basis of personal experiences and abilities;
2. to maintain and introduce these changes;
3. to notice how these new strategies influence the client's present life;
4. to create a context in which clients choose what is and what is not good for them;
5. what will and will not be continuing; and
6. what will be introduced.

We are talking here about changes that appear on the level of acting, of doing things *(euhérésis).*[2]

At this stage, clients use "scaling" and "self-observation" to:

- define what in the chosen area of life is working out in a sufficient way, with what they can be satisfied;
- remember the times when it was better and look for these elements that helped to make those moments better;
- on the basis of their own experiences and achieved knowledge, use the experiences of other members of the group, "support team," important persons, or therapists with whom they plan "small steps" to introduce in the near future;
- observe to what degree introducing new strategies influenced their lives, self, and environment;
- decide what is working in sufficient ways and is therefore worth continuing, and what is not working out sufficiently and therefore must be changed.

When working with "Deck of Trumps," the client and therapist use the following techniques: creating a picture of the "preferred future" both near and a long time ahead; looking for and identifying "exceptions": times when there was not a problem, a problem was less intensive, when there was a full solution working, or when a solution was created and utilized to some degree; complimenting; scaling; self-observation; and acting on choices.

By using the above techniques, changes occur as redescriptions of the client's reality *(eusémie)* and on the level of client's behaviors *(euhérésis).*

When reading the questions and giving the answers, you will notice that clients refer to their experiences from the past and present that are positive and constructive. These experiences are used as a basis to build on and to introduce further steps in the process of creating solutions. When using these formulas (in the first and second stage) with clients, it is recommended that you try to elicit as many details as possible from both internal and external lives at the times when clients functioned in a better way. You also need to avoid the danger of analyzing the nature and the causes of the client's problems. (That would be another game, maybe the "Deck of Low Cards"!) Instead, keep your focus and concentrate on what worked in the past, what is working now, and what can work in the future.

The presented procedure needs to be treated in a very flexible way so as to adjust to each individual client's needs and goals. It is good to remember that every time you offer this procedure, it is only a proposition. Letting your client make the decision about the eventual use of this procedure will let you keep the responsibility for change on the right side.

Furthermore, it is important to remember that introducing changes must be done with respect for the client's ability and readiness to do new things that lead to changes in his/her reality. The process of keeping change in the frame of a client's acceptance will allow him/her to keep a proper level of safety and orientation. With such flexibility and working "slower than clients," therapists are able to create situations in which subjective feelings of continuity between past, present, and future are supported in the process of introducing changes *(transcontinuite)*.[3]

POSSIBILITIES OF APPLICATION

To make my experience with applications of the Deck of Trumps more objective, I asked other therapists who have used the procedure about their experiences and ideas, particularly about ways of application and effects. Below I quote some of their ideas.

1. The Deck of Trumps was used in a variety of areas of providing psychological help to people who need it. Mainly, the following situations were mentioned: mental health problems, chemical addictions, family violence, family and couple dysfunctions, social disability problems, parenting problems, children and adolescent disabilities.
2. The procedure also was used as a tool in the process of teaching and supervising other professionals in the area of helping people.
3. It was used with adults, adolescents, and, after providing some changes in the outlook and content, with children.
4. In group settings, it was applied either as one of the propositions or as main scenario.
5. Within individual therapy, clients worked with particular formulas independently, coming to the sessions after responding to one area. The therapist helped the client to answer questions during the session or a formula was used as a framework for conducting a solution-focused session.
6. Deck of Trumps was offered to clients as a way to broaden therapeutic programs provided so far, or was used as a way of reinforcing the process of solution-focused therapy.
7. Cognitive behavioral therapists used elements of the procedure in preparing "expert" programs of therapy for clients.
8. Depending on clients' needs and therapist readiness, Deck of Trumps was used at different times during the process of therapy from the very

beginning moments up to work with people who are at the end of the process or in "aftercare" programs.
9. It was applied in residential and ambulatory health care programs, in public and private institutions, at social care systems, at juvenile systems, and school settings.

This procedure has been used with many issues because it is aimed at what the client wants to achieve from therapy and what he or she wants to improve. It keeps the focus on creating and introducing possible solutions instead of focusing on the nature of the problem–a basic idea for solution-focused therapists.

ADVANTAGES/EFFECTS

Based on the experiences of those professionals who used Deck of Trumps, two kinds of advantages have emerged: first, those experienced by clients and second, those perceived by therapist themselves. Clients' advantages/effects generally include: growing feelings of self-esteem; changes in self-perspective, from seeing oneself as "not able, not capable" into a person who "is able, can do"; greater readiness to talk about problems and to change problematic behaviors; increasing the amount and quality of constructive behaviors; reinforcement of the feeling of having impact on one's life; strengthening hope connected with therapy; developing abilities in creating and introducing desired strategies; improving the quality of relationships with other people; better preventing of relapses; shortening periods of the relapse's duration and its intensity; higher motivation to participate in therapy programs. Other advantages/effects for clients include: after preparing formulas, finding answers to solution-focused questions easier to obtain; faster specifying of goals, exceptions, and resources; maintaining a solution-focused perspective between sessions.

Therapist's advantages/effects include experiencing decreased levels of client resistance to the therapy process; increasing possibilities of cooperation with clients; higher subjective feelings of self-efficacy; strengthening of the therapist engagement in the workplace; broadening therapists' perspective of new possibilities and solutions; changing attitudes toward clients to much more friendly and optimistic feelings, particularly toward so called "difficult clients"; making it easier to conduct solution-focused sessions and to keep the focus on solutions instead of problems.

The above advantages and effects were quoted by many therapists, many of whom were not solution-focused ones. Most of these are very common for people who were trying to use SFBT even to some degree. So, I can say it is not likely to be the advantage of using the Deck of Trumps, but that using Deck of Trumps is useful for many on the basis of SFBT's principles. In such a perspective, it is a helpful tool to introduce SFBT's techniques into one's therapeutic practice and for clients to find effective way to achieve their goals and meet their needs in a safe and respectful way.

NOTES

1. Eusémie-Greek: *eu*-well, good; *seme*-sign, meaning.
2. Euhérésis-Greek: *eu*-well, good; *haeresis*-choice.
3. Transcontinuite–the concept of *transcontinuite* is described by Luc Isebaert and Marie Cristine Cabie in their book, *Pour uné therapie brève*.

REFERENCES

Isebeart, L., & Cabie, M-C. (1997). *Pour une thérapie brève*, Edition Erès.
Metcalf, L. (1998). *solution-focused group therapy*. New York: The Free Press.
Berg, I. K., & Miller, S. D. *Working with the problem drinker*. New York: Norton.
Berg, I. K., & Reuss, N. H. (1997). *Solutions step by step*. New York: Norton.

APPENDIX

DECK OF TRUMPS
ME . . . WORKING EFFECTIVELY IN A SOLUTION-FOCUSED WAY
(This part of Deck of Trumps was created in cooperation with Piet Rademakers)

In the following formula you can consider your functioning in your professional work. I hope that this exercise will be useful for you in improving the quality of, and, when necessary, introducing changes in the way you are working in a solution-focused way. Please focus your attention on everything connected with that, looking for the moments when you thought it was better, when you did things better, and when you were more satisfied with you working in a solution-focused way.

1. Which aspects of your work show you that you are working effectively in a solution-focused way? Give examples of your work, like questions, interventions, and reactions to the client.

2. Describe several situations when you worked, even to some degree, in a way you've characterized above. Times when you could say: "I was really and effectively working in a solution-focused way!"

3. On the basis of the above examples and other ones you may have in mind, try to fill out the following table. What have you, in the course of years, learned about what you are capable of? What abilities did you develop? What kind of personality features can you show that are helpful in working effectively in a solution-focused way in a way that you like, and like you described in Items 1 and 2. If necessary, ask someone to help you to fill out this table!

What was I able to do?	What abilities did I show in that situation?	What features of my personality did I show?

4. What was helpful and useful to you to work in such a way?

Inside yourself	Outside of you

5. Please estimate your present way of working professionally on a scale from 1 to 10, where 1 stands for "I am working a little bit effectively in a solution-focused way now" and 10 stands for "I am working almost always effectively in a solution-focused way."

1	2	3	4	5	6	7	8	9	10

"DECK OF TRUMPS"–FORMULA FOR CHANGE–1

In the preceding formula (one of the Deck of Trumps exercises) you answered many questions. The 1st question was devoted to considering how you imagine yourself functioning well and constructively in the chosen area. In the 2nd question, you reminded yourself of some of the moments in your life when you behaved in the way you would like, when you had been able to act constructively. By doing this exercise, you proved that you have the abilities to do this. Maybe you're not a master yet, but time is at your disposal! By giving answers to the 3rd question, you defined your own abilities, skills, talents, and advantages that could be helpful to you in achieving your stated goals. In the answer to the 4th question, you clarified what "inside and outside" you is helpful for you to behave in the way you would like. The answer to the 5th question is an attempt to estimate your present level of functioning in the chosen area. If you want to continue preparing and introducing further changes in the process of improving your functioning, you may go on to the questions specified in the following formula.

1. Please rewrite your score you had chosen on the scale from 1 to 10 in formula of "Deck of Trumps–part "........." (your answer on Question 5 in the formula you worked on):

1	2	3	4	5	6	7	8	9	10

2. Consider now what already exists in that area. What let you estimate that situation on the level of .... (your valuation from point 1), and not lower about 1 or 2 points? When answering, try to think and write about what you're doing, thinking, feeling, what others are doing, what other things exist–what factors contribute to placing the present moment at that level. Try to write about what "is" happening, not what "is not" happening.

3. Now, remind yourself of some past moments in your life when your score could have been even higher than you gave it in Question 1 above. Think and write about what you were doing, thinking, feeling, what others were doing, what other things were existing–what placed that moment at that level. Try to write in terms of what "was," not what "was not."

4. Imagine a moment in the near future when you'll be able to estimate your situation a little bit higher that you've estimated in Question 1. Think and write in what way that situation will be different from the present. What will you be doing, thinking, feeling, what will others be doing, what else will there be, what will place that moment on a higher level than it is now?

| |
| |

5. Now on the basis of your answers on Questions 3 and 4, consider and write what will be your next two or three steps toward point 10 on the scale, steps which in the near future make it possible to say: "I'm a little bit higher than I was a short time ago!" Write about what you'll be doing, where, when, how, in what way, who will help you and how, which of your thoughts and feelings will be helpful in such an enterprise.

| |
| |

If you now know what to do, put down that formula in a safe place and go do it! After all, you're able to influence some things in your life! Try to notice even the smallest signs of change—these are small parts of a big change. Do what works!

"DECK OF TRUMPS"–FORMULA FOR CHANGE–2

With this formula you can work on introducing changes and observing if/in what way these changes are good for you, or work well for you. You can decide whether it is worthwhile to continue what you do, and what needs to be changed on the way to achieving your goals!

In accordance with my planned steps, I've undertaken the following activities, which have brought the following changes:

What I've done and how	Changes influenced by my activity

2. Presently I estimate my situation on a scale from 1 to 10 to be at a:

1	2	3	4	5	6	7	8	9	10

3. Write in a few sentences which of your abilities, strengths, features, or advantages you used and how you did it when you took the steps you mentioned in Item 1.

4. Now, please imagine into the near future a moment when you'll be able to estimate your situation a little bit higher that you've done it in Item 2. Think and write in what way that situation will be different from the present one. What will you be doing, thinking, feeling? What will others notice? What else will happen? What will place that moment on a higher level than it is now?

5. Now on the basis of your answer on Item 4, consider and write what will be your first two or three things you can do to move you up on the scale. These are steps which make it possible to say in the near future: "I'm a little bit higher that I was a short time ago!" Write about what, where, when, how, in what way you'll be doing things differently, who will help you and how, and what sort of thoughts and feelings you have that will be helpful in taking these steps.

Do you want to introduce more changes into that area of your life?	Yes	No
Is it possible to introduce more changes into that area of your life?	Yes	No

If you answered, "Yes" two times, please take new copies of "Formula for Change–1 and 2" and continue your work on introducing desired changes and achieving your goals!
We wish you good luck!

Playing Trumps Scenario:
One of Many Possibilities!

Tomasz Switek

KEYWORDS. Solution-focused, training

This exercise is used in trainings with professionals who are familiar with basic techniques and questions of SFBT. These participants should at least be familiar with the ways of looking for resources, creating pictures of preferred future and goals, looking for exceptions, and using scales. The aim of this exercise is to help them use and shift between different techniques that are used in SFBT.

We introduce this exercise by describing SFBT as one of many possible ways of doing therapy–just one of them–like different kinds of playing cards exist and are used. So today we're going to play a solution-focused game. To play this game, we'll need some rules: we can talk "only" in four directions:

- looking for resources, possibilities;
- talking about needs, hopes, goals, and preferred futures;
- looking for exceptions; and
- scaling the present situation.

Tomasz Switek is a therapist and trainer, Polish Solutions Focused Team, Solutions Focused Therapy Institute, Inowroclaw, Poland.

Address correspondence to: Tomasz Switek, Szarych Szeregow 7a/6, 88-100 Inowroclaw, Poland.

[Haworth co-indexing entry note]: "Playing Trumps Scenario: One of Many Possibilities!" Switek, Tomasz. Co-published simultaneously in *Journal of Family Psychotherapy* (The Haworth Press, Inc.) Vol. 16, No. 1/2, 2005, pp. 103-105; and: *Education and Training in Solution-Focused Brief Therapy* (ed: Thorana S. Nelson) The Haworth Press, Inc., 2005, pp. 103-105. Single or multiple copies of this article are available for a fee from The Haworth Document Delivery Service [1-800-HAWORTH, 9:00 a.m. - 5:00 p.m. (EST). E-mail address: docdelivery@haworthpress.com].

Available online at http://www.haworthpress.com/web/JFP
Digital Object Identifier: 10.1300/J085v16n01_26

We divide the group into teams of 3 or 4 where one person is a client, one is a therapist, and one or two are observers.

The "client" introduces some issue, personal or based on professional experience, and from the beginning is ready to work in a cooperating type of relationship. We remember that we are not doing therapy but are in a training workshop, so our main purpose is to practice some particular abilities.

Every therapist has in front of him or her, four color cards taken from the Playing Trumps. These are to help remember, choose, and follow the four possible ways of conducting consultations in the solution-focused way. Every time the therapist asks a question of the client, she/he takes one of the four cards to stress in which direction she/he is going to conduct the consultation.

The therapist and observers also have an empty sheet of "Playing Trumps Work." Their task is to write down all the details that are available during the consultation about the client's abilities, goals, preferred future, exceptions, etc.

After 20-30 minutes of conversation, we break. Therapists and observers prepare "Expert's Stance" feedback for the client. The clients prepare feedback for the therapists about what was helpful and useful during that conversation, what the therapist did in useful ways for the client, and what the client would like to see more of from the therapist.

Finish the exercise with a short discussion about other aspects of this experience.

APPENDIX

playing trumps!

Client's strengths, abilities, and other resources CLIENT'S POSSIBILITIES	Client's hopes, needs, and goals. Picture of the "Preferred Future" *Let's take a look at the future!* CLIENT'S HOPES AND DREAMS

Exceptions *Let's take a look at the past!* CLIENT'S EXPERIENCES	What is already OK? -scales- *Let's take a look at the present!* CLIENT'S ACQUIRED POSSESSIONS

Please write a short message for the client:

THERAPIST'S "EXPERT STANCE"

Scaling in Action

Brenda Zalter
Heather Fiske

KEYWORDS. Brief therapy, solution-focused, termination, training

TYPE OF AUDIENCE

- Students, workshop participants at any level, supervisees
- Clients in individual, group, family or couple treatment

Group Size: 1-? We have used this method with groups of up to 300.
Experience Level: Introductory to advanced; no experience with solution-focused ideas or applications is necessary

PURPOSE OF THE EXERCISE

- As a warm-up
- To begin right away utilizing solution-focused methods in the learning process
- To facilitate individual goal-setting and goal-monitoring in a group learning environment

---

Brenda Zalter is affiliated with Credit Valley Hospital, Mississauga, Ontario, Canada.

Heather Fiske is a psychologist and has a private practice in Toronto, Ontario, Canada.

Address correspondence to: Brenda Zalter, 35 Pirie Drive, Dundas, ON, Canada L9H 6X5 or Heather Fiske, 35 Scarborough Road, Toronto, ON, Canada M4E 3M4.

[Haworth co-indexing entry note]: "Scaling in Action." Zalter, Brenda, and Heather Fiske. Co-published simultaneously in *Journal of Family Psychotherapy* (The Haworth Press, Inc.) Vol. 16, No. 1/2, 2005, pp. 107-109; and: *Education and Training in Solution-Focused Brief Therapy* (ed: Thorana S. Nelson) The Haworth Press, Inc., 2005, pp. 107-109. Single or multiple copies of this article are available for a fee from The Haworth Document Delivery Service [1-800-HAWORTH, 9:00 a.m. - 5:00 p.m. (EST). E-mail address: docdelivery@haworthpress.com].

Available online at http://www.haworthpress.com/web/JFP
Digital Object Identifier: 10.1300/J085v16n01_27

- To get a range of group opinions
- To introduce scaling
- To practice scaling and get a taste for its utility
- To practice developing a picture of a more positive future
- To liven people when they are getting droopy (This exercise is literally a "warm-up," gets people moving, thinking, talking, often laughing and connecting as well. We are convinced that talk flows more easily and people are more engaged when they move their bodies.)
- As a check-in to evaluate progress/goal achievement
- To involve less verbal participants
- To demonstrate how solution-focused methods can be adapted and integrated.

Experiential Level of the Exercise (1-10): Instructions aside, this exercise is a 10.

Time Frame for the Exercise, Debriefing: As an introductory exercise, it can be completed comfortably in as little as 15 minutes; 20-25 is more typical.

Instructions: We ask participants to imagine that there is a line drawn down the middle of a room, a scale from 1 to 10. 1 is at *this* end and stands for _____ and 10 is at *that* end and stands for _____. (We will often walk along the line as we talk.) We then say:

- Stand up, and place yourselves where you are on this scale right now.
- (If not 1) How did you get to where you are now?
- Where do you want to be on this same scale? Move to that place.
- Imagine that you have in fact done what you needed to do to achieve that goal. Turn to the people around you and tell them one thing that is different now that you are where you wanted to be on the scale.
- From that same place, where you want to be on the scale: What was the very first small step you took that got you on track to where you wanted to be? Tell the people around you the first step you took.
- Other questions, e.g., What difference did that step make? What did you discover as you moved up the steps? . . .
- Thank you, sit down. During the rest of the workshop we invite you to attend to whatever may help you to move to where you want to be on the scale.

List of Sample Questions: On this scale from 1 to 10:

- How solution-focused is your practice right now?
- How prepared/confident/ready/skilled are you to deal with your most difficult client?

- How prepared/confident/ready/skilled are you to deal with a _____ client? (traumatized, suicidal, under 5, etc. . . . usually related to particular content of course/workshop)
- How well is the course meeting your learning needs so far?
- (At end of workshop/course) How prepared/confident/ready/skilled are you to deal with your most difficult client?
- How helpful has this workshop/course been for you?
- Ask the first question (i.e., where you are on the scale right now). Have the person highest on the scale and the person lowest on the scale trade places *and roles*, and then answer as each other. That is, the person who was lowest and is now "highest" is asked, "How did you get to this level?" and person who is lowest is asked, "What do you need to do to move higher on the scale?" etc.
- After first question, ask, "What is working well for you about where you are right now? What is there about where you are that you want to have continue?"
- Ask the first question and then invite participants to ask further questions of the group in the same format.
- Have participants role-play their clients' responding to questions about how helpful therapy is, etc.

Handouts: None specific to the exercise; we would include a handout on scaling with examples of verbal and nonverbal applications.

Closing Comments: Used early in the training process, this exercise sets a tone for the learning process that is active, spontaneous, relaxed, participatory–and *fun*. It facilitates group interaction while helping learners to focus on their individual needs and goals. And as trainers, we have found the experience of literally seeing people move forward to be highly rewarding.

A Scaling Walk

Paul Jackson

KEYWORDS. Solution-focused, training, scaling

Type of audience: Learners of the principles and practices of solution-focused work.

Group size: Any. I've run this with group sizes from 5 people in a training session to around 100 at conferences.

Experience level: Any from beginners to the most experienced.

Purpose of the exercise: To bring scaling to life through experience and discussion of all its main features.

Experiential level of the exercise: Nine. Mostly experiential, some questioning by the facilitator and some discussion at the end.

Time frame for the exercise, debriefing (if appropriate): 15-30 minutes

Instructions (pre and post): This is an opportunity to reinforce the concept of scaling by getting the group to physically experience different points on the scale. Ask everyone to think of a sport or hobby that they currently engage in and would like to be better at. "10 represents your performing consistently at your personal peak, in your chosen hobby, 0 is you regularly and stuckly at the worst you imagine it can be for you. Where are you now? Let's call that *n*."

Set out a scale in the room from 0 at one end to 10 at the other. Line the group up first at *n* on the scale, somewhere in the middle of the room. "Simply by placing yourself on a scale, you have implications of potential movement

---

Address correspondence to: Paul Jackson, 23 Bloomfield Road, Bath, BA2 2AD, England.

[Haworth co-indexing entry note]: "A Scaling Walk." Jackson, Paul. Co-published simultaneously in *Journal of Family Psychotherapy* (The Haworth Press, Inc.) Vol. 16, No. 1/2, 2005, pp. 111-112; and: *Education and Training in Solution-Focused Brief Therapy* (ed: Thorana S. Nelson) The Haworth Press, Inc., 2005, pp. 111-112. Single or multiple copies of this article are available for a fee from The Haworth Document Delivery Service [1-800-HAWORTH, 9:00 a.m. - 5:00 p.m. (EST). E-mail address: docdelivery@haworthpress.com].

Available online at http://www.haworthpress.com/web/JFP
Digital Object Identifier: 10.1300/J085v16n01_28

and therefore possible progress. If this is where you are now, what do you see when you look towards 10 (possible future) and towards 0 (know-how, counters, exceptions). You've used your know-how to get you to n.

"Let's now visit 0 on the scale." Move the group to that end of the room and ask questions like, "What's significant about 0?" "What do we need to know about 0?" "How much detail do we need to have of what 0 looks/feels like?"

Now move the group to 10 on the scale, the other end of the room. Ask, "What does 10 represent?" "How much detail do we want about 10?" "What's the point of mentally visiting 10 on the scale?" "Who has been at 10, for real, for a period, a moment, one swing of a golf club?" (That's the source of useful know-how.)

Take the group back to n on the scale and ask what's different now about looking to 10. Often people say they feel inspired, motivated, they know something they didn't know before. "Where do we go from here?" "Do we go straight to 10?" No, we look at the know-how we've used to get to n, we look at what we've learned about 10, we collect the know-how we need to advance up the scale and we move to $n + 1$. Getting to 10 in one step is probably too big a step or you'd probably have done it by now anyway. If not, then do it.

Ask the group to take the step up to $n + 1$. Looking at 10, what can they say about 10 now? What have they learned? (New counters and momentum from going from n to $n + 1$.)

Ask the group to return to their seats, ask any questions they have about scaling and make any notes they need to in their workbooks.

Notes from Rayya

Rayya Ghul

KEYWORDS. Solution-focused brief therapy, miracle question

To help workshop participants understand how the miracle question can work, I say, "If I asked each of you what is the first thing you'd notice, you might all say, 'I'd have won the lottery/had loads of money'"–watch for the head nods. "That's not particularly useful, is it?" Then I say, "But if I then said, 'what difference would that make?,' how many different answers do you think I'd get?" I then lead into a discussion about how people use symbols for what they want (be rich, be thin, live somewhere different) and sometimes forget why they want those things, so focus on the symbolic goal rather than making goals for what they really want (and what is probably more attainable).

Rayya Ghul is a member of the Institute of Learning and Teaching, Lyminge, Kent, England.

Address correspondence to: Rayya Ghul, Allied Health Department, Canterbury Christ Church University College, Canterbury CT1 1QU, England.

[Haworth co-indexing entry note]: "Notes from Rayya." Ghul, Rayya. Co-published simultaneously in *Journal of Family Psychotherapy* (The Haworth Press, Inc.) Vol. 16, No. 1/2, 2005, p. 113; and: *Education and Training in Solution-Focused Brief Therapy* (ed: Thorana S. Nelson) The Haworth Press, Inc., 2005, p. 113. Single or multiple copies of this article are available for a fee from The Haworth Document Delivery Service [1-800-HAWORTH, 9:00 a.m. - 5:00 p.m. (EST). E-mail address: docdelivery@haworthpress.com].

Available online at http://www.haworthpress.com/web/JFP
Digital Object Identifier: 10.1300/J085v16n01_29

The State of Miracles in Relationships

Insoo Kim Berg

KEYWORDS. Miracle pictures, vision of solutions, client's vision, social context

What is it? Rather than explaining the value of the miracle question (MQ), it is useful to have the training and workshop audience to experience the state of miracle as well as the usefulness of the relationship questions. Combining these two questions with a single exercise is an efficient and effective use of training time. Not only does the exercise afford the opportunity to imagine the MQ, but also other important people in participants' lives are brought into the discussion; therefore, clients can also experience a state of solutions and how others in their lives will behave toward them in response.

Type of audience. General introductory level of audience and those who may be reluctant and/or not yet convinced about the usefulness of the MQ and the relationship question. Even for those who may have used the MQ for some time, it is a good idea to have them experience what it feels like to go through this exercise and then participate in a debriefing discussion, using a list of questions described below.

Time frame. This exercise comes in two parts; the first part takes about 4 minutes and the second part takes about 15-20 minutes to debrief and discuss the implications. It often leads to related questions and comments.

Insoo Kim Berg is affiliated with the Brief Family Therapy Center, Milwaukee, WI.

Address correspondence to: Insoo Kim Berg, 1907 Wauwatosa Ave., Milwaukee, WI 53213.

[Haworth co-indexing entry note]: "The State of Miracles in Relationships." Berg, Insoo Kim. Co-published simultaneously in *Journal of Family Psychotherapy* (The Haworth Press, Inc.) Vol. 16, No. 1/2, 2005, pp. 115-118; and: *Education and Training in Solution-Focused Brief Therapy* (ed: Thorana S. Nelson) The Haworth Press, Inc., 2005, pp. 115-118. Single or multiple copies of this article are available for a fee from The Haworth Document Delivery Service [1-800-HAWORTH, 9:00 a.m. - 5:00 p.m. (EST). E-mail address: docdelivery@haworthpress.com].

Available online at http://www.haworthpress.com/web/JFP
Digital Object Identifier: 10.1300/J085v16n01_30

INSTRUCTIONS

1. Set the stage for the exercise. I often use this at the end of the first day of a two-day workshop, but this exercise can also be adapted to fit into a one-day or even half-day training session, which will be described later in the discussion section. Workshop leaders may need to improvise and adapt it to fit the setting and needs of the audience.

2. You may have already explained the uses, phrasing, and how to follow-up on the MQ during the training session. At the end of the first day or training segment, I give the audience some "homework" and of course many are surprised at this and I use a lot of humor about having to do homework between the end of the first day and the second segment of the training.

3. Some participants may not go home and if I know this in advance, I ask them to pretend they are going home at the end of the day. The homework is given as following:

   > The moment you step outside the door to go home now, there will be a miracle dropping from the sky and will land on your head. The outcome of this event is that all your frustration and aggravation related to your job is all solved. It means no more budget problem, no more paperwork, no more bad boss or administrators. Your task is to stay in this state of mind until you return tomorrow morning to this workshop. I will ask lots of questions about this homework when you return for the second half of this training.

4. The next morning, before you begin the second half of the training, set aside about 20-30 minutes to go through the following set of questions.
   a. I joke how some may have not remembered the homework. If so, just pretend you did the homework, since nobody will know the difference of whether you did or not.
   b. I set a rule that I will assume their partner is a male because it is easier to use single sex in formulating questions, rather than repeating him/her, his/hers, throughout the following sequence.
   c. They also are to pretend that they have children even though some may not have any. Dog or cat will easily replace children, also.
   d. The audience is free to answer aloud, but this is not necessary if they are not so inclined. However, they are asked to answer the questions in their own mind and follow through silently. The questions will build on previous questions; therefore, it will be useful for them to follow through because this is what the client is asked to do when we suggest that they pick a day and pretend that a miracle happened on that day. The following questions are asked in a slow pace, allowing the audience to answer the questions in silence, if they prefer. I further explain that I am not interested in the content of the answer but

the process of what it is like to imagine the miracle picture. Many in the audience like to write down the list of questions while they are thinking at the same time. Therefore it seems important to ask the question slowly with long pauses between each question. The room becomes very quiet and peaceful.

QUESTIONS

1. Suppose I ask your family member what he noticed different about you when you returned home yesterday from this workshop that told him that there was a miracle for you and all your problems related to your job were all solved; what would he say about how he could tell there was miracle for you without your telling him this?
2. What would he say was a difference this made to him, seeing these changes in you?
3. What would he say what difference this made between you and him the rest of the evening?
4. What would he say your life would be like when this difference continues for a week, two weeks, or even a month?
5. Suppose I ask your children what they noticed different about you and them that told them that a miracle happened to you and your frustration related to your job is all solved; what would they tell me?
6. What would they say about the kind of impact this had on them?
7. What would they say their life would be like when this continues for a week? A month?
8. Suppose I ask your colleagues, how could they tell that a miracle happened to you and . . . ? continue with the rest of questions,
9. Suppose I ask your best friend . . . continue with the questions.
10. Suppose I ask your clients (supervisor, administrator, and so on) . . .

DEBRIEFING QUESTIONS

1. Again, I remind the audience that I am not interested in the content of solutions but what were they aware of going on inside as they were trying to answer these questions. What else? Anything else? What else?
2. Then I ask whether they were aware that all the questions were framed as someone else's perspectives. What impact did this have on them as they were trying to answer these questions?

DISCUSSION AND HIGHLIGHTS OF THE EXERCISE

The most frequent answers I get from audiences are:

    a. Small change can create big ripple effects.

    b. I can see the pictures of myself in details before my eyes.

    c. I can feel positive feelings in my body as I imagined the miracle.

    d. It's all up to me to decide to have a pleasant evening or a miserable one.

    e. I became sad that I didn't know I had so much control (influence) over myself and my family.

    f. Why didn't I know I had so much control over what happens to me?

It is good to discuss the usefulness of the relationship questions, especially for those clients who see themselves as victims of what others are doing to them. Because of adaptation to suit each client's unique needs and situations, it can have powerful influences on those who feel helpless to change the situations they are in.

The MQ can also be adapted to fit a limited time available for training, for example, 3-hour session, during which you may want to introduce the MQ even though you may have no plan to follow-up. Have them experience the miracle pictures as soon as they go back to work and have them debrief what it felt like and what they take from this exercise. Since the MQ demands a great deal from clients, that is, to focus and describe vivid images of their life without problems, it can be quite challenging. It is not 100% foolproof, however, since some clients would refuse to participate in it or do not have the time. In these circumstances, it is better to use scaling questions to learn how much progress the client has made toward his/her goal already and ways to maintain the progress, first, and then to move up a notch.

APPLICATION TO OTHER SETTINGS AND GROUP SIZES

I have adapted the MQ to fit in a variety of settings such as group therapy, business, and organizational consultation of various natures. I have applied this combination of questions to a group of 150 participants in one organization because they knew what the concerns and issues were. If one can imagine working with a large family group, one can easily adapt it to different size groups as well as the nature of the business or functions.

"Picturing the Future" Exercise

Janet Campbell

KEYWORDS. Solution-focused brief therapy, training, future focus

Introduction: This exercise was developed in e-mail conversations with Josée Lamarre of Montreal, Canada. Josée had written for suggestions to aid students in learning how to help clients switch from problem talk to future talk. It is based on a dialogue with Harry Korman of Malmö, Sweden, in the mid-'90s when he was a visitor sitting behind the mirror during a solution-focused meeting with a client. Harry related that he will not move on in a conversation with a client until he has a picture in his mind of what the client's life will look like when the problem that brings them to counseling is no longer a problem.

Type of audience: Any group of people learning SFBT, including those wanting a refresher course.

Group size: Groups of 5 can be made from a larger group. Groups can be as small as 3.

Experience level: Participants would benefit by having an idea of the basic principles of SFBT.

Janet Campbell is affiliated with the Center for Solutions, Walden, NY.

Address correspondence to: Janet Campbell, Center for Solutions, 175 So. Montgomery St., Walden, NY 12586.

[Haworth co-indexing entry note]: " 'Picturing the Future' Exercise." Campbell, Janet. Co-published simultaneously in *Journal of Family Psychotherapy* (The Haworth Press, Inc.) Vol. 16, No. 1/2, 2005, pp. 119-121; and: *Education and Training in Solution-Focused Brief Therapy* (ed: Thorana S. Nelson) The Haworth Press, Inc., 2005, pp. 119-121. Single or multiple copies of this article are available for a fee from The Haworth Document Delivery Service [1-800-HAWORTH, 9:00 a.m. - 5:00 p.m. (EST). E-mail address: docdelivery@haworthpress.com].

Available online at http://www.haworthpress.com/web/JFP
Digital Object Identifier: 10.1300/J085v16n01_31

Purpose of the exercise: To help participants move the conversation with a client from talking about problems to talking about solutions while actively listening to a client's responses.

Experiential level of the exercise: 9

Time frame for the exercise: 30-40 minutes depending on group size

Instructions: Participants are briefly informed about the purpose of the exercise. Participants are asked to break into groups of 5 with the following constituents: one role playing a client, one being an observer, and the rest role playing therapists.

The therapists' goal is to get a picture in their minds of what the client wants for her/himself and to build on this picture with each question asked. Each therapist takes a turn and asks one question of the client that adds more details to the picture of what the client's life will look like when the problem that brought them to therapy no longer exists. The first therapist to ask a question starts with, "How will you know that coming here and talking today had been helpful to you?" (This question may be written on a handout or a blackboard.)

The picture developing in the therapists' minds from the client's descriptions is to include what the client will be doing as well as what others in the client's life will be noticing different about the client when things are better. Each question asked by a therapist should relate to the client's last response.

The observer's job is to notice how well the therapists' questions create a detailed picture in the observer's mind of a better life for this client. The observer is also to notice how well each therapist's question relates to the client's last response.

Therapists continue to ask questions of the client for 10 minutes. At this time all reconvene into the large group.

Therapists are asked the following questions: "How clear in your mind was your picture of the client's future without the problem?" "What were the hardest and the easiest parts of the exercise?"

Observers are asked: "What did you notice about how the picture of the future developed? How clear did it become in your mind?" "How did the therapists' questions relate to the client's responses?"

Clients are asked: "What did the therapists do or say that was most helpful to you?" "How clear was the picture in your mind of a future without the problem?"

All are asked: "Was there anything that surprised you about this exercise?" "What did you learn from this exercise?"

Discussion: The picture in each participant's mind of the client's description of the future will not be the same. It is important to note that the only picture that is truly relevant is the one in the client's mind.[1] The ultimate usefulness of the exercise is to help the client get more and more details of their life without the problem.

NOTE

1. See "The Listen and Describe Approach to Training in Solution-Focused Brief Therapy" by Dan Gallagher in this volume.

A Solution-Focused Group Message

Heather Fiske
Brenda Zalter

KEYWORDS. Brief therapy, solution-focused, training, feedback

TYPE OF AUDIENCE

- Students, workshop participants at any level, supervisees
- Groups

Group Size: This exercise can be done effectively with any number; in groups larger than 20, participants must be divided into smaller groups.

Experience Level: Introductory to advanced; no experience with solution-focused ideas or applications is necessary.

PURPOSE OF THE EXERCISE

- To practice what we preach
- To provide participants with the opportunity to receive a solution-focused message and experience its impact

Heather Fiske is a psychologist and has a private practice in Toronto, Ontario, Canada.
Brenda Zalter is affiliated with Credit Valley Hospital, Mississauga, Ontario, Canada.
Address correspondence to: Heather Fiske, 35 Scarborough Rd., Toronto, ON, Canada M4E 3M4.

[Haworth co-indexing entry note]: "A Solution-Focused Group Message." Fiske, Heather, and Brenda Zalter. Co-published simultaneously in *Journal of Family Psychotherapy* (The Haworth Press, Inc.) Vol. 16, No. 1/2, 2005, pp. 123-125; and: *Education and Training in Solution-Focused Brief Therapy* (ed: Thorana S. Nelson) The Haworth Press, Inc., 2005, pp. 123-125. Single or multiple copies of this article are available for a fee from The Haworth Document Delivery Service [1-800-HAWORTH, 9:00 a.m. - 5:00 p.m. (EST). E-mail address: docdelivery@haworthpress.com].

Digital Object Identifier: 10.1300/J085v16n01_32

- In some variations, to provide practice in constructing solution-focused messages
- To illustrate utilization

Experiential Level of the Exercise (1-10): This exercise is sometimes a 10; in its most basic form the participants are not "doing" anything obvious beyond listening, but they are *experiencing* a solution-focused message.

When participants construct the message, the exercise is a 7 because there is a component of "teaching" the construction of solution-focused messages.

TIME FRAME FOR THE EXERCISE, DEBRIEFING

- For a group of 20 or less, with the instructor developing the message, 5 minutes to deliver the message and 10 minutes at breaks for the instructor to construct the message.
- For the participants to construct, deliver, and debrief their own messages, 30-45 minutes.

INSTRUCTIONS

Basic Format: At the end of the class/course/workshop, the instructor delivers a solution-focused message (compliments, bridge, task) to the group of participants, utilizing (if available) the resource list from the Name Game for compliments and incorporating language, goals and positive events from the training experience.

Variation #1: Following the instructor's modeling of a solution-focused message (see "basic format"), the group(s) can be challenged to construct and deliver a message for the instructor.

Variation #2: The participants construct and deliver a solution-focused message for themselves as a group. Usually the instructor spends a few minutes (5 or less) reviewing the elements of a solution-focused message.

Handouts: Fiske, H. "Post-Break Message to Client" (see Appendix)
Closing Comments: Everyone leaves feeling good.

APPENDIX
Post-Break Message to Clients

1. *Compliments*
   - must be sincere and honest
   - affirm:
     - patient's hard work
     - difficulty of task
     - what they do that works
   - assign "positive blame"
   - reinforce coping
2. *Bridge*
   - rational explanation
   - in the client's language
   - within the client's world view
   - Examples: −"I agree that it is time to try something specific . . ."
     −"Because you have shown me how much you want to change things . . ."
     −"Since it is clear that what you are already doing is making a difference . . ."
     −"Since you don't feel that what you are doing so far is working . . ."
     −"It seems to me that there is so much happening in your life that some important things may be getting missed . . ."
3. *Task ("suggestion")*
   - should fit with level of motivation/readiness for change
   - can be: (a) active;
     (b) passive, reflective; or
     (c) simply an invitation to return

(Also consider Chevalier's formula:
Intervention = client view + client compliments + homework task)

−H. Fiske, 2001

Solution-Focused Scavenger Hunt

Heather Fiske
Brenda Zalter

KEYWORDS. Brief therapy, solution-focused, training

Type of Audience: Students, workshop participants at any level, supervisees
Group Size: This exercise can be done effectively with any number; in groups larger than 20, participants must be divided into smaller groups.
Experience Level: Introductory to advanced; some exposure (minimal, e.g., one day) to solution-focused ideas or applications is necessary

PURPOSE OF THE EXERCISE

- To have fun; to "play" with the training material
- To practice identifying and utilizing basic components of the solution-focused model

Experiential Level of the Exercise (1-10): (Instructions aside) this exercise is a 10.

Heather Fiske is a psychologist and has a private practice in Toronto, Ontario, Canada.
Brenda Zalter is affiliated with the Social Work Department, Credit Valley Hospital, Mississauga, Ontario, Canada.
Address correspondence to: Heather Fiske, 35 Scarborough Rd., Toronto, ON, Canada M4E 3M4 or Brenda Zalter, 35 Pirie Drive, Dundas, ON, Canada L9H 6X5.

[Haworth co-indexing entry note]: "Solution-Focused Scavenger Hunt." Fiske, Heather, and Brenda Zalter. Co-published simultaneously in *Journal of Family Psychotherapy* (The Haworth Press, Inc.) Vol. 16, No. 1/2, 2005, pp. 127-129; and: *Education and Training in Solution-Focused Brief Therapy* (ed: Thorana S. Nelson) The Haworth Press, Inc., 2005, pp. 127-129. Single or multiple copies of this article are available for a fee from The Haworth Document Delivery Service [1-800-HAWORTH, 9:00 a.m. - 5:00 p.m. (EST). E-mail address: docdelivery@haworthpress.com].

Available online at http://www.haworthpress.com/web/JFP
Digital Object Identifier: 10.1300/J085v16n01_33

TIME FRAME FOR THE EXERCISE, DEBRIEFING

One to several hours. Debriefing, scoring, and prize-giving will probably require at least an hour as well, depending on extent and volume of the hilarity produced.

This exercise can be done on a single occasion or over several days of a course or workshop. It can be assigned as homework to be debriefed either at the next meeting or at the end of the training.

Instructions: Find a story[1] about or example of:

- a small change leading to a larger change
- a person's unique solution to a problem
- how looking ahead to a more positive future helped someone change
- a solution-focused song (may be an existing song or one written by you–extra points for team performance)
- a time when someone (client, you, anyone) surprised you by:
    - recovering more quickly than you had thought possible
    - demonstrating strengths you didn't know they had
- doing something different that made a difference
- adaptations of SF methods
- being part of someone's solution
- making a solution-focused approach or strategy part of your "tool kit" (extra points for concrete representations or symbols)

Scoring: Points are awarded and prizes given on a team basis. Extra points for:

1. demonstrations, pictures, performances, documentary evidence (show and tell)
2. having at least one item for each of the categories. Points are awarded for every story/example in each category.

PRIZE IDEAS

Magic wands
Stress balls
Toys ("something to help you do something different")
Key chains with keys ("keys to change")
Chocolate coins (can be used for coin toss homework assignments)
"Occam's razors" (plastic disposables with blades removed)
Printed licenses–to do something different: to take small steps; to look

for miracles; 007 (out of 10) . . .
Printed awards for creativity, courage, unique solutions, thinking outside the box, black belts in humor, shamelessness, group bonding . . .

Shopping Tip: Dollar stores are an excellent and heuristic source of prize possibilities (see "Solution-Focused Shopping" article in this volume for further information).

Closing Comments: We think laughter and play are both aids to memory and ways of helping trainees to "own" the material. One of the hazards of adult learning is attending courses or workshops, being interested and even inspired, and then never thinking about the material again once we start, or get back to, our jobs in the real world. Your students will not forget this exercise, and we think they may be a little more likely to notice solution-focused "opportunities" around them.

NOTE

1. Stories/examples may be a person's own, someone else's, real or fictional, from books, movies, plays . . .

Group Gift Exercise

Brenda Zalter
Heather Fiske

KEYWORDS. Brief therapy, solution-focused, termination, training

TYPE OF AUDIENCE

- Students, workshop participants at any level, supervisees
- Groups, families

Note: Participants in this exercise should know one another somewhat; ideally, they should have been working together for at least one day.

Group Size: This exercise can be done effectively with any number. In groups larger than 20, participants must be divided into smaller groups. We often use the group gift as a closing exercise, with trainees in the working groups in which they have participated for the duration of the training.

Experience Level: Introductory to advanced; no experience with solution-focused ideas or applications is necessary.

Brenda Zalter is affiliated with Credit Valley Hospital, Mississauga, Ontario, Canada. Heather Fiske is a psychologist and has a private practice in Toronto, Ontario, Canada.

Address correspondence to: Brenda Zalter, 35 Pirie Drive, Dundas, ON, Canada L9H 6X5 or Heather Fiske, 35 Scarborough Rd., Toronto, ON, Canada M4E 3M4.

This exercise is not original to the authors; it is a solution-focused adaptation of a family/group gift-giving game.

[Haworth co-indexing entry note]: "Group Gift Exercise." Zalter, Brenda, and Heather Fiske. Co-published simultaneously in *Journal of Family Psychotherapy* (The Haworth Press, Inc.) Vol. 16, No. 1/2, 2005, pp. 131-133; and: *Education and Training in Solution-Focused Brief Therapy* (ed: Thorana S. Nelson) The Haworth Press, Inc., 2005, pp. 131-133. Single or multiple copies of this article are available for a fee from The Haworth Document Delivery Service [1-800-HAWORTH, 9:00 a.m. - 5:00 p.m. (EST). E-mail address: docdelivery@haworthpress.com].

Available online at http://www.haworthpress.com/web/JFP
Digital Object Identifier: 10.1300/J085v16n01_34

PURPOSE OF THE EXERCISE

- Closing/termination exercise
- Compliments in action

Experiential Level of the Exercise: Instructions aside, this exercise is a 10.
Time Frame for the Exercise, Debriefing: Depending on group size and number of layers (compliments) on the gift, 15-30 minutes.

INSTRUCTIONS

Instructions for Facilitator: Choose a gift that can be shared by the group; food treats or novelty souvenirs are often good choices. Wrap the gift in layers of paper (we recycle used newspapers). On each layer, glue or tape a direction.
Instructions for Group: This group gift is wrapped in layers of paper. On each layer is a direction. Read the direction OUT LOUD, and give the gift to the person in the group who matches the direction. When you receive the gift, unwrap one layer, read the next direction, and continue passing and unwrapping until you reach the last layer and the gift is unwrapped. Feel free to ask for or give explanations for your choices.
Sample Directions (this set is one we have used with practitioners graduating from a solution-focused training program):

- Someone who makes you laugh
- Someone who taught you something
- Someone compassionate
- Someone who asked the miracle question sincerely
- Someone who asked the miracle question creatively
- Someone who knows how to make numbers talk
- Someone for whom compliments come naturally
- Someone who notices strengths in others
- Someone who thinks in terms of possibilities
- Someone who is patient with silence
- Someone expressive
- Someone with a "big ear"
- Someone who believes everyone has their own solutions
- Someone good at giving homework assignments
- Someone who practices what they preach
- Someone curious
- Someone Columbo-like
- Someone who knows how to get a person's attention

- Someone who can interrupt a negative story
- Someone who can integrate what works for them with something new
- Someone who has tried something new
- Someone who has dared to do different
- Someone open to miracles
- Someone who can see through the eyes of a child
- Someone who can walk in another person's shoes
- Someone hopeful
- Someone ready to be surprised
- Someone whose laugh is contagious
- Someone who showed a rich imagination
- Someone easy to talk to
- Someone trustworthy
- Someone who can comfort
- Someone who is a "10" in motivation
- Someone who is a "10" in energy
- Someone who celebrates positive change
- Someone focused on exceptions
- Someone who values coping
- Someone goal-oriented
- Someone looking for what's better
- Someone who can build on small changes
- Someone who can deal with "I don't know"
- Someone who invites hopeful conversation
- Someone who wants to talk about what the other person wants
- Someone who can build bridges from compliments to tasks
- Someone who asks relationship questions
- Someone who is a real team player

Note: Directions can (and probably should) be tailored for the particular group. With younger groups or groups who know one another less well, directions may be more concrete. With some younger groups, it may be important to say that everyone should get the gift at least once. I usually begin with "someone who smiled at me today" and end with "someone generous."

List of Questions: How is this exercise solution-focused?

Closing Comments: Everybody leaves feeling good.

Exercise of Appreciation

Frank Thomas

KEYWORDS. Appreciation, affirmation, competencies, experiential, resources, strengths

TYPE OF AUDIENCE

1. experientially oriented
2. for people who know each other well, they should be on positive or neutral terms with each other;v
3. for people who have just met, they should have spent most of the day together talking and sharing or this will be a bust!

Group size: Each group should be 3-5, no more than 5.

Experience level: n/a

Purpose of the exercise: Appreciation for the contributions of others; validating colleagues; creating a positive, affirming context; highlighting competencies, gifts, and value. As a competency-based trainer who does a lot of workshops on resiliency and solution-focused therapy and supervision, this is a great fit.

Experiential level of the exercise: 4-6

Frank Thomas is affiliated with the Reunion Institute, Salesmanship Club Youth and Family Centers, Dallas, Texas.

Address correspondence to: Frank Thomas, Salesmanship Club Youth and Family Centers, Inc., 106 E. 10th St., Dallas, TX 75208.

[Haworth co-indexing entry note]: "Exercise of Appreciation." Thomas, Frank. Co-published simultaneously in *Journal of Family Psychotherapy* (The Haworth Press, Inc.) Vol. 16, No. 1/2, 2005, pp. 135-136; and: *Education and Training in Solution-Focused Brief Therapy* (ed: Thorana S. Nelson) The Haworth Press, Inc., 2005, pp. 135-136. Single or multiple copies of this article are available for a fee from The Haworth Document Delivery Service [1-800-HAWORTH, 9:00 a.m. - 5:00 p.m. (EST). E-mail address: docdelivery@ haworthpress.com].

Digital Object Identifier: 10.1300/J085v16n01_35

Time frame for the exercise, debriefing: This exercise should take 10-15 minutes and is best when near the end of an all-day (or 2-day) retreat. Debriefing could take place after a short break. I like to do this mid-afternoon, come back after a break for some debriefing and comments, and draw a workshop to a close.

INSTRUCTIONS (PRE AND POST)

1. *PRE:* People should be encouraged to participate throughout the day by saying the following: *"Notice strengths, resources, and positives about the people in your group throughout the day. There will be a QUIZ!!"* I check up on them periodically through the workshop by saying, *"Have you written anything down about your colleagues in the past 30 minutes? If not, take a moment to do so now."*

2. *THE EXERCISE/POST:* See Appendix for the exercise instructions.

Handouts: The Appendix can be a PowerPoint slide or an overhead, but it should be left up during the exercise so folks can refer to it.

Closing comments: People–both long-term colleagues and new relationships–have found this exercise affirming and valuable. Please do *not* force this to fit a workshop–if it fits and if it makes sense, then it can be powerful!

APPENDIX

Overhead transparency or PowerPoint slide:

Sharing Perspectives of Strengths

➤ Stay in your day-long groups of 3, 4 or 5.

➤ One person sits in a chair, facing away from the others. Others gather around behind her/him in a semi-circle.

➤ *Each standing member:* Speak your view of that person's strengths, as you've seen/heard/thought today while *others come close to 'eavesdrop'/listen.* Speak 'into' the back of the head of the seated member as though speaking into a microphone.

➤ *Seated person:* You are *not* to give feedback to the speakers . . . just listen to their words. Don't speak or nod.

➤ Rotate so each person becomes the 'microphone.'

Solution-Focused Shopping

Heather Fiske
Brenda Zalter

KEYWORDS. Solution focus, shopping

What you buy tells you what you were shopping for.

–adapted from S. de Shazer

Type of audience: Anyone who loves to shop can participate; the target population however is anyone who hates to shop. We believe in miracles.

Group size: Size doesn't matter; it's who you are inside that counts.

Experience level: We do recommend that this program be facilitated initially by experienced shoppers (or, as Insoo would say, shopping gurus. We ourselves prefer the more traditional terminology, "shopping goddesses"). As acolytes (or "trainees") acquire basic safety skills in this area, short solo expeditions are recommended in the company of a solution-focused shopping consultant (cash only).

Heather Fiske is a shopping consultant, Toronto, Ontario, Canada.

Brenda Zalter is a catalogue buyer, Mississauga, Ontario, Canada.

Address correspondence to: Heather Fiske, 35 Scarborough Rd., Toronto, ON, Canada M4E 3M4 or Brenda Zalter, 35 Pirie Drive, Dundas, ON, Canada L9H 6X5.

Author note: With (unwitting) contributions from Laura Champion, Nancy Latimer, Ruth Bruce, Thorana Nelson, Josée Lamarre, and, of course, our mothers.

[Haworth co-indexing entry note]: "Solution-Focused Shopping." Fiske, Heather, and Brenda Zalter. Co-published simultaneously in *Journal of Family Psychotherapy* (The Haworth Press, Inc.) Vol. 16, No. 1/2, 2005, pp. 137-140; and: *Education and Training in Solution-Focused Brief Therapy* (ed: Thorana S. Nelson) The Haworth Press, Inc., 2005, pp. 137-140. Single or multiple copies of this article are available for a fee from The Haworth Document Delivery Service [1-800-HAWORTH, 9:00 a.m. - 5:00 p.m. (EST). E-mail address: docdelivery@haworthpress.com].

Available online at http://www.haworthpress.com/web/JFP
Digital Object Identifier: 10.1300/J085v16n01_36

PURPOSE OF THE EXERCISE

- Opportunities for creative complimenting
- Self-esteem enhancement
- Meeting personal shopping goals, e.g., speed, focus, budget, precision, artistry, flair, knocking 'em dead . . .

Experiential level of the exercise (Scale from 1-10): We keep telling you: it's who you are inside that counts. And besides, Marilyn Monroe was a size 14. Trainees at any level of experience may benefit. (See our 2005 article, "Solution-Focused Feng Shui," for an extended discussion of this point.)

PRINCIPLES

Shopping is always happening; our task is simply to collaborate with and build on the person's existing ways of shopping.

- Work with the person where they are (even if it's a Kmart)
- Small changes lead to larger changes (and large steps lead to smaller sizes–BZ)
- Compliments are a powerful tool for change

Time frame for the exercise: A lifetime is too short. Any available time slots in the scheduling of workshop/training events are an opportunity. Utility of the opportunity may vary with location; workshops held in malls obviously expand possibilities; those held in more remote locations may necessitate emergency procedures such as resorting to the shopping channel.

Debriefing: Here, experience may make a difference; shopping gurus/goddesses can extend debriefing of even a "simple" postcard purchase over years; neophytes may need several questions to get them started (see below); gifted amateurs have been known to exceed even our own capacity. Because it is non-pc to comment on gender differences in this area, we will not.

Instructions: Accessorize (trivia matter)

LIST OF QUESTIONS

- How will you know that you never have to go shopping again?
- If a miracle happens and there is still credit left on your card, how will that make a difference for you?
- What will your husband see that will tell him you have met your shopping goals?

- And what else?
- And what else? . . .
- What is the first thing you will notice that will let you know that you got a great deal?
- How will you know that it's a scratch 'n save day?
- How will this make a difference for you–in your home life?–in your work life?–in your sex life?
- How will your pet know that this was a scratch 'n save day for you?
- What difference will it make for him/her?
- On a scale from 1 to 10 (or 10 to 20, size *really* doesn't matter!), if one number stands for "worst possible" and the other number stands for "best possible":
    - where were you on the scale when you first saw the mannequins in the window?
    - . . . when you tried on a bathing suit in February?
    - . . . after your solution-focused consultation?
    - . . . after your discount?
    - where are you on the scale when you consider that this purchase is:
        - Refundable?
        - Reversible?
        - Washable?
        - Packable?
        - A match for the sweater Aunt Trudy gave you eight years ago and which has sat in your closet ever since?
    - Really *really* you?

INTEGRATING HELPFUL APPROACHES FROM OTHER PARADIGMS

- Release your inner shopper. (Bradshaw)
- Your purchase is ok and my purchase is better. (whatshisname)
- Shop in the here-and-now. (Buddha)
- Buy what your mother would have bought. (Freud)
- Buy what your mother would never have bought. (Freud)
- Understand your motivations, thoughts, and desires before buying (i.e., buy 20 years from now). (post-Freudian)
- Buy what your older sister doesn't have. (Adler)
- Buy mythically. (Jung)
- Is shopping more like an enemy or a friend? (White)

Handouts: Catalogues

Resources for followup: Homework assignments:

Notice what difference it makes when you have had a successful shopping experience. What difference does it make in:

- Your mood?
- Your speed on the highway?
- Your lunch?

Closing comments: Closing times vary of course, but some department and grocery stores are now open 24 hours. Shopping is *always* occurring.

TRAINING WORKSHOPS

Training in solution-focused brief therapy comes in many forms: working with students, supervision, and workshops. These articles present outlines and exercises for full workshops.

Clinical Training
in Solution-Focused Therapy

Josée Lamarre

KEYWORDS. Training, solution-focused, supervision

The *Centre de psychothérapie stratégique* in Montréal offers a two-year training course comprised of nine classroom days per year to mental health professionals, including psychologists, social workers, physicians, and guidance counselors. Some participants bring much experience to the proceedings, while others come with relatively little. However, all participants generally seek to acquire a more effective and efficient intervention model that allows them to better respond to the needs of their clients within their particular time constraints, thereby achieving greater job satisfaction.

André Grégoire and I, Josée Lamarre, founded the Centre in 1992 after having integrated the solution-focused approach into our brief therapy clinical practice. It soon became clear that this approach, which is centered on client strengths and based on their collaboration, was needed in Québec, and so we set out to make it better known. Today, our training emphasizes the need to build client competency, forge collaborative solutions and construct a positive vision of the future. Our challenge lies in bridging the gap between partici-

---

Josée Lamarre is affiliated with the *Centre de psychothérapie stratégique*, Montréal, Québec, Canada.

Address correspondence to: Josée Lamarre, 2160 Boul Perrot, Notre-Dame De L'ile, Perrot, Quebec J7V 8P4, Canada.

[Haworth co-indexing entry note]: "Clinical Training in Solution-Focused Therapy." Lamarre, Josée. Co-published simultaneously in *Journal of Family Psychotherapy* (The Haworth Press, Inc.) Vol. 16, No. 1/2, 2005, pp. 143-148; and: *Education and Training in Solution-Focused Brief Therapy* (ed: Thorana S. Nelson) The Haworth Press, Inc., 2005, pp. 143-148. Single or multiple copies of this article are available for a fee from The Haworth Document Delivery Service [1-800-HAWORTH, 9:00 a.m. - 5:00 p.m. (EST). E-mail address: docdelivery@haworthpress.com].

Available online at http://www.haworthpress.com/web/JFP
Digital Object Identifier: 10.1300/J085v16n01_37

pants' pre-knowledge and what our program provides. To smooth the learning curve, we suggest that participants try to make connections between our presentations and the techniques they currently employ; making such links allows them to more easily comprehend the new method. Participants frequently confirm that becoming aware of what they do during their interventions allows them to subsequently make better use of their techniques. This corresponds to a clinical situation in which the client under treatment reveals an exception which, once recognized and understood, can be put to effective use.

The *Centre de psychothérapie stratégique* uses various professional training procedures–intensive training sessions and days of working in small, supervised groups–that employ a range of pedagogical tools such as lectures, videotaped interviews, role-playing, guided readings, and case discussions. Training groups have a maximum of 25 participants, while supervised groups are made up of no more than 15.

Training days are structured around a predefined timetable. We begin by presenting the basic concepts of brief therapy: its systemic approach, constructivist framework, future-focused orientation, emphasis on client collaboration, and interactive process. Following this, the themes addressed include finding and using exceptions to the problem, enhancing the client's overall abilities, visualizing a better future, and prescribing therapeutic tasks. We emphasize techniques for optimizing relations with the client and facilitating his or her empowerment. Course notes are provided to each participant. These include information on the themes addressed, specific readings, and a bibliography with which participants can continue their learning. Throughout the course's theoretical component, "learning by doing" is given primary importance, and specific indications are provided on *how* and *when* to intervene. The exercises and videotapes bring the course experiential level to approximately 3/10.

Following is an example of our training methods. The following exercise, which I often propose to participants, modifies their perception of reality, and allows them to realize that exceptions do exist, even if they are not immediately identifiable. I begin by suggesting a short test of their powers of observation. I have them put down their pencils and then ask them to observe and memorize all the objects–walls, ceiling, clothes, etc.–of a certain color, the color chosen being the dominant color of the room. After a moment or two, I have them shut their eyes and name all the objects in the room that are not of this dominant color but are instead of an *unusual* color–pink, for example. Here, participants are in a situation that parallels that of the client who is being questioned about exceptions. Indeed, certain participants have informed me that they conducted the same test on their clients when exceptions could not be found: their clients came away believing that exceptions do exist, even if they couldn't be readily identified. In short, this exercise is an excellent way to prepare clients to note exceptions between therapy sessions.

Changing the practitioner's focus during client interviews is one of the main challenges we face in our program. The majority of participants are university trained and, as such, have generally learned to focus on the pathological aspects of the client, who is analyzed accordingly. Learning to direct their attention towards the client's abilities, which manifest themselves at the same time as the problems, constitutes a significant change for many therapists. To promote solution-focused listening and empowerment-based intervention, we suggest the following exercise: In pairs, participants take turns playing the role of client and therapist. The "client" has three minutes to discuss a real-life problem. Given the length of the exercise, I recommend bringing up problems of a lesser intensity than, for example, the participant's recent divorce or recurring paranoia. The "therapist," listening attentively, must be sure to compliment the client on a perceived strength or good intention revealed while recounting the problem. The exercise is subsequently repeated with the roles reversed. Once this second stage is complete, we review the exercise, and I point out that each participant has successfully provided positive feedback in the face of a lament. As a result, participants begin to develop skill in perceiving the positive within the negative. It is interesting to note that the "clients" always seem to feel that they have been heard, even if the "therapist's" comment takes them by surprise. In fact, this element of surprise effectively reframes the problem; from that moment on, the client cannot help but see the situation differently. For the most part, the therapist's compliment provides a sense of hope and allows the client to feel that all is not as black as it might have seemed.

With regard to supervision days, whose experiential level is 8/10, the content is much more flexible. In general, we begin with a round of "good tricks." We ask participants to relate an instance in which they successfully used a solution-focused therapy tool. Participants briefly outline the client's situation, describe how they used the technique in question and explain how the client reacted. For example, a psychiatric nurse described his use of a scale with a client diagnosed as manic-depressive. On this scale, 1 represented the most depressed state of mind, 10 the most agitated and 5 a kind of middle ground. When asked to situate himself on this scale, the client was better able to judge his mental state. The most interesting response emerged from the question, "Where on the scale would you wish to live permanently?" The client responded, "6." While "5" was deemed to be too tedious, the client knew that too much exultation brought a higher risk of depression. This admission led the intervener to enlist the client's help in seeking ways to determine when he was at "6" and how to stay there. The sharing of "good tricks" is always very enriching for all participants.

The round of "good tricks" is in fact an applied use of the solution-focused approach, which emphasizes successes rather than failures. After helping participants to clarify their "good tricks," the supervisor expands the field by posing different questions. For example, "How did you come to say that?" "What made you persist in this direction, despite the client's uncertainty?" It is important to give a name to the different techniques employed, since participants are not always entirely conscious of their operative methods. Their abilities, creativity, capacity for bringing to light the client's strengths, etc., are also highlighted. In the second year, participants are responsible for identifying the different techniques used by themselves and others, thus gaining more insight into how they may best respond to their clients. The supervisor might also provide indications as to how participants can deepen their understanding of the process.

Next to be addressed are the "bugs," the places where the therapist admits to not having known how to elicit solutions from the client, highlight his or her strengths, or direct questioning toward a constructive vision of the future. Here too, we utilize the solution-focused approach by asking the participant with the "bug" how they resolved the situation and what they would do in the future should a similar situation arise. It often happens that, even while asking for help, the participant holds elements of the solution within him- or herself. In addition, calling on other participants to suggest new ideas stimulates everyone's creativity. All findings are subsequently supplemented with our own suggestions and with variations on the techniques in use.

Case discussions can follow, either via brainstorming sessions or through role playing. Here, to direct the process most effectively, we ask that participants who submit cases for discussion should name their objectives. Role playing allows strengths and weaknesses to be observed through the course of an intervention. We emphasize the strengths of the therapist and we can make suggestions on avoiding difficulties we have observed without necessarily attributing the difficulty to any one person in particular. This avoids discrediting the participant; many therapists have been traumatized by criticism incurred during supervision in university. We believe that clinical skills are best developed on the basis of participants' strengths.

At the beginning of the training year, participants receive a list of the skills associated with the solution-focused approach (see Appendix), and are asked to conduct a self-assessment based on a scale linked to each of these skills. Our aim here is to help participants recognize their strong points. We also ask that they set themselves a modest goal in a skill area of their choosing. They are also required to specify how they will know when they have advanced one point further up the scale pertaining to their goal. This method brings the candidate's desired improvement within range. A follow-up of these objectives is conducted at the end of each year.

At the end of the second year, we ask participants to draft a case study including all the interventions, real or speculative, that they considered or carried out. This case study allows them to review all aspects of the solution-focused approach and to synthesize their learnings.

After two years of training, certain groups continue to meet regularly to discuss cases, develop work tools, share readings and so on. Sometimes they organize additional sessions through us around a particular theme. Every year we also arrange workshops with experts in solution-focused brief therapy such as Insoo Kim Berg, Yvonne Dolan, and Ben Furman. Those who have followed our training often attend these workshops, and come away stimulated and with renewed energy. In addition, we publish a free online journal, *L'EFFET SPIRALE VIRTUEL* (available in French only) which presents case studies and articles on a given theme or technique. Scales, questionnaires, and translated work tools can be distributed through the journal. In sum, *L'EFFET SPIRALE VIRTUEL* is a source of regular input following training. Some participants may be asked to write articles, depending on their particular area of expertise.

We also work with organizations seeking custom training for their employees; we develop personalized programs that include both training and supervision. Companies with a limited budget who cannot afford the two-year option are nevertheless recommended to select at least as many days of supervision as of training so that the learning can be fully integrated. In Québec over the last 10 years, we have helped train members of diverse fields including education (primary and secondary), community health (CLSCs [local community service centers] and crisis centers) and protection (*Centres Jeunesse* [youth centers]), psychiatry (residence and external clinics), and organizations such as Suicide-Action Montréal.

For me, training is an all-consuming passion; in my career, I have passed from being the expert to being the one seeking participants' expertise. This position is not always easy, because participants continue to perceive my colleagues and me as the authoritative figures. But solution-focused therapy and supervision frees us from having to know all the answers; we seek them in the participants instead, who quickly learn when the accent is placed on their capabilities. The resulting empowerment provides them with the motivation to integrate the other elements of the method. We believe that, while participants may learn to use the techniques during the first year, it is during the second year that they truly acquire a solution-focused spirit. This can free them to develop their own solution-oriented vision in which the applied techniques are integrated with other tools they might already possess.

In conclusion, I would like to share one of the most satisfying comments made by a participant in evaluating their two years of training: "This is the first time I have felt competent all the way through a training course!"

APPENDIX

Centre de
psychothérapie
stratégique

C.P. 236
Succ. De Lorimier
Montréal (Québec)
H2H 2N6

SUPERVISION GOALS TO BECOME **A GOOD SOLUTION-FOCUSED THERAPIST**

	0	1	2	3	4	5
Good relationship (empathy, respect, authenticity)	|____|____|____|____|____|
Positive and global vision of the client	|____|____|____|____|____|
Not-knowing posture	|____|____|____|____|____|
Empowering, positive feedback, compliments	|____|____|____|____|____|
Adjustment to client motivation	|____|____|____|____|____|
Language: Yes set, client's words and metaphors	|____|____|____|____|____|
Leading from behind	|____|____|____|____|____|
Problem description	|____|____|____|____|____|
Decrystallisations	|____|____|____|____|____|
Relational questions	|____|____|____|____|____|
Reframings	|____|____|____|____|____|
Well formed goals	|____|____|____|____|____|
Miracle question	|____|____|____|____|____|
Scales, small steps	|____|____|____|____|____|
Pre-session change	|____|____|____|____|____|
Exceptions finding and amplifying	|____|____|____|____|____|
Transfer of competencies	|____|____|____|____|____|
Prescriptions messages	|____|____|____|____|____|

Three Case Studies

Joel Simon

KEYWORDS. Training exercise, case studies, changing perspective, problem versus solution focus, meaning making

INTRODUCTION

The origin of solution-focused brief therapy (SFBT) began with the very simple question of what do therapists do that is helpful to clients? Later, this question was expanded to: What do therapists and clients do together that clients say is helpful? This question logically leads to training that emphasizes practical techniques that have proven to work over time. My own experience initially as a trainee and currently as a trainer is that the clear majority of time spent in training is on introducing solution-focused questions and how to use them to construct conversations that are helpful to clients.

Those who have trained and have persisted in practicing SFBT report that they think very differently about their own and their clients' roles. Personally, as I practiced SFBT, I began to question how I defined my work, the work of the people who sought my services, and the assumptions I was making about the process.

Although this process occurs over time and is the result of the experiences the trainees have using the approach, I had come to hypothesize that it may

Joel Simon is affiliated with the Center for Solutions, Walden, NY.
Address correspondence to: Joel Simon, 7 Ivy Lane, Walden, NY 12586.

[Haworth co-indexing entry note]: "Three Case Studies." Simon, Joel. Co-published simultaneously in *Journal of Family Psychotherapy* (The Haworth Press, Inc.) Vol. 16, No. 1/2, 2005, pp. 149-154; and: *Education and Training in Solution-Focused Brief Therapy* (ed: Thorana S. Nelson) The Haworth Press, Inc., 2005, pp. 149-154. Single or multiple copies of this article are available for a fee from The Haworth Document Delivery Service [1-800-HAWORTH, 9:00 a.m. - 5:00 p.m. (EST). E-mail address: docdelivery@haworthpress.com].

Digital Object Identifier: 10.1300/J085v16n01_38

prove useful to challenge the traditional ways in which trainees think about the conversations they have with clients and to incorporate exercises in my trainings that may serve to challenge their thinking. I had devised the following exercise for that purpose.

INSTRUCTIONS

The exercise is especially suited for groups of eight to 20 people. I have used it not only for multiple day trainings, but also for presentations that last for two or more hours. The exercise typically takes about one hour to complete. I have found it a useful starting point for discussion and therefore is quite suitable as an introductory exercise. The exercise assumes a certain amount of clinical knowledge; however, I have found that most people have enough experience and training to promote a useful outcome. The group is divided into two subgroups and it is best if the subgroups can meet in separate spaces. They are asked to choose a group leader whose job is to keep the group on task and a recorder who will report the group's findings. Each subgroup is given an identical set of three case descriptions.

CASE ONE

The client is a 17-year-old white, single, male. Client was seen with his parents. Client was attending his senior year of high school when he experienced what his family physician described as a "nervous breakdown." According to referral information, the client is isolative and presents as easily distracted and anxious. He is described by his teachers as a poor student who has difficulty concentrating, is easily distracted, and is "a problem in class." The mother removed him from school and placed him on home schooling.

Developmentally, the mother describes a significant lag in speech development. The father discussed his son's lack of friends and expressed disappointment in his son's lack of athletic ability and poor school performance. Both parents report odd mannerisms. The mother stated that her son invented his own religion and chants hymns to himself. In an apparent attempt to find the correct words to describe their son, the parents stated, "He is different."

CASE TWO

The client is a 17-year-old male accompanied by his mother. The referral was suggested to the mother by the client's teacher who described him, according to the mother, as "mentally ill." According to the mother, this opinion is shared by both relatives and neighbors although the mother emphatically insists that her son is normal.

The client's school performance is marked by disruption and poor grades. The client stated to the interviewer that he hated school. In fact, according to the mother, one of the teachers strongly suggested that the client leave school because "his very presence destroyed the other students' respect for the teacher." Previous evaluations describe the mother as "domineering, demanding and pessimistic."

According to the mother, the client does not have many friends, and does not enjoy playing with his peers; she described him as "lonely." According to the parents, the client is prone to violent temper outbursts. The only significant history gleaned is that the client was born with a "large head" and the family experienced the death of three children prior to his birth.

CASE THREE

The client is a 16-year-old female currently being raised by her maternal grandmother. The mother separated from the father who is now deceased; according to the grandmother, he suffered from alcoholism. The grandmother reports that the client's mother is rejecting of the child, calling her "homely" in the client's presence and complaining that the child lies and steals candy.

The client characterized her relationship with her father as "warm." According to the referral material, "[The client] lives in a fantasy world where she is her father's mistress." This fantasy appears to be of long duration.

This appears to be a family of long-term dysfunction. The maternal uncle also is described as alcoholic, left the family, and his current location is unknown. There is a maternal aunt living with the grandmother who is described as depressed and who spends her days sequestered in her bedroom. Several other aunts and uncles live in the home who, according to the grandmother, are "out of control."

It is evident that the grandmother is attempting to compensate for her perceived ineffectiveness with her own children by over-protecting and controlling the client. The client is not allowed to play with peers, she is required to wear a brace to improve her posture, and the grandmother refuses to send her to school. During the interview, the client presented with clothing chosen by the grandmother, which, in the interviewer's opinion was inappropriate for her age.

EXERCISE

The group is divided into two and each subgroup is given a different set of instructions.

Subgroup I: Following are 3 case studies. These are actual patients with known outcomes. For each case, adhere to the following procedure:

1. Formulate a problem statement including, where appropriate, etiology and problems within the social environment (e.g., family dysfunction, possible history of or tendency for sexual abuse).
2. Based upon the above, suggest a range of possible diagnoses from the most benign to most chronic.
3. Given the problem as stated above, diagnoses, and assuming no treatment, predict the most probable course of the clients' lives in adulthood.

Subgroup II: Following are descriptions of 3 individuals. These are actual people with known outcomes. In each case, the individual through hard work and creative use of their own resources surprised the experts and lived lives well beyond expectations. Expected to be failures, they became successes. Your job as a group is to have fun and see if you can guess on the basis of this information, how they fooled the experts. How did they become successful? Remember, this is not meant to be a case conference and therefore avoid discussions regarding pathology or problems. Have Fun!!!!!

Both groups are given 20 minutes to complete the task. It is very common for Subgroup II to complete the task significantly faster than Subgroup I. My own admittedly subjective observation is that there is usually more levity in the latter group as well. I have found it occasionally necessary to sit in on Subgroup II to keep them on task. Especially when there is a preponderance of clinicians, there is a tendency to revert back to familiar conversations, i.e., the traditional problem-focused case conference.

Once the respective subgroups have completed the task, the group is reassembled. As each subgroup reports their findings, the leader writes a side-by-side comparison. It quickly becomes evident to the group that there is something amiss and they first guess that the case descriptions differ. When it is demonstrated that the descriptions are identical, they next deduce that each group was assigned different tasks.

EXAMPLE

In this example, a group of between 10 and 15 students is in an undergraduate social work class. The instructor of the course invited me to talk about solution focus; this was the first contact that the students had with me. The students had a brief introduction to solution focus given by the instructor but had a minimal idea about the approach. The students' own experiences varied: one was working as a counselor in an alcohol treatment program, another worked for Big Brothers/Big Sisters, several had no experience working in mental health or related fields.

Once the group had reassembled, they reported the results. Tables 1, 2, and 3 show a side-by-side comparison of the two subgroups for each case. The group quickly surmised that the introductions were very different. The actual

TABLE 1. Case Example #1

	Subgroup I (Problem-Focused)	Subgroup II (Solution-Focused)
Problem	Parent problem Inability to cope Demoralizing family Lacking peer involvement Family dysfunction	Not applicable
Diagnoses	ADHD Phobia Sexual abuse Drug involvement	Not applicable
Possible Outcomes	"Self-fulfilling prophecy"	Religious leader Scientist Diplomat/mediator Intellect Spiritual healer Creates an open school for creative thinkers Gandhi Albert Einstein

TABLE 2. Case Example #2

	Subgroup I (Problem-Focused)	Subgroup II (Solution-Focused)
Problem	Disruptive in school Lack of family support Controlling mother Mother in denial regarding her son's serious problems	Not applicable
Diagnoses	Fetal alcohol syndrome Developmentally disabled/retarded Mental illness	Not applicable
Possible Outcomes	Jail Institutionalization	Comedian Social worker Professional wrestler Advocate Attorney "Hat Model" Circus entertainer Cop Jerry Seinfeld

TABLE 3. Case Example #3

	Subgroup I (Problem-Focused)	Subgroup II (Solution-Focused)
Problem	Alcoholism Dealing with father's death Controlling grandmother Incest Family dysfunction	Not applicable
Diagnoses	PTSD (sexual abuse) PTSD (physical abuse)	Not applicable
Possible Outcomes	Prostitution Alcoholic Recluse Repeating same pattern as her own mother	Actress Owner of a bar and grill Psychic Trashy novel writer Social worker Model

identities of the case examples were then revealed. The first case describes Thomas Alva Edison; the second case, Albert Einstein; and the third case is Eleanor Roosevelt.

The students were asked what meaning the exercise had for them. One of the class members stated her understanding that the kind of questions that are asked will determine how the client will be perceived. There was a lively discussion regarding how cases were presented with the focus on problems and as a result, a narrow, selective and pathology-based orientation to the individual. Several currently working in the field reported that the process of Subgroup I is very similar to what they experience in their respective agencies' case conferences. There was a remark that although Subgroup II took much less time than Subgroup I, their results more closely paralleled actual outcome.

DISCUSSION

Although case examples for Thomas Alva Edison, Albert Einstein, and Eleanor Roosevelt were used, it is possible to create case studies of most famous individuals as long as biographical information is available. These can be readily found in libraries.

The number of individuals who have approached me requesting a copy of the case examples attests to the interest that the exercise generates. The exercise has had three common results: (1) It engenders a discussion regarding the way in which language influences outcome; (2) It results in a dialogue about the effect that diagnosis has on the practitioner's view of the individual and the individual's view of himself or herself; and (3) It calls into question the usefulness of the traditional case conference methodology.

Five Small-Group Exercises
for Experiential Learning of SFBT

Heather Fiske

KEYWORDS. Scaling, solution-focused brief therapy, training

These five exercises are designed to provide an almost completely interactive, non-didactic format for conveying the basic principles and methods of solution-focused work. They are the direct result of opportunities I have had to teach solution-focused methods to service providers who work with the homeless. As a group, these students are remarkable for two things: first, the intensity of their interest in whatever may be helpful to their clients and their eagerness to learn; and second, the educational challenges they present to an instructor.

These challenges arise both from these students' working conditions and also from their linguistic and educational diversity. In terms of working conditions, there are the obvious challenges of working with "multiproblem" (multisolution?) clients; limited environmental supports; largely unstructured helping interactions often conducted in inconvenient, uncomfortable, sometimes dangerous conditions; and in addition, the fact that from one-third to one-half of my students have worked all night before coming to class and

Heather Fiske is a psychologist and has a private practice in Toronto, Ontario, Canada.
Address correspondence to: Heather Fiske, 35 Scarborough Rd., Toronto, ON, Canada M4E 3M4.

[Haworth co-indexing entry note]: "Five Small-Group Exercises for Experiential Learning of SFBT." Fiske, Heather. Co-published simultaneously in *Journal of Family Psychotherapy* (The Haworth Press, Inc.) Vol. 16, No. 1/2, 2005, pp. 155-158; and: *Education and Training in Solution-Focused Brief Therapy* (ed: Thorana S. Nelson) The Haworth Press, Inc., 2005, pp. 155-158. Single or multiple copies of this article are available for a fee from The Haworth Document Delivery Service [1-800-HAWORTH, 9:00 a.m. - 5:00 p.m. (EST). E-mail address: docdelivery@haworthpress.com].

Available online at http://www.haworthpress.com/web/JFP
Digital Object Identifier: 10.1300/J085v16n01_39

many will work all night between the first and second days of a two-day course.

Cultural and linguistic diversity is a common feature of any classroom in Toronto (officially the most multicultural city in the world), but still this group is exceptional. In all of the groups I have taught, English is not a first or even second language for more than half the class; I had one group of 14 students with 12 languages of origin and *42* languages in total. In terms of educational background, while Master's degrees in counseling or social work are becoming more common in this field, the range is extreme, from limited or no formal education–there has been at least one functionally illiterate student in each of my classes–to multiple PhDs–also true of at least one student in each of my classes.

The conventional educational approaches–lecture, reliance on readings and on slides or overhead notes of printed materials–are simply not an option with this group, even as an adjunct. Therefore, these exercises were my attempt to utilize two of the outstanding strengths of this group of practitioners–their own human experience and their deep interest in helping their clients–to facilitate their learning.

Exercises were conducted in small groups of four to six, with group members interviewing each other in turn. In addition to the five exercises below, I also use the Scaling Conversation exercise, where group members get to know each other and/or solicit one another's views on a theme(s) using only scaling questions. Scaling questions would already be somewhat familiar from use of the "Scaling in Action" warm-up/goal-setting exercise (Zalter & Fiske, this volume).

Following each exercise, debriefing conversations are conducted with the whole group, giving me an opportunity to highlight and reinforce solution-focused principles and practices. I also invite them to tell stories of how similar approaches have already been helpful with their clients and of homeless clients' unexpected strengths, resources, and successes.

EXERCISES A-E

What Makes a Difference: Exercise A

Think about someone who has had a positive impact in your life. This person may not have been someone who was around a lot, but in some small or large way, they made a difference to you. It may be someone who you haven't seen for a long time.

Respond to the following questions:

1. Who was this person? How did you know them?
2. What did this person say or do that was special to you?
3. What difference did it make to you at the time?
4. What difference has it made to you since then?
5. How do you continue to show the positive impact this person had on you in your life today?
6. How do you want to keep building on this?
7. Give one or two words to describe what it was this person did or said that made a difference for you.

How Change Happens: Exercise B

1. Describe a change you have made in your life: an accomplishment or progress that you are proud of.
2. How did you do it?
3. Did this happen step by step or all at once?
4. If it happened all at once, were there things that led up to it?
5. When did you know that this was something that you wanted?
6. What was the very first step you took that led to this change?
7. What does it tell you about yourself that you were able to do this?

Thinking About a Better Future: Exercise C

Think of your most challenging recent or current client. Imagine that one year from now, someone asks them how you were helpful, and they have a positive answer. Role-play the question and their answer. Then respond to the following questions:

1. What do you think you will have done or said that that allows this client to say this about how you were helpful?
2. What have you already begun to do or say that could contribute to this positive outcome?
3. What can you do to build on what you have started?
4. What might you want to do differently?
5. Give one or two words for what it is that you can say or do to make a difference for this client.

The Miracle Question: Exercise D

Think about a problem that you have now, not something too personal, perhaps a work-related problem (paperwork? shifts? time?). Then respond to the following:

1. Suppose that tonight, while you are sleeping, a miracle happens. The miracle is that this problem that has been bothering you is solved, just like that [snap fingers]. But, because you are asleep, you don't know that this miracle has happened. So, tomorrow, after you wake up, what's the very first thing you will see that will tell you, something is different?
2. . . . And what difference will that make?
3. And what else? And what else?
4. What will you be doing or saying that you are not doing now?
5. Who in your life will be the first to notice that something has changed?
6. What will that person see that will tell him or her, something is different for you?
7. What difference will seeing that change in you make for that person?
8. When was the most recent time that even a small part of this "miracle picture" already happened?

The Power of Compliments: Exercise E

Part A. Respond to the following:

1. Describe one of the best compliments you have ever received.
2. How did it affect you?
3. What difference did it make to you then and later?
4. What difference does it make to you now as you tell us about it?
5. Sometimes people have trouble believing compliments–What made this compliment believable to you?
6. When will it be most helpful for you to remember this compliment again?

Part B. What is the most recent compliment you received?

1. How did it make a difference in your day?
2. When will be a good time for you to remember this again?
3. How will it make a difference then?

Brief Training in Brief Therapies

Steve Myers

KEYWORDS. Youth justice, solution-focused therapy, involuntary clients, training, criminology

Having attended voluntary agency conferences in the UK on Youth Crime for a number of years, presenting workshops on a variety of issue, but predominantly about the sexual misbehaviour of young people, I have begun to introduce elements of Solution-Focused and Narrative work in this field. The opportunities afforded by having perhaps a maximum of one and a half hours to introduce any topic are limited, but certainly hone the mind in thinking about the most effective methods to impart key points that are understandable, stimulate interest in further study, and are rooted in practice. The participants in the workshops are from a wide variety of backgrounds, disciplines, and experiences. However, they are all involved in work with children and young people who are in the criminal justice system at some point. This allows for some commonalities of experience and a presumption that they may actually want the best for the young people with whom they work. In the UK, the age of criminal responsibility (at which a child can be held fully responsible in law

Steve Myers is affiliated with the School of Community, Health Sciences and Social Care, University of Salford, Salford, England.

Address correspondence to: Steve Myers, School of Community, Health Sciences and Social Care, University of Salford, Allerton Building, Frederick Road, Salford, M6 6PU, England.

[Haworth co-indexing entry note]: "Brief Training in Brief Therapies." Myers, Steve. Co-published simultaneously in *Journal of Family Psychotherapy* (The Haworth Press, Inc.) Vol. 16, No. 1/2, 2005, pp. 159-162; and: *Education and Training in Solution-Focused Brief Therapy* (ed: Thorana S. Nelson) The Haworth Press, Inc., 2005, pp. 159-162. Single or multiple copies of this article are available for a fee from The Haworth Document Delivery Service [1-800-HAWORTH, 9:00 a.m. - 5:00 p.m. (EST). E-mail address: docdelivery@haworthpress.com].

Digital Object Identifier: 10.1300/J085v16n01_40

for criminal behaviour) is 10, and the Youth Justice system manages young people from this age to 17 with a range of community-based, state-funded provisions available. Children within this age range may also be imprisoned. The overwhelming majority of participants are not familiar with Solution-Focused or Narrative approaches.

The field of crime and criminology is dominated by positivist and determinist ideologies that have popular as well as institutional support. A cursory glance at the media-led anxieties about youth crime as well as the research base that has informed legislative and governmental policy/practices in the UK demonstrates a reliance on rather crude notions of causality and difference about young people who commit offences (Goldson, 2000). This has led to practices that are prescribed by directives from central government through protocols and preferred 'evidence-based' approaches (Muncie, 1999). These have a tendency to locate the problem of offending within a psychological construct, specifically the notion of 'wrong-thinking,' which has led to the dominance of cognitive behavioural approaches in practice in the UK, influenced by the more psychopathologising approaches popular in the US.

As a former practitioner and current lecturer in this area, I am fairly familiar with the issues involved and the prevailing culture(s) involved in tackling youth crime. I think this allows some reflection and acknowledgement of the current pressures and priorities placed upon workers, who are under enormous moral and institutional pressures to prevent young people from offending, which is a Sisyphean task. I have found it useful to have this grounding in the 'realities' of their work to target the sessions in a way that will resonate with their needs and experiences, but also enable them to take a critical stance on their current knowledge. Finding the keys to holding their attention and making the ideas relevant to them is both respectful and inherently subversive in the prevailing 'thin storied' climate of crime-work.

An early exercise is one that allows them to identify their notions of causality and the significance of this in affecting outcomes in work with young people. I present a pre-prepared case study that has almost a complete range of potential reasons why the young person may have committed an offence, ranging from Attention Deficit Hyperactivity Disorder (a current and hopefully fleeting moral panic) to ethnic and sexual identity to socio-economic deprivation. The case is dragged from the depths of my experience and imagination. Participants are invited to consider the case and then to share their thoughts as to why the young person committed the offence. This generates a range of ideas that are equally (in)valid and often contradictory (for example, ADHD and Social Learning Theory) and allow participants to consider how their preferred ways of understanding events may lead to particular responses and outcomes. I lead discussion about the nature of responses based on each of the notions of causality and the consequences of these. It also is useful to reflect that most of the answers about causality are based on notions of deficit within the person be they biological, psychological, or social explanations.

This exercise provides a good introduction for the principles of Solution-Focused and Narrative approaches in problematising the significance of causality in moving forward. It allows the notion of 'truth' about a person to be destabilised and made multi-faceted, which is useful in questioning dominant ways of thinking. I have a specific interest in and concern with identity and this is also an opportunity to reflect on what White (1995) called the 'thin' identities such theorising can produce. This is particularly useful when I am using sexual misbehaviour as the theme, because 'the sex offender' is a powerful construct that often terrifies people into narrow responses.

A further exercise that is useful in engaging people in the importance of language is to pair participants up and, using the case study, ask them to decide who is going to be the interviewer and who the young person. The notion of role play is usually met with groans but I am clear about the boundaries of this, including a very strict time limit of say, three minutes. The interviewer is requested to ask the young person why they committed the offence as if they were meeting them for the first time in a mandated setting. Youth crime participants tend to enjoy playing the recalcitrant young person, which fits nicely with the intended outcome. When I ask how the young person responded to the exercise, I inevitably receive a chorus of 'Don't Know,' 'Dunno's,' or other regionally specific phrases. At this point I am able to dramatically flourish a pre-prepared flip chart paper with the words, 'Don't Know' written on it and we are able to discuss the feelings generated by the question, 'Why,' including blame and frustration, felt both by the interviewers and the 'young people.'

This exercise enables the participants to reflect on the usefulness of causality as a tool in working with young people and links in with their practice experience. Many will talk about the futility of asking 'Why' in 'real' cases, when they can see that they do not know the answer themselves, or recognise that there are many answers. It also allows reflection on their preferred model of understanding problem behaviour, linking the initial 'explanations' exercise with causality-seeking questioning.

The exercise is repeated after discussion with a prohibition on using the question, 'Why.' Participants are encouraged to use 'What,' 'When,' 'How,' and 'Where' in framing their questions. This usually elicits a much richer response in the young person and a feeling of movement with the interviewer. The difference between the two approaches is compared and contrasted and participants become clearer that the way a person is approached through constructions of language will impact on the outcome. Interestingly, some participants have voiced that they do this anyway in their practice, but that it did not have a name before. I remain unsure of this because I think they usually refer to the more general, positive nature of the approach, rather than acknowledgement of the specific centrality of the language used. However, in the time allotted, I tend not to care because the outcome is a raised awareness of the principle of the importance of language, which is the desired outcome.

In assisting participants to understand the notions of Scaling Questions and Miracle Questions (de Shazer, 1988), I have given them two copies of a pre-prepared form that act as workshop evaluations and as aide memoirs to take home. Very simply, the forms ask participants to scale their knowledge of Solution-Focused and Narrative approaches at the beginning of the session and at the end. A further question invites them to consider what it would take to move them one point further up their scale and how they would achieve this. The Miracle Question is also simple: 'What would be different if they woke up the next day and their knowledge of Solution-Focused and Narrative approaches was complete? How would I know that they had achieved this? What would they be doing differently?' This allows them to reflect on what it would take based on the information given in the session. Pointers for further reading are included in the written information.

The above are very simple and straightforward exercises and can be accused of being simplistic and not acknowledging the complexity of some of the techniques and ideas. However, if we are considering a basic introduction and motivating participants to undertake their own further studies within a very limited time frame, I have found these exercises to be helpful as have the participants. Experience has demonstrated that participants find it easier to access the techniques of Solution-Focused approaches, which are in essence more straightforward than the more challenging concepts of Narrative ideas. Participants need much more time than the space allocated to really absorb the concepts because the fundamentals of the approaches confront some deeply held positions. However, demonstrating *how* these ideas may work, rather than concentrating on *why* they may work fits in with the approaches and allows busy, pragmatic workers to have the beginnings of another set of tools for working with young people. I also have the subversive hope that they will be able to use the ideas to challenge some of the totalising and monolithic discourses within which they work.

REFERENCES

de Shazer, S. (1988). *Clues: Investigating solutions in brief therapy.* New York and London: Norton.

Goldson, B. (Ed). (2000). *The new youth justice.* Lyme Regis, UK: Russell House Press.

Muncie, J. (1999). *Youth and crime: A critical introduction.* London: Sage.

White, M. (1995). *Re-authoring lives: Interviews and essays.* Adelaide, Australia: Dulwich Centre Publications.

Doing Something Different

Judith Milner

KEYWORDS. Problem free talk, "expert" knowledge, client resources, solution-focused therapy training

As I suspect is the experience of most trainers, students who are completely new to therapy find it easiest to grasp the philosophy and practice principles of solution-focused brief therapy. Those with prior training and practice in other approaches find it hard to give up old habits. Even where questions asking them what they hope to gain from the training reveals that they are completely stuck with their clients and eager to do something different, they often say they hope to acquire more expertise. Pre-course work asking them to identify existing skills (see, for example, Sharry, Madden, & Darmody, 2001, pp. 16-21) actually makes it harder for them to yield expertise because they often identify skills that are embedded in the original method (for example, 'I am good at relapse prevention') or so vague as to be almost meaningless (for example, 'I'm a good listener'). As they begin to practice the techniques, they find it hard to resist the lure of problem talk and the editing of conversations which are then reproduced in their own professional languages.

As solution-focused therapists, we know that it is much harder to stop doing something than it is to start doing something so I devised a set of linked exer-

Judith Milner is affiliated with the Northorpe Hall Child and Family Trust, Mirfield, England.

Address correspondence to: Judith Milner, Northorpe Hall Trust, Northorpe Lane, Mirfield WF12 OQL, England.

[Haworth co-indexing entry note]: "Doing Something Different." Milner, Judith. Co-published simultaneously in *Journal of Family Psychotherapy* (The Haworth Press, Inc.) Vol. 16, No. 1/2, 2005, pp. 163-167; and: *Education and Training in Solution-Focused Brief Therapy* (ed: Thorana S. Nelson) The Haworth Press, Inc., 2005, pp. 163-167. Single or multiple copies of this article are available for a fee from The Haworth Document Delivery Service [1-800-HAWORTH, 9:00 a.m. - 5:00 p.m. (EST). E-mail address: docdelivery@haworthpress.com].

Available online at http://www.haworthpress.com/web/JFP
Digital Object Identifier: 10.1300/J085v16n01_41

cises that would give students an experience of what it felt like to be listened to at the level of the word and have their strengths and resources identified through ongoing problem free talk. The latter is a skilled process and I find that students experience three difficulties as they begin practising it:

- difficulties in timing the shift from problem to solution talk, with a tendency to become solution-forced rather than solution-focused (O'Connell, 2001);
- a tendency to keep problem free talk at the social chit chat level; and
- not exploring widely enough clients' resources, creativity, imagination and dreams.

This latter difficulty seems to be grounded in a rather strange belief about 'not setting the client up to fail'; however, students who are unable to recognize that solution-focused therapy sets clients up to succeed will struggle with the whole approach. Where students have been schooled to classify problems, categorise people, and identify deficits–usually within an 'expert' language–it is hard for them to see their clients as resourceful, creative people. And because clients will construct and share their language according to the audience for whom their stories are intended, they are highly likely to tell the therapist a problem story. The ensuing conversation may use ordinary language but therapists will interpret what the client says within the 'expert' story they have in their head. The ensuing conversation not only reduces the likelihood of the client's talking about strengths and resources but also blows up problems. One way out of this is for students to change their language and focus by practicing using what Jacob describes as having two buckets of words: one full of jargon for talking with colleagues and an empty one to receive the client's words. The first exercise I ask students to undertake aims to develop conversations which move away from 'expert,' problem stories to stories of resourcefulness.

EXERCISE 1

Part 1. In order to demonstrate an 'expert,' dominant story, I write up my 'official' qualifications as a trainer on the flip chart. I then comment on that story's potential to limit the way in which they would introduce themselves in that it sets an agenda for what can be talked about in the way of skills, one that has the unfortunate side effect of highlighting deficits. I cross out all I have written, take a fresh sheet and write my 'thick' story, one that describes resourceful qualities and strengths. This includes details of my hobbies, proudest achievements, hopes and dreams, etc., commenting as I go along on what these things say about me in terms of personal qualities.

Part 2. I ask the students to interview each other in pairs, to elicit at least one skill, ability, resource, etc., that they did not previously know that person had. They are asked to listen carefully to the words used and take notes because they will be asked to report back on what they have heard.

Part 3. The students report back to the whole group the one thing they have discovered that they did not previously know, why that particular thing impressed them, what resonances it has for them, and how they think it will add to the interviewer's performance as a counsellor. During this reporting back, I ask the interviewees if they felt listened to (because they invariably say that they did, this prevents criticisms that solution-focused brief therapy's emphasis on questions means that it is not empathic) and if they knew this about themselves (they usually say that they had not known this and express real pleasure in the discovery).

This exercise produces extraordinarily richer descriptions of students' skills and abilities that are talked about throughout the course as others are curious to know more. Students discover that qualities such as integrity, tenacity, humor, courage, resilience, etc., have as much, if not more, value than the 'official' skills of therapy and this encourages them to search more thoroughly for competencies away from 'the problem' when they practice taking a history of hope and possibility. They also have become used to asking the question, 'did you know that about yourself' and thus have a grasp of several solution-focused techniques at an early stage of the training. Breaking down problem free talk into three stages of the telling, the retelling, and the feedback on the retelling eases the students into listening at the level of the word, helps them make the important distinction between the giving of compliments and praise, and ensures that they do not close down clients' stories.

EXERCISE 2

This exercise is done in four parts, reflecting the main parts of a solution-focused interview. This breaks up the flow somewhat but provides the students with the opportunity to practice one technique at a time and start again when they get stuck. I find that I am called on for advice most in the first two stages but that, with growing confidence, the second half of this exercise needs little input from me.

The students practice using the miracle question, scaling, etc., in the same pairs, using a 'problem' that has some meaning for them. This can be something they want to change about the way they work or something they want to change about themselves, commonly health-related issues such as dieting.

They are asked to take verbatim notes to slow them down and continue listening at the level of the word, and read back these notes when summarising–checking the accuracy of what they have heard. They are also asked to evaluate the interview at regular intervals by asking questions such as, 'is this conversation helpful to you? Are we talking about things that are interesting for you or should we be talking about . . . ? What would I have been asking you if I had been more helpful?' At the homework-setting stage of this exercise, they are asked to tailor this to the skills and abilities they discovered during the first exercise.

EXERCISE 3

The students are introduced to the recording format described by Berg and Reuss (1998, p. 167) and given an example to read. They are then asked to write their own solution-focused session note on the interview they have completed, check it for accuracy with the interviewee, and then present them with it.

I find that this exercise has several advantages. First, the students find it relatively simple to do and become more enthusiastic about recording. Second, the record is obviously valued–the students invariably fold it neatly and tuck it away safely, underlining the point that clients will appreciate a record that demonstrates that they have been listened to, that they are valued, and that they are seen as people with the resources to find their own solutions to problems.

EXERCISE 4

At the beginning of the second day, students are invited to answer the question, 'what's better?' before the session on second sessions. I find that many of them report considerable success in solving the 'problem' they identified during exercise 2. This helps them realise how much movement is generated through a solution-focused approach and the possibility of incorporating the philosophy into their own lives.

The rest of the training is taken up with dealing with second session responses when things are the same, nothing is better, etc., more skills-identification, and follow-up consultancy arrangements.

Many trainers will already be doing much of what I describe here. What I have learned from doing training this way is that the intertwining of personal competency-finding throughout the training enables students to give up expertise and trust the client more, and realise how hard the client works with a solution-focused approach; that is, solution-focused work may be simple but it isn't easy. Most of all, the students learn what a good experience therapy can be.

REFERENCES

Berg, I. K., & Reuss, N. H. (1998). *Solutions step by step. A substance abuse treatment manual*. New York and London: Norton.

O'Connell, B. (2001). *solution-focused stress counselling*. London: Continuum.

Sharry, J., Madden, B., & Darmody, M. (2001). *Becoming a solution detective*. London: B. T. Press.

Introducing Solution-Focused Thinking: A Half-Day Workshop

Rayya Ghul

KEYWORDS. Solution-focused, solution-focused thinking, training, workshop

TYPE OF AUDIENCE

This exercise was originally developed for second year undergraduate social work students and has been used with occupational therapy undergraduates as well. The students would have some understanding of approaches to working with individuals and families from human psychology and systems theories, but would not have had in-depth training in any particular model. They also would have had some fieldwork experience.

GROUP SIZE

Ideally, a minimum of 12 people are required. It has been used successfully with a group of 80.

Rayya Ghul is a member of the Institute of Learning and Teaching, Lyminge, Kent, England.

Address correspondence to: Rayya Ghul, Allied Health Department, Canterbury Christ Church University College, Canterbury CT1 1QU, England.

[Haworth co-indexing entry note]: "Introducing Solution-Focused Thinking: A Half-Day Workshop." Ghul, Rayya. Co-published simultaneously in *Journal of Family Psychotherapy* (The Haworth Press, Inc.) Vol. 16, No. 1/2, 2005, pp. 169-174; and: *Education and Training in Solution-Focused Brief Therapy* (ed: Thorana S. Nelson) The Haworth Press, Inc., 2005, pp. 169-174. Single or multiple copies of this article are available for a fee from The Haworth Document Delivery Service [1-800-HAWORTH, 9:00 a.m. - 5:00 p.m. (EST). E-mail address: docdelivery@haworthpress.com].

Available online at http://www.haworthpress.com/web/JFP
Digital Object Identifier: 10.1300/J085v16n01_42

EXPERIENCE LEVEL

This exercise works with people who are complete beginners to solution-focused brief therapy, but who have at least some experience of working with people.

PURPOSE OF THE EXERCISE

This exercise was developed as an introduction to solution-focused brief therapy as a result of the author's experience of teaching solution-focused brief therapy for 5 years. It had been noticed that beginners tended to become over-focused on the 'classic' solution-focused questions and were more concerned with asking the questions in the right way at the right time than working in tune with the client. This often led to 'solution-forced' practice, which then had to be modified. Additionally, the context in which the author was teaching solution-focused brief therapy meant that the students or participants already had a professional practice such as social work, nursing or occupational therapy and that solution-focused brief therapy would need to be integrated into rather than replace existing practice. Building on the ideas of clinical reasoning (Mattingly & Fleming, 1994), the author considered how the thinking behind solution-focused questions could be introduced as a clinical reasoning tool from which the questions would flow naturally.

Experiential level of the exercise: 9

TIME FRAME FOR THE EXERCISE

Will depend on the size of the group, but it is essentially a 2-3 hour workshop.

MATERIALS REQUIRED

Overhead projector, large whiteboard or large space to put up flip chart paper. Ideally, four different colour pens should be used. The room should be suitable for people to work in small groups, i.e., not a banked lecture theater. Prepared overhead transparencies (OHT) with the four stages of solution-focused thinking.

INSTRUCTIONS

The workshop is preceded by a very short introduction to solution-focused brief therapy to credit the people who developed it and to say when and where it was developed (e.g., de Shazer, 1991; 1994). The rest of the workshop is separated into 5 stages plus time for debriefing. The participants will need a break during the workshop. When this takes place is probably best left to the discretion of the workshop leader. The author usually takes it after Stage 4.

An Overhead Transparency was put up of the 'essence of solution-focused brief therapy' (George, Iveson, & Ratner, 1999), which is the author's preference.

- To work with the person rather than problem
- To look for resources rather than deficits
- To explore possible and preferred futures
- To explore what is already contributing to those possible futures
- To treat clients as the experts in all aspects of their lives (George et al., 1999).

The workshop is then introduced as a way of bringing these statements to life. Participants are told they are going to 'invent' solution-focused brief therapy. They will be taken step by step through the thinking (clinical reasoning) process and see how it translates into the questions they ask. Participants are asked to form themselves into groups of four.

WORKSHOP STAGE ONE

Overhead Transparency:

- *What do the stakeholders want?*
- *How will the stakeholders know that the desired change has taken place? What will they notice?*
- *What difference does each stakeholder think the desired change will make?*

The participants are told that these are the questions that the therapist is asking themselves; this guides what they need to elicit from the client. Participants are asked to work in their small groups for 10 minutes to develop questions they could ask their clients that would answer the questions on the OHT. For this first stage, it is useful to move between the groups to find out how they are getting on and give suggestions or encouragement. Often they feel the 'easy' question is not good enough, or need encouragement to be creative.

After 10 minutes, ask the groups to give you the questions they have come up with. With a large group, ask each group for one question in turn. Write all the answers on a whiteboard or flip chart in writing large and clear enough to be read by everyone. If you use a whiteboard, split the board into four sections and do not rub out the questions at each stage—you will need them all for Stage Five. Check that the whole group thinks the questions meet the criteria of the OHT. Compliment the room on their creativity! The time this section takes depends on the number of people in the room, but allow 10 minutes at least.

STAGE TWO

Overhead Transparency:

- *What is already happening?*
- *What aspects of the desired change are taking place already, however small?*
- *If it is happening in one domain, can it be transferred to another?*

Repeat the same process as Stage One. If possible, use a different colour pen.

STAGE THREE

Overhead Transparency:

- *Existing strengths and resources?*
- *What strengths and/or resources (skills) are needed to enable the desired change to take place?*
- *Are any of these present already?*
- *Is everyone willing to collaborate to enable the desired change to take place, even in a small way?*

Repeat the same process for preceding stages. If possible, use a different colour pen.

STAGE FOUR

Overhead Transparency:

- *How do we get started?*
- *What is the first small step that needs to take place that will let people know the desired change is happening?*
- *Is that step small, measurable, achievable and defined in time and space (when and where)?*

Repeat the same process for preceding stages. If possible, use a different colour pen.

STAGE FIVE

You should now have either a whiteboard full of questions from all four stages, or four (or more) sheets of flip chart pinned up so everyone can see them. The participants are then told that their small group is now a therapy team. Ask one member of each small group to take the role of a client. They can use their own experiences or can role play a client they know. Discourage them from using their most 'difficult' client!

The therapy team now must role play a therapy session but they can only use questions from the lists they have created. Stress that it is important that these are the only questions they can use. Because you are a generous workshop leader, you give them two additional questions they can use. These are:

- What else?
- What difference would that make?

They should aim to work through the questions in the order of the stages but can use as many questions from each section as they wish. They have 15 minutes to carry out the therapy session.

DEBRIEF

Ask the 'clients' how they found the process? Was it useful? Ask the 'therapists' how they found the process? Did they think it was useful for the client? Answer questions.

FOLLOWING UP

Participants are given a handout with 'classic' solution-focused questions. They are invited to look at them and see how they compare with the ones that they came up with. If this workshop is part of a course, this can be done in subsequent sessions.

COMMENT

This is an exciting workshop to run. Participants come up with really good questions. The workshop seems to promote a sense of ownership of the process and when the classic solution-focused questions are introduced they already have a context in which to be fitted and where they make sense. Feedback from this workshop has been extremely positive. Participants appear confident in using the approach and also to adapt it to their own profession.

REFERENCES

George, E., Iveson, C., & Ratner, H. (1998). *Problem to solution: Brief therapy with individuals and families* (revised). London: BT Press.

Mattingly, C., & Fleming, M.H. (1994). *Clinical reasoning: Forms of inquiry in a therapeutic practice*. F.A. Davies.

de Shazer, S. (1991). *Putting difference to work*. New York: W.W. Norton.

de Shazer, S. (1994) *Words were originally magic*. New York: W.W. Norton.

SOLUTION-FOCUSED TRAINING AND SUPERVISION

Solution-Focused Training
for Social Workers

John Wheeler

SUMMARY. This article describes one solution-focused trainer's efforts to learn more about how solution-focused therapy is practiced in different contexts in different parts of the world. Exercises for a training workshop are included. *[Article copies available for a fee from The Haworth Document Delivery Service: 1-800-HAWORTH. E-mail address: <docdelivery@ haworthpress.com> Website: <http://www.HaworthPress.com> © 2005 by The Haworth Press, Inc. All rights reserved.]*

KEYWORDS. Social work, training, solution focus

INTRODUCTION

I first encountered Solution-Focused Brief Therapy (SFBT) at a time when I was reasonably happy with the practice theories at my disposal, but not fully so. As I heard about the possibilities of this newer approach, my interest grew. In particular, the approach appeared better able to deliver the respect, useful-

---

John Wheeler is a social worker/family therapist with the Child and Mental Health Service, Gateshead, UK.

Address correspondence to: John Wheeler, 5 Runhead Gardens, Ryton, NE40 3HH, England.

[Haworth co-indexing entry note]: "Solution-Focused Training for Social Workers." Wheeler, John. Co-published simultaneously in *Journal of Family Psychotherapy* (The Haworth Press, Inc.) Vol. 16. No. 1/2, 2005, pp. 177-187; and: *Education and Training in Solution-Focused Brief Therapy* (ed: Thorana S. Nelson) The Haworth Press, Inc., 2005, pp. 177-187. Single or multiple copies of this article are available for a fee from The Haworth Document Delivery Service [1-800-HAWORTH, 9:00 a.m. - 5:00 p.m. (EST). E-mail address: docdelivery@haworthpress.com].

Available online at http://www.haworthpress.com/web/JFP
© 2005 by The Haworth Press, Inc. All rights reserved.
Digital Object Identifier: 10.1300/J085v16n01_43

ness and empowerment I, as a social worker in a child mental health service, had been looking for from therapeutic models. Initially I assumed my social work colleagues in statutory settings would see what I was seeing, and proceeded to tell them what I had found through conversations and in-service training. Ironically, I was yet to apply solution-focused thinking to my solution-focused training. Given the nature of the material, some did become as excited as I, but some didn't, and the proportion of course participants who actually went away and tried it out was usually small.

Following the third rule of Brief Therapy, "if it doesn't work do something different," I gradually figured out how to be more solution-focused in my training. This change was substantially assisted by a small research conversation with trainers from various countries, exploring what worked for them. This account, firstly, outlines the outcome of that research and then gives details of three exercises which have become reliable companions when I seek to introduce solution-focused practice to my social work colleagues now. The exercises typically fall at the beginning, middle and near the end of two days of training, which would usually be followed by a review day a month later to explore what has worked.

Research

To make contact with trainers from around the world, I posted a set of questions to the Solution-Focused List (SFT-L@MAELSTROM.ST.JOHNS.EDU)*, an Internet-based discussion group accessed by around 850 people from a variety of professions, including social work. I used five main questions to explore the use of SFBT in social work in different countries, connections to legislation, and ideas on promoting the approach to social workers.

In total, eight people replied: a social worker in the US who had left agency practice in order to better enhance his potential as a solution-focused trainer, practitioner, consultant and supervisor; a social worker in Sweden who had written a number of articles on SFBT; a social worker in Australia who taught SFBT in social work courses; a CEO from a voluntary agency working with children and families in Australia, who had provided training to social workers in Australia and New Zealand in SFBT; a Professor from a School of Applied Social Science in the US who had pioneered research into SFBT across a range of professions and settings; a social work researcher and trainer from Finland, who had taught SFBT to social workers and researched the effects of this on their practice; a UK social worker who worked in a voluntary agency and ran a local support group for professionals using SFBT; and another UK social worker who was running a project for a voluntary agency working with children and families, who had also trained other social workers in SFBT.

In general, participants' comments indicated that the interest in SFBT amongst social workers was developing at different rates in different countries. Respondents could only comment on their impressions; no one knew of any formal auditing of the approaches used by social workers. The positions of respondents may thus have influenced their estimates of the use of SFBT amongst social workers. For my own part I believe there is growing interest in the UK, but then I often choose to meet with social workers who are interested, so this will also influence my view.

When I asked what had helped the incorporation of SFBT into social work practice, responses suggested that this varied quite substantially from country to country. Efficacy and benefits for the worker were thought to be important in the US. Meeting the needs of a young profession seemed to matter in Sweden. Fitting well with the culture was reckoned to be important in Finland and a good fit with social work values was thought to be most important in Australia. In practice, it may be that to some extent or another, all of these factors have been important in each country, with culture and the context of social work practice determining which matters most.

When I asked whether particular government policies had helped, most respondents, apart from those from the US, saw a good fit between SFBT and legislative changes in their country. In my view, solution-focused practice relates well to most legislative trends in the UK. It is to be hoped that there is a global trend towards working in partnership with service users and working in a manner that enhances users' strengths and confidence. If this is so, this should help to ensure that solution-focused practice is increasingly relevant to what social workers are expected to do.

When I asked whether there were particular constraints to the acceptance of SFBT amongst social workers in their countries, respondents pointed to the importance of professional credibility as a contextual factor when social workers are considering a new approach to practice. In the UK, for example, Social Work has had to work hard to achieve credibility amongst other professions such as Medicine, Psychology, and Law, which all have lengthier formative training compared to Social Work. Criticisms of the profession in the media in the UK are also an ongoing influence on the levels of confidence in the profession as a whole.

When I asked what participants had found to be the best way of working with any constraints they had come across, each respondent, not surprisingly, recommended that the assumptions of SFBT should also guide how the approach is presented. Social workers come to training with experience and knowledge and it is important to invite participants to consider SFBT as something they might incorporate into their practice, not something they accept as an entire alternative to their current practice.

In drawing conclusions, it must, of course, be held in mind that I only conversed with trainers with Internet access, and those who were reasonably fluent in English. The methodology inevitably excluded those who do not have such facilities. All respondents were from developed countries, so the study was not fully international. It also is important to bear in mind that whilst participants drew on a wealth of experience, each inevitably spoke from their own perspective. A conversation between eight participants and I could not represent a full account of social work in five different countries. Nonetheless, hearing from practitioners from several other countries, who I might not otherwise have encountered, greatly helped to refine my thinking on how I might best share solution-focused practice with social workers.

When figuring out what to do differently, I came to the following conclusions.

- When training social workers, it is important to be sensitive to the context within which social workers find themselves, both locally and nationally. In particular, I needed to be more appreciative of the culture of social work in the UK and the general level of confidence in the profession.
- It is important to try to meet participants where they are and, where possible, to link the training material to their positions, much as a gardener would graft a shoot onto a growth point in the branch the graft is being joined.
- Participants come to training with a wealth of practice and life experience. What they already know about effective practice is likely to fit quite easily with solution-focused thinking, because the approach itself has been developed out of what works.
- Participants can be left and trusted to do their own figuring out, just as clients do. This is more likely to happen if training opens up spaces for thinking to happen and for participants to engage in learning which is uniquely useful to them.

POWER-WITH VS. POWER-OVER EXERCISE

Background

This exercise was introduced to me by St. Luke's, Anglicare, Australia, and I am thankful to them for giving permission to share this adaptation. The exercise is designed to fall at the beginning of training, to prepare the ground for people to hear about the assumptions and techniques of SFBT. In the busyness of social workers' lives, it can be difficult to step outside of the patterns of interaction that emerge with clients. In particular, it can be difficult to always appreciate the extent to which professional power contributes to users' actions. Although social workers may not necessarily have been formally trained in an interactional view of behaviour, all will have had some experience of being on the receiving end of power. The exercise is suitable to participants with a wide range of experience and can work with small to large groups. Although the exercise is participatory, its success depends on careful steering and facilitation by the trainer throughout. In total, the exercise lasts 20 to 30 minutes depending on the degree of discussion it generates.

Step 1

Invite participants to recall being thirteen and at school. After a pause for some savoring of memories, ask if they saw any signs that teachers had power over them. How could they tell that teachers had power? When participants provide examples, it helps the exercise if you can agree on descriptions that could apply to anyone in authority. "Put me on detention" can thus be worded as "controlled our time." "Told our parents" can become "drew on other sources of authority." These are then listed on the top left hand corner of a large flip chart. This takes five minutes or so.

Step 2

Participants are then asked whether they recalled everyone going along with this or whether they saw examples of rebellion or defiance. As examples are given, again, for the sake of the exercise, it's useful to agree on wordings which might also describe the actions of others in subjugated positions. "Didn't hand in homework" can become "didn't complete tasks." "Truanting" becomes "not being there." Humor and a degree of ice-breaking can be introduced if the trainer shares some extraordinary memories of their own. Write these on the top right hand corner of the flip chart. Again this takes five minutes or so.

Step 3

Now point to the list of teacher behaviours and ask, "what sort of assumptions must they have had about 13 year olds to treat them in those ways?" Assumptions can be hard to specify, so sometimes the trainer will need to push for clarity by asking, for example, "what words would they have used to describe us?" A third list, usually including assumptions such as "ignorant and unable to learn without being made to," "uncivilised and needing to be told how to behave" is then written at the bottom of the flip chart. This takes another five minutes or so.

Step 4

Now draw circles around each list. Point to the list of pupil behaviours and ask, "when teachers saw us behaving like this, what did that do to their assumptions about us?" Participants easily see that the pupil behaviours reinforce the teacher assumptions. The trainer can then draw arrows between the three lists to indicate the potential for the teacher behaviours to reinforce the pupil behaviours, which in turn reinforce the teacher assumptions, which in turn reinforce the teacher behaviour. The trainer then names this as a power-over dynamic. This takes a couple of minutes.

Step 5

Pointing at the list of pupil behaviours, the trainer then asks if participants have ever seen clients behaving like this. Usually they have. This then allows the trainer to propose a hypothesis that when clients behave in rebellious and defiant ways, this may be in response to the power they perceive in the social worker's position, whether or not this is evidenced by the worker's actions. Interestingly, sometimes you can look at the list of teacher behaviours and see connections to common social work actions. This takes five minutes or so.

Step 6

The trainer then asks participants to think of good outcomes with clients and figure out what they contributed to this. Depending on the time available, this can be done in a large group or with people in small groups to give more people a chance to speak. Typically, participants will name "listening," "offering choices," "being honest" and so on. The trainer can then name these as the ingredients of a power-with dynamic. At this point the trainer may need to acknowledge that although statutory social workers often cannot drop their power to a level equal to the client, there are ways they can make the differential as small as possible and invite collaboration.

Step 7

The ground is now usually ready for an introduction to the assumptions of solution-focused brief therapy, which usually fits well with what people are already recognizing as elements of their own, or others' good practice. If time permits, participants could also be shown the table produced by Amundson,

Stewart, and Valentine (1993) which highlights the shift to collaborative practice within family therapy that corresponds well both to most social workers' ideas of what constitutes good practice and to SFBT.

A Word of Caution

The original exercise was based on Australians' knowledge of the power-over dynamic between white settlers and the indigenous peoples. The early stages of the above adaptation can seem unfairly critical of teachers and sometimes it is necessary to clarify that that's not the purpose of the exercise, but rather that the trainer is drawing on common experience to illustrate a point.

PANNING FOR GOLD EXERCISE

Background

When my children were young, we shared a holiday in France with French friends. Michel, the father in the French family, was employed as a geological surveyor at the time. One morning Michel announced that he was taking us to a river to pan for gold. Once there, adults and children alike explored the silt for signs of gold. Whilst the adults quickly gave up, the children persevered. Unlike the adults, the children really believed in the possibility of finding gold. Somehow, those of us who have grown up in a western culture have learnt to look out for what isn't working, and when we train as professionals this often becomes an emphasis on deficits. White (2002) has recently referred to "the dramatic growth of the phenomenon of personal failure" (p. 43), arguing that this is a manifestation of current processes of social control and normalisation. Whilst social workers do endeavour to find strengths and do seek to empower service users, they nonetheless are influenced by this cultural preoccupation with the broken bits of people's lives. There can also be a tendency in social work to seek to find what's broken with a view to being the person who fixes it.

I use this exercise to sharpen participants' skills in noticing qualities and abilities. Usually I locate the exercise after a day of training. Typically, participants are settling into solution-focused thinking, though not necessarily with a lot of confidence. Participants usually are more successful with this task than they expect, which helps to raise participants' belief in their potential to use the approach as a whole. The exercise also tends to demonstrate the usefulness of taking a break. The exercise works with any number of participants, though participants usually find it easier to generate their ideas in small groups and the number of groups would determine how much time would be needed for a plenary feedback. Responsibility for the exercise is shared between trainer and participants with the trainer providing the material and a task and participants working on the task as set. Overall, the exercise takes about half an hour, depending on the number of groups.

Step 1

Show participants a short extract of videtape where the presentation looks gloomy. I choose between a three-minute excerpt of a parent who speaks despondently about her children and the future or a short excerpt of a teenager voicing despondency about what's happening in her life and difficulties with her family. A transcript of the interview can be helpful because participants usually need to read between the lines in a very real sense.

Step 2

Participants are then asked to work together for about ten minutes to identify the strengths and qualities implied, if not actually stated, by the service user. Often participants will sit in silence, staring at the transcript, and only start talking to each other when invited to do so. This later provides an opportunity to appreciate why breaks are recommended in SFBT to enable the worker to step out of the potential negativity of an interview and identify compliments to end the session with.

Step 3

Participants then share their discoveries with the whole group. The wealth of evidence that is usually shared often surprises participants, especially because the excerpt has been very short and, on the face of it, they've only had a day's training. This helps to amplify the point that if you expect to find strengths and qualities, you are more likely to find them, just like panning for gold. In both situations, these are clients I came to know well over a period of time. Participants are particularly fascinated when they hear that strengths they glimpsed showed up more distinctly later on.

A Word of Caution

Only once have I encountered a participant who declared that she saw no strengths or qualities. In practice I found it best not to make an issue out of this person's position and moved on to hear what others had noticed. I assumed that being in a minority of one provided its own opportunity for reflection and learning.

REASONS TO STOP NOW EXERCISE

Background

Before using this exercise, I would often meet up with participants for a review day to explore what had been useful, only to find that although most had liked SFBT, they had not used it. On exploring this further, I typically found that participants had a host of good reasons for not doing so. Typically, these reasons came from a variety of positions: personal stories, voices from the local professional culture, voices from the professional culture at large, and so on. O'Hanlon (2001), for example, has referred to a colleague who, every time he tries something new, hears the voice of his father saying, "so who do you think you are?" White (1997) has outlined the variety of "voices" that can powerfully undermine practitioners' confidence and constrain them from trying out new practices. Turnell and Edwards (1999) have written more specifically on the highly charged and risky context in which statutory child care social workers usually work. It finally struck me that if these good reasons were going to be around it would be more useful, from a training point of view, to encounter them before people left the training, to see if we could reduce their impact.

The exercise may be particularly relevant to people new to SFBT, calls for a degree of trust between participants and requires determined facilitation by the trainer. The exercise usually provides a further opportunity for people to use a scaling question and recognize the perniciousness of negative thinking. Sometimes the exercise releases a wave of critical ideas that have been voiced for the first time in the training. There is a risk that when participants take well to SFBT, this is at the expense of adequately acknowledging doubts and concerns. Once participants are away from the camaraderie and excitement of successful solution-focused training, they may encounter these ideas on their own. Again, I believe it makes more sense to name the demons when participants are still together and in a position to assist each other. Overall, the exercise takes 30 minutes or so, depending on the discussion.

Step 1

Ask participants to scale their current confidence over using SFBT with 10 as the maximum and ask them to write the number down.

Step 2

Invite people to go into pairs, imagine themselves with a client and just about to use something new from SFBT, notice any awkward thoughts that pop into their heads, and then share these with each other. This takes 10 minutes or so.

Step 3

Ask people again to scale their confidence in using SFBT and compare it to the previous number. Then ask people to say whether the number changed. Usually the number goes down and this is a further experiential opportunity to acknowledge how encountering negative thinking has affected them.

Step 4

Invite people to share their awkward thoughts in the large group. Participants may voice ideas like, "I'm not a therapist, so I shouldn't be doing this." "I might cause harm by dabbling." "I might get out of my depth." "My clients might notice I'm doing something different." Whilst the trainer may be able to address these ideas directly, it is more useful if the trainer invites other participants to say how they would help the participant with that particular concern, or how they would address that idea if it occurred to them. Usually these intellectual pests are particular to only a few participants at a time, which means that others can think creatively about them, even if they can't think creatively about their own. There is then scope for the trainer to check confidence levels again to see if the discussion has helped.

A Word of Caution

Sometimes the wave of criticism is huge, and threatens to destroy all that the training group have achieved up until that point. Be ready to wade through it, confident that there are ways of addressing most awkward ideas that arise. If an idea cannot be addressed, then the participant can be invited to see what they end up doing about it if it does pop up. Once a group told me that their confidence had gone up after discovering their doubts. When I asked how this had happened, it turned out that they had anticipated the Step 4 discussion, and had already found their own answers. As in practice, you can never know what people will do with a task until they try it out.

CONCLUSION

Thomas (2000), addressing the complexities of supervision, proposes three supervisor positions: guru, gatekeeper, guide. From the position of guru, the supervisor imparts expert knowledge on practice and supervisees seek to copy. From the position of gatekeeper, the supervisor arbitrates over whether supervisees will belong to the community of practitioners. From the position of guide, the supervisor collaborates with the student to foster learning that will elicit their unique version of practice. Experience is teaching me that the same options can arise in training. One of the most frustrating evaluation comments I received said, "loved the approach, couldn't possibly do it myself, but I know who to refer people on to." When gurus shine, their disciples can be left in the shadows. When participants try to copy a guru they usually find they can't. I'm finding that social workers in training often take much more from each other's inspiring practice than mine. Disagreements, misunderstandings, and mistakes can all tempt a trainer to be a gatekeeper and point out the error of a participant's thinking. Nowadays when I'm inclined to tell participants how it should be, I try to switch to curiosity. "Tell me more about that idea? How were you thinking that would be helpful?"

I suspect we all have to become our own guru and I believe most of us can be a reliable gatekeeper to our own good practice. In using the word guide, Thomas (2000) explains that he is thinking in particular of a *sherpa*, a guide who knows the mountains, but leaves the walkers to decide on their own route up. As a trainer, I can have ideas about how SFBT might be useful to other social workers. Only they can work out how it is.

REFERENCES

Amundson, J., Stewart, K., & Valentine, L. (1993) Temptations of power and certainty. *Journal of Marital & Family Therapy, 19*(2), 111-123.

O'Hanlon, B. (2001). Possibility Therapy workshop. Newcastle, UK. September 2001.

Thomas, F.N. (2000). Mutual admiration: Fortifying your competency-based supervision experience. *RATKES: Journal of the Finnish Association for the Advancement of Solution and Resource Oriented Therapy and Methods, 2*, 30-39.

Turnell, A., & Edwards, S. (1999) *Signs of safety: A solution and safety oriented approach to child protection casework.* London: W.W. Norton.

White, M. (1997). *Narratives of therapists' lives.* Adelaide. Dulwich Centre Press.

White, M. (2002). Addressing personal failure. *The International Journal of Narrative Therapy and Community Work, 3*, 33-76.

Becoming Solution-Focused:
Some Beginning Thoughts

Lee Shilts
Kaisha A. Thomas

SUMMARY. This preliminary paper addresses how therapists, students, and professionals go about the business of learning to accept the concepts and philosophy of becoming brief, solution-focused therapists. What is it that "clicks" for them to make that paradigmatic shift? This paper is a beginning exploration to this overarching question as we research therapists' experiences in moving from one model of therapy into the solution-focused approach. We incorporate an open dialogue between ourselves as we begin the process of exploring how individuals become solution-focused therapists. This paper is offered as a starting point. We hope to continue to collect data from a wide variety of individuals as they reflect on their personal journeys in becoming brief, solution-focused therapists. *[Article copies available for a fee from The Haworth Document Delivery Service: 1-800-HAWORTH. E-mail address: <docdelivery@haworthpress. com> Website: <http://www.HaworthPress.com> © 2005 by The Haworth Press, Inc. All rights reserved.]*

Lee Shilts is affiliated with Nova Southeastern University, Ft. Lauderdale, FL.

Kaisha A. Thomas is a PhD candidate at Nova Southeastern University, Ft. Lauderdale, FL.

Address correspondence to: Lee Shilts, Nova Southeastern University, 3301 College Ave., Ft. Lauderdale, FL 33314 or Kaisha A. Thomas, Nova Southeastern University, School of Humanities and Social Sciences, 3301 College Ave., Ft. Lauderdale, FL 33314.

[Haworth co-indexing entry note]: "Becoming Solution-Focused: Some Beginning Thoughts." Shilts, Lee, and Kaisha A. Thomas. Co-published simultaneously in *Journal of Family Psychotherapy* (The Haworth Press, Inc.) Vol. 16, No. 1/2, 2005, pp. 189-197; and: *Education and Training in Solution-Focused Brief Therapy* (ed: Thorana S. Nelson) The Haworth Press, Inc., 2005, pp. 189-197. Single or multiple copies of this article are available for a fee from The Haworth Document Delivery Service [1-800-HAWORTH, 9:00 a.m. - 5:00 p.m. (EST). E-mail address: docdelivery@haworthpress.com].

Available online at http://www.haworthpress.com/web/JFP
© 2005 by The Haworth Press, Inc. All rights reserved.
Digital Object Identifier: 10.1300/J085v16n01_44

KEYWORDS. Knowledge structures, knowledge acquisition, model observation

INTRODUCTION

I (L.S.) recently watched Insoo Berg do a workshop on brief, solution-focused therapy. As often happens, one of the audience participants questioned the validity and effectiveness of the model particularly as it related to families with substance abuse problems. The audience member was coming from a traditional medical model (AA) regarding substance abuse. Insoo did a marvelous job of not getting into a symmetrical battle with the participant. She gently demonstrated respect by curiously talking with the participant about her particular stance with such families. Insoo did not negate the participant's position on working this way nor did she advocate that there was one right way to conduct therapy. Rather, she kept an open mind and allowed the participant to voice her concerns about solution-focused therapy. As I watched and listened to the interchange unfold between Insoo and the audience member, my thoughts and reflections of the process went something like the following.

The audience member's concern and question could have been viewed as "resistance" toward Insoo and the solution-focused model. I think Insoo took a more productive stance by viewing the participant's position as one of curiosity; it was her "best" way of cooperating at that particular time. Thus, the ideas and philosophy had not started "clicking" for her. There were no exceptional moments that caused a shift for the participant to begin to look at the families' problems through a solution-focused lens.

Once that shift occurs, I believe the participant and Insoo may have been able to agree that the family may have needed to "do something different" in relationship to how they were organized around the substance use. This is just a working hypothesis that both parties could have plausibly agreed to.

However, there was still a sharp path of divergence between the two parties. The audience participant felt she knew from a position-of-knowing what the family needed to do and wanted to "prescribe" her fix-it answer. Insoo's response, I believe, would be that families normally do not respond well to such an approach. Insoo's path would be something like this: for difference or change to occur, the family must come up with their own unique "prescription." Otherwise, the change would not be meaningful and produce a "difference that makes a difference" (Bateson, 1983) for the family system.

This example is somewhat typical, we believe, of how people go about the business of "learning" to do brief, solution-focused therapy. Conversely, exploring these "exceptional moments" may have a profound impact on how teachers, trainers, and supervisors go about the business of helping other professionals learn the techniques and philosophy of solution-focused therapy. This is our overarching goal: to find ways and means for helping make the model "click" for people in their own unique ways.

The following paper is a collaborative effort of the two authors and they therefore share equal authorship. The first author is a professor of marriage and family therapy at Nova Southeastern University. During the development of this project, he was providing supervision of supervision (SOS) to the second author. The second author was in the third year of her doctorate studies at the same university. Both were engaged in providing solution-focused therapy supervision to other graduate students training at the university's brief therapy clinic.

NEW APPLICATIONS
OF THE SOLUTION-FOCUSED APPROACH

Solution-focused therapy traditionally has been used within the disciplines of marriage and family therapy. However, new applications have been found in other, less conventional venues (Webb, 1999). The basic premises and philosophy of the model have spread and are used in pediatrics (Klarr & Coleman, 1995), gerontology (Ingersoll & Radner, 1993), schools (Bonnington, 1993; Metcalf, 1998; Murphy & Duncan, 1997; Rhodes, 1993), nursing (Mason, Breen, & Whipple, 1994; O'Brien & Bacca, 1997), child protective services (Berg, 1994; Corcoran, 1999), group work (Coe & Zimpfer, 1996; LaFountain & Garner, 1996; Metcalf, 1999), employee assistance programs (Cyzewski, 1996), and corporations (Jackson & McKergow, 2002; Priest & Glass, 1997).

A hallmark of solution-focused therapy is that the relationship between the therapist and the client is cooperative, collaborative, and respectful (Berg, 1994). This is based on the therapeutic assumption that the client is the best expert on themselves (Berg & Miller, 1992; Berg, 1994) and that they have the resources to resolve their complaint (Berg, 1994). We have also found that seeing the clients as the best expert upon themselves and assuming that they have the resources to resolve their own complaints translates well to both supervision and training. It is therefore our belief that unlocking the key to how professionals go about learning brief, solution-focused therapy may have a profound and positive influence on how we teach, train, and supervise others in becoming solution-focused therapists.

MUSINGS ON BECOMING SOLUTION-FOCUSED: KAISHA

Having never considered myself a solution-focused therapist, I was not sure what I had signed up for when I decided to do a supervision practicum with Lee Shilts. In fact, prior to my experience in the practicum, my training thus far, coupled with my experience of observing students who considered themselves solution-focused, left me feeling that the model was very contrived, predictive, and, quite honestly, simplistic. However, my understanding of solution-focused therapy changed when, one night during a different practicum, my supervisor at the time called in Lee for a consultation on a potentially volatile case. Sitting behind the mirror with Lee, I was fascinated when in only a few minutes he was able to conceptualize the entire case and offer an intervention that hit the nerve center of the family. I was immediately fascinated by how he was able to do that. This one single event made me want to know more about this approach and how Lee made sense of therapy and, by extension, the solution-focused model. It was at that point I decided to sign up with him for practicum as a supervisor-in-training.

That first practicum experience was so powerful that I decided to sign up with him for yet another semester practicum. Luckily for me, Lee agreed to have me join his team again, even though many of my colleagues also wanted the chance to work with him. Two practicums later, I have no regrets. I have thoroughly enjoyed my experience and have learned more than I expected in a relatively short period. The following will outline some of the high points for me and the moments when I felt "aha, I think I get it."

The single most important factor in my learning over the past two semesters has been watching a therapist skilled in solution-focused therapy at work. Knowledge can be thought of as being in two levels–acquiring new knowledge and remodeling existing knowledge. Acquiring new knowledge can be thought of as adding new blocks to the building. The miracle question comes to mind–if you were to wake up tomorrow and a miracle were to happen, what would be the first thing that you would notice is different? For me, this was learning the solution-focused model in the classroom, extensively reading de Shazer, journal articles, and other textbooks on the subject. I had a good knowledge base, but it was not until I was placed into this practicum experience and saw solution-focused therapy in practice that I started to make sense of what I was reading. This changed my epistemology, and can be thought of as remodeling existing knowledge–in other words, remodeling the existing blocks. Watching this clinician, his ability to bond and develop an immediate rapport with the clients, his confidence, and his command of the model has been inspiring. Lee might humbly account for this by having twenty plus years of experience, but it seems to me that there is more to it than that. Whether that ability is part of the solution-focused model or simply his innate skills/qualities as a clinician, I cannot tell, but it is truly fascinating to watch. I think it is that belief in the model that comes across when he delivers an intervention.

I have observed other clinicians deliver similar messages to a client that falls flat. What is the difference? One part of that, I think, is that there is not a full understanding of the model so that when the clients do not latch on to the idea, the therapist does not know how to salvage the intervention or where to take it. Additionally, many neophyte therapists know the questions to ask–the exceptions, the miracle question, and the scaling question–but are unsure of why they might be asking them or what to do once they have been answered. These sorts of questions were exactly why I thought the model was so contrived. In my prior experience, everyone who went into the room was asking those questions; the funny thing was that absolutely no one knew why they were asking the question or what to do with the answer. However, watching the model at work over the past year has left me with this impression: You must understand the overall philosophy behind the model, not just know the questions to ask, and use that as the overarching umbrella that informs your questions and guides your curiosity. Reading about the model is quite simply not enough. It does not do justice to the model and, in my opinion, leaves you with the questions to ask, but not the essence of the model.

Admittedly, my initial learning of the model was not from a solution-focused therapist. Was that the difference that made the difference (Bateson, 1983)? Could very well be; it could also be that my first semester at Nova Southeastern University (NSU) was and still is a blur. Be that as it may, for many of my colleagues, for which the first semester was not a blur and who considered themselves solution-focused, all agree, seeing the solution-focused model in practice, from someone who really knows and understands the model, is far more effective than reading about it. Students do not have enough opportunities to see their professors–master clinicians–perform in the therapy room. This is truly our loss. Additionally, we do not have the opportunity to have visiting masters in the field demonstrate their skills in our clinic. At the very least, for me, watching someone who truly understands the model in the room has been *the* most significant learning experience over the past year. I can now say I truly feel I have a better understanding and command of the model. I am by no means an expert; after all, doesn't it take twenty years? However, I feel more confident in my knowledge from the conversations behind the mirror. Watching the supervision and interventions on cases and listening to the feedback, I have a clearer understanding of the model.

I would recommend that all practicum professors be required to take on a case during the course of that practicum. Most people learn by seeing and at the very least, it concretizes what they are reading in their books. Additionally, many students, especially at the masters' level and some at the doctoral level, have no practical experience. All of their knowledge is derived from books. However, many of the books and teachings of solution-focused therapy leave the impression on many therapists that this model is too "positive" and does not give the clients a chance to really describe the problem, but rather discounts the clients' experience. One of the criticisms of the model suggests that therapists move too fast in trying to find exceptions and solutions. What I have come to realize is that that is not necessarily so. In fact, solution-focused therapists listen very closely to the problem, but in so doing are looking for the times when there is something different going on–when there is an exception. This is a powerful learning tool that helps students actually see what they are reading about put into practice, with real people and real problems. So, finally, in answer to your question, what helps neophyte therapists learn the model? For me at least, it is watching someone that understands and believes the philosophy and has a great command of the model put it in practice.

KNOWLEDGE STRUCTURES/KNOWLEDGE ACQUISITION

Understanding how family therapy students respond to anomalous data is essential to understanding knowledge acquisition in family therapy training centers. Chinn and Brewer (1993) postulate that there are seven distinct forms of response to anomalous data, only one of which is to accept new data and change theories. Thus, the encounter with contradictory information is at the heart of knowledge acquisition in family therapy, particularly as it relates to new models of brief therapy. However, students typically resist giving up their pre-instructional beliefs. It is clear that a key to improved family therapy education is to find better ways of encouraging students to change their pre-instructional theories in response to new, contradictory ideas.

In educational psychology, two different learning perspectives have been categorized for research purposes, but, of course, are really not true categories, but more of a continuum. They are: (a) building new knowledge structures called schemas or schemata; and (b) restructuring existing knowledge structures or schemas. When relating these schemas to brief solution-focused therapy, the former would be akin to building new knowledge structures. Examples of this would be teaching the miracle question, scaling questions, and exception questions to a student who was unfamiliar with them. This is fairly easy. It is like beginning to build a new house. The contractor prepares the landscape, builds the foundation, brings in new materials, and begins to build the house according to the blueprint. The second category, restructuring schemata, is more like a total remodeling job. This is much more difficult. It is comparable to teaching students how to collaborate with the client in building/ rebuilding meaning, or when and how to use the miracle question effectively. The foundational epistemologies of the student may need to change from the belief that truth exists to truth being perceived. It is possible that restructuring epistemologies is the real challenge of teaching solution-focused brief therapy because most students have been entrenched in tacit beliefs about the nature of knowledge and the position of knowledge relative to the knower that are at odds with the effective use of solution-focused brief therapy.

First, the individual must be unhappy with some aspect of his or her current belief either because it does not explain some experience he or she has had or because, when following a model based on the prior beliefs, the results were unsatisfactory. Second, an alternative belief must be available and understandable and does what the original belief does not. Third, it is helpful if the person can "deeply process" the whole thing. In other words, compare and contrast the two theories. If any of these steps are missing, the likelihood is that the individual will not totally restructure the schema, but react somewhere between ignoring/rejecting to peripheral change while retaining the core belief. In the previous section, one of the authors (K.T.) shared her journey in becoming a brief solution-focused brief therapist. Hopefully, her story will illustrate that the journey is more than just learning new concepts. It should also entail a deep process that challenges one's existing epistemologies.

CONCLUSION

This paper offers some initial thoughts on becoming solution-focused in one's brief therapy approach. The authors suggest that learning to become a solution-focused therapist is an ongoing process including, but not limited to, building new knowledge structures as well as restructuring existing schemas. The second author offers some "musings" in her exploration with the model as a doctorate student in a family therapy program. Her journey into learning solution-focused therapy appears to parallel some of the ideas behind acquiring new knowledge structures as articulated in the work on scientific revolutions by Thomas S. Kuhn (1970). Initially, she states that she struggled to respond to anomalous data and felt an urge to return to her pre-instructional beliefs, i.e., her roots with traditional psychology theory and techniques. It took more than just building new schemata for her to make a paradigm shift to a new way of thinking about and doing therapy. What was necessary for her was the idea of restructuring existing structures or schemas. This was only accomplished through the actual shift in her current epistemologies about therapy. For example, it was not enough to just read about and learn how to recite the miracle question to a client. It was further necessary for her to watch and observe over a length of time how the first author with more experience went about utilizing the miracle question in his clinical work. If this process was not accomplished, there was a good likelihood that there would not have been a total restructuring of existing schema and a meaningful shift to a new knowledge structure. In general, one may say a shift occurred in the "foundational epistemology" of the second author while working with the first author that allowed her to incorporate solution-focused therapy principles into her work. As always, more data collection is needed to fully understand this process. This paper is offered as only a beginning. We encourage more re-search in this area to help teachers, trainers, and supervisors in their work in helping others become brief, solution-focused practitioners.

REFERENCES

Bateson, G. (1983). *Steps to an ecology of mind.* Chicago: The University of Chicago Press.

Berg, I. K. (1994). *Family based services: A solution-focused approach.* New York: Norton.

Berg, I. K., & Miller, S. (1992). *Working with the problem drinker: A solution-focused approach.* New York: W. W. Norton & Company.

Bonnington, S. B. (1993). Solution-focused brief therapy: Helpful interventions for school counselors. *The School Counselor, 41*(1), 126-127.

Chinn, C. A., & Brewer, W. F. (1993). The role of anomalous data in knowledge acquisition: A theoretical framework and implications for science instruction. *Review of Educational Research, 63*(1), 1-49.

Coe, D., & Zimpfer, D. (1996). Infusing solution-oriented theory and techniques in group work. *Journal for Specialists in Group Work, 22*(1), 49-57.

Corcoran, J. (1999). Solution-focused interviewing with child protective clients. *Child Welfare, 78*(4), 461-479.

Cyzewski, K. M. (1996). Rapid EAP: Solution-focused therapy in employee assistance. *EAP Digest, 16*(2), 16-19.

Ingersol, D. B., & Radner, J. (1993). Searching for solutions: Mental health counselors in nursing homes. *Clinical Gerontologist, 13*(1), 33-50.

Jackson, P., & McKergow, M. (2002). *The solutions focus: The simple way to positive change.* London: Nicholas Brealey Publishing.

Klarr, H., & Coleman, W. L. (1995). Brief solution-focused strategies for behavioral pediatrics. *Family-Focused Pediatrics, 41*(1), 131-141.

Kuhn, T. S. (1970). *The structure of scientific revolutions* (2nd Ed.). Chicago: University of Chicago Press.

LaFountain, R. M., & Garner, N. (1996). Solution-focused group counseling: The results are in. *Journal for Specialist in Group Work, 21*(2), 128-143.

Mason, W. H., Breen, R. Y., & Whipple, W. R. (1994). Solution-focused therapy and inpatient psychiatric nursing. *Journal of Psychosocial Nursing, 32*(1), 46-49.

Metcalf, L. (1998). *Solution-focused group therapy: Ideas for groups in private practice, schools, agencies, and treatment programs.* New York: The Free Press.

Murphy, J., & Duncan, B. L. (1997). *Brief interventions for school problems: Collaborating for practical solutions.* New York: The Guilford Press.

O'Brien, R. A., & Bacca, R. P. (1997). Applications of solution-focused interventions to nurse home visitation for pregnant women and parents of young children. *Journal of Community Psychology, 25*(1), 47-57.

Priest, S., & Gass, M. (1997). An examination of "problem solving" versus solution-focused facilitation styles in corporate settings. *Journal of Experiential Education, 20*(1), 34-39.

Rhodes, J. (1993). The use of solution-focused brief therapy in schools. *Educational Psychology in Practice, 9*(1), 27-34.

Webb, W. (1999). *Solutioning: Solution-focused interventions for counselors.* Philadelphia: Taylor & Francis Company.

Success Enhancing Supervision

John R. Briggs
Gale Miller

SUMMARY. In this paper, the authors posit that therapists (beginning and experienced) have a propensity for being self-deprecating and critical. Following Bandura's (1977, 1986) theory of perceived self-efficacy, when this becomes reinforced by a supervisor, therapists lose their sense of self-efficacy as a therapist, and their competence suffers accordingly. In an effort to foster improved perceived self-efficacy, the authors apply solution-focused and constructive methods of therapy to the context of clinical supervision. Several case illustrations are presented compromising goal construction and the development of the supervisory relationship, co-constructing competence and confidence, circumventing impasses, the role of teaching and education in supervision, and the potential paradox of evaluation. *[Article copies available for a fee from The Haworth Document Delivery Service: 1-800-HAWORTH. E-mail address: <docdelivery@haworthpress.com> Website: <http://www.HaworthPress.com> © 2005 by The Haworth Press, Inc. All rights reserved.]*

KEYWORDS. Supervision, counseling, therapy, solution-focused, solution-oriented, constructive

---

John R. Briggs is affiliated with the Solutions Behavioral Health Group, Wauwatosa, WI.

Gale Miller is affiliated with Marquette University, Milwaukee, WI.

Address correspondence to: John Briggs or Gale Miller, Solutions Behavioral Health Group, 10702 W. Burleigh Street, Wauwatosa, WI 53222.

[Haworth co-indexing entry note]: "Success Enhancing Supervision." Briggs, John R., and Gale Miller. Co-published simultaneously in *Journal of Family Psychotherapy* (The Haworth Press, Inc.) Vol. 16, No. 1/2, 2005, pp. 199-222; and: *Education and Training in Solution-Focused Brief Therapy* (ed: Thorana S. Nelson) The Haworth Press, Inc., 2005, pp. 199-222. Single or multiple copies of this article are available for a fee from The Haworth Document Delivery Service [1-800-HAWORTH, 9:00 a.m. - 5:00 p.m. (EST). E-mail address: docdelivery@haworthpress.com].

Available online at http://www.haworthpress.com/web/JFP
© 2005 by The Haworth Press, Inc. All rights reserved.
Digital Object Identifier: 10.1300/J085v16n01_45

Therapists, like many artists, can be their own worst critics. Less experienced therapists are especially prone to excessive self-deprecation, thereby creating unnecessary anxieties about their development into competent therapists. Hale and Stoltenberg (1988) suggest this anxiety is amplified by evaluation apprehension–the fear of negative evaluation by one's supervisor. Duval and Wicklund (1972) described this anxiety as objective self awareness. A therapist *under* supervision experiences an increased level of self-focus when being audiotaped, videotaped, or observed by a supervisor and/or treatment team, which contributes to a heightened degree of anxiety.

Stoltenberg and Delworth (1987) point out that approaches to supervision often mirror approaches used in working with clients. Constructivist approaches to therapy are designed to construct a sense of competence with clients (Hoyt, 1994, 1996). Accordingly, it makes intuitive sense that the same principles could be applied to supervision to construct a sense of competence and confidence with the therapists we supervise.

Like problem-focused therapies, problem-focused approaches to supervision reinforce a therapist's feelings of inadequacy and confusion. The supervisee will quickly learn to identify him or herself as a "trainee who makes mistakes" rather than as a "clinician who has successes" (Wetchler, 1990, p. 131). A solution-focused approach to supervision does the opposite. Just as the solution-focused therapist positions him or herself "to be in a state of *being informed* by the client" (Anderson & Goolishian, 1992, p. 29), we position ourselves in a state of *being informed* by the therapist as opposed to expecting the therapist to position him- or herself in a state of *being informed* by the supervisor.

The focus of this paper is on identifying strategies and practices that enhance clinicians' senses of themselves as competent and successful professionals. We use the name *Success Enhancing Supervision* to emphasize how supervisors assist therapists in building, augmenting, extending, and/or accentuating the therapists' clinical strengths, skills, and successes. We draw heavily from aspects of solution-focused and solution-oriented therapy in developing our success enhancing orientation to supervision. The paper also shows that we have learned much from the writings of other constructivist therapists, managers, and coaches.

We believe the goal of supervision is to facilitate the development of a competent therapist, which will ultimately affect his/her efficacy with clients. We place special emphasis on the word *facilitate*. To facilitate is to make easy or easier (Webster, 1990). Accordingly, the supervisor is a facilitator who works *with* the therapist to identify and amplify the therapist's competencies. This is very similar to the ideas behind Goolishian and Anderson's (1992) description of social construction in which the dialogical process of constructive conversation reveals a 'newness' that heretofore existed undiscovered. It follows Bateson's (see O'Hanlon & Weiner-Davis, 1989) notion that the therapist's job is to identify and amplify change.

It is undoubtedly clear, then, that we recognize and value the fact that therapists possess, as a preexisting condition, many competencies that will allow them to be effective. With these preexisting competencies, the supervisor's responsibility is to encourage the therapist's ability to utilize those strengths as he or she facilitates change in the client. By maintaining such a positive and constructive focus, we believe much of the self-criticism and self-deprecation that therapists 'under' supervision experience can be avoided. Success Enhancing Supervisors redirect therapists' focus/energies by identifying and amplifying the therapist's strengths and successes–striving to construct a sense of competence.

Although this position is quite consistent with our ultimate goal of improving client outcomes, the primary focus of supervision is on the therapist rather than the client. This, we believe, aligns our approach to supervision in stark contrast with others that focus on the client and/or therapist 'mistakes.' We have often observed that supervision of a therapist actually becomes a "case study" of the client with whom the therapist is working. As a result, "supervision" becomes client and situation specific. When the focus of supervision is on the client and his or her problems, the therapist is less likely to generalize whatever is gleaned from that supervisory session to other clients and situations. By focusing on the therapist's strengths and successes (which tend to be more global), we believe the usefulness of supervision will generalize more across clients and situations. Accordingly, we strive to only shift our attention to the client in an effort to highlight (amplify) how the therapist is affecting a positive change in that client or to help the therapist recognize the impact of his or her interventions (or lack thereof) from the client's frame of reference.

The importance of a constructive supervisory relationship based on the discovery of therapist strengths cannot be overstated. Research shows that therapist burnout (Bush, Powell, & Herzberg, 1993) and career changes (Cherniss, 1989) can be traced back to less than effective supervision. These researchers contend that traditional supervision models have not been effective in developing a positive sense of perceived self-efficacy (Bandura, 1977, 1986). They further contend that developing positive perceived self-efficacy in the therapist is essential to constructing competency in those therapists (Bandura, 1977, 1986; Bush et al., 1993; Cherniss, 1989). A focus on strengths and successes in supervision creates a climate of comfort and safety which contributes to therapist confidence, and we believe therapist confidence contributes to therapist competence.

When a therapist is lacking in confidence and is overly concerned with the potential for severe (even if only perceived) criticism in forthcoming supervision sessions, it becomes difficult to focus on the task at hand while participating in therapeutic conversations with clients. It is not uncommon for therapists in these situations to attempt to focus on two events simultaneously while conducting therapy sessions–the client in that session and the supervision that will follow. These, we believe, are incompatible tasks. We want to construct a supervisory relationship whereby the therapist is able to confidently approach and conduct sessions with an undistracted focus on the client and his or her frame of reference.

An additional benefit of a success enhancing orientation to supervision is that it reminds supervisors that there is no single, "always correct" way to do therapy. Each of us finds our own path to success. Supervisors get in trouble when they assume that what works for them must also work for the therapists they supervise. Such supervisors forego opportunities to learn from the competencies and successes of the therapists that they supervise. One lesson that we have learned from observing, reading, and listening to other therapists is that different therapy approaches share far more common ground than is often acknowledged by fundamentalist proponents of various therapy approaches (Miller & Briggs, in press).

SUPERVISION AS A JOB

We see Success Enhancing Supervision as consistent with *therapy as a job orientation* defined by Miller and de Shazer (1998). They explain that

> The job rubric is useful in highlighting the practical side of therapists' professional activities and relationships. Therapists ask questions and make suggestions that are designed to help clients improve their lives. Doing this job is basic. Again, it is necessary to repeat the question, "Does it work?" Therapists who fail at this job fail at therapy, no matter what else they may accomplish in the process. (p. 367)

Approaching supervision as a job is a simple, but not simplistic, orientation to the purpose and contexts of supervisory relationships. The purpose of Success Enhancing Supervision is to serve the therapist by enhancing the therapist's knowledge, skills, and related competencies. The client is only indirectly involved in supervision, and the supervisor is only indirectly involved in therapy. It is the therapist's job to serve the client. Effective Success Enhancing Supervisors assist therapists in doing a better job of serving their clients. This is the most important criterion that we use in evaluating supervisors. Supervisors who are unclear about who is the therapist can make already strained therapist-client relationships even worse. This is a major way in which supervisors fail to do their jobs.

The sections that follow might be seen as a job description for Success Enhancing Supervision. We begin with an overview of the process of success enhancement in supervision and then discuss three cases that illustrate different aspects of the approach. We build on the overview and case illustrations in later sections by discussing how and when Success Enhancing Supervisors take directive stances toward the therapists they supervise, how this supervisory approach can be further extended and adapted to include additional elements, and how we use a formal evaluation instrument to assess the progress of our supervisory relationships.

OVERVIEW

As alluded to earlier, the process of Success Enhancing Supervision closely parallels that of solution-focused therapy (Berg & Miller, 1992; Berg & DeJong, 1996; DeJong & Berg, 1998; de Shazer, 1985, 1988, 1991, 1994). While the following describes the typical approach used when a therapist brings a video or audio tape to the supervisory session, a similar process takes place while supervising a "live" interview, a group of therapists, and/or when the supervision is merely (without video or audio tape) a conversation about the therapist's work.

The therapist is asked to bring a video or audio tape to each supervision session, schedule a live interview, or come prepared to discuss her or his work. At the beginning of each supervisory session we ask some version of the goaling question:

- What is your goal in coming to supervision today?
- What would you like to accomplish in supervision today?
- What would you like to have happen during the next hour, so you don't find yourself looking back and saying, "Wow! That was a waste of time?"
- What are your best hopes for today's meeting?

These questions are designed to communicate the supervisor's assumption that the therapist wants to accomplish something in supervision, as well as the expectation that the therapist is prepared to begin to work on accomplishing his or her goals. Additionally, at the beginning of the supervisory relationship, we ask several goaling questions that focus beyond the session at hand, such as, "Once all of our meetings are done and you look back on them, what would you like to say that you accomplished" or, "What are your best hopes for how supervision will help you to become the kind of therapist that you want to be?" (see Marek, Sandifer, Beach, Coward, & Protinsky, 1994 and Thomas, 1996).

Then, depending on where the therapist leads us, we begin to look for strengths, successes, and exceptions to problems. Some of the questions we might ask include:

- What are the strengths that you demonstrated in this session we are about to watch (that you just conducted, that we are about to discuss)?
- I appreciate your clear description of the times when therapy isn't going as well as you'd like. This is useful information for me. Also, could you tell me about times when you are not experiencing these difficulties?
- What is different about the times you seem to be having successes with this or similar clients?

In asking these questions, we are drawing the focus away from the client and toward the therapist. Additionally, we are communicating our assumption that the therapist has observable strengths and successes. Therapists' answers to these questions are the foundation from which Success Enhancing Supervisors construct affirmative evaluations of therapists. The evaluations might compliment therapists on the content of their answers (such as, "I am patient," "I go slow," or "I focus on what the client is saying") or the affirmative evaluations might call attention to the therapist's insight into her or his strengths as a therapist (e.g., "Wow, how were you able to notice that about yourself?").

After having a conversation about the therapist's goals and strengths, the therapist is asked to present his or her case (start the tape). We work diligently to ensure that the therapist realizes he or she is in control of the session. Even subtle events help communicate this. For example, when watching a videotape, the therapist is given the remote control to start and stop, forward and reverse the tape as he or she pleases. We have observed some pleasant looks of surprise on the faces of therapists when passing this baton.

As the tape/session is presented, the supervisor and therapist work together to identify and amplify the therapist's strengths and successes. The therapist is asked to point out observable events in the session that he or she did well. Initially, the supervisor may have to take the lead in pointing out the positives. This is one way in which Success Enhancing Supervisors use their distinctive position in the supervisory relationship as a positive resource for enhancing therapists' future success. We find, however, that the therapist quickly joins in and takes the lead shortly thereafter. Of course, we also do our share of cheerleading, which is another way of saying that we do a lot of affirmative evaluation of therapists.

- That was really good, how did you know to do that?
- Wow! The client is really responding to you there!
- That's excellent! Very cool! How did you do that?

When the therapist focuses on a problem, we listen and might even agree with the therapist's assessment, but then we ask some version of the exceptions question. Another useful question asks, "So, how were you and your client able to work your way out of this short-term difficulty?" The point is that knowing how to recognize and recover from pitfalls in therapy is important. This is especially true for beginning therapists, but even the most experienced and successful therapists encounter unanticipated difficulties form time to time. Part of being a competent therapist is having confidence that whenever unanticipated issues emerge, you and your client will find a way to get beyond them. This is important, because for us, confidence is not so much an internal feeling as it is something we do. We convey confidence to others through our actions and reactions to them. Our confident behaviors also invite others to share our confident presumption that there is no reason to worry, things will work out in the end.

When the therapist focuses on the client, we redirect that focus by asking about the client's perspective through the therapist's lens.

- What would you have liked to have done instead?
- Tell me about the times you don't have that problem.
- What might have you done differently?
- When you do that (When that happens), what do you suppose the client is thinking?
- What, do you think, would the client like to see you do differently?

Ideally, the process of identifying and amplifying strengths will roughly conform to the following pattern. The therapist identifies strengths with the supervisor's encouragement, the client's perspective (of those strengths) is obtained through the therapist's lens, the supervisor corroborates the strengths noted by the therapist and the "client" (thus creating a three-way consensus), and a statement of generalization is made. For example, the supervisor might ask, "I wonder how something like this might work in other situations and with other clients?"

Sometimes therapists are unable to quickly identify their strengths and successes. A useful supervisor response is to periodically pause the tape and to ask,

- What do you suppose the client thinks you are doing at this point in the session?
- What could you do differently (instead)?
- How would you do that?
- How would the client probably have responded had you done that?

Again, the supervisor corroborates, affirmatively evaluates, and adds comments of generalization.

Occasionally, the therapist or supervisor may recognize a "mistake" that "must" be commented on. In writing this, we are mindful of de Shazer's axiom that "Being solution-focused does not mean being problem phobic!" (personal communication). Accordingly, we ask the therapist to pause the tape or interrupt the conversation and ask questions such as:

- What do you think you did there?
- What were you trying to accomplish there?
- How would that have been useful?
- What would you have liked to have done differently (instead)?
- How would you have done that?
- How do you think the client would have responded if you had done that?

It is very important to conclude discussions of problems with compliments that credit therapists with recognizing that problems exist and with having good ideas about how to effectively deal with them. Dorothy Loeffler, one of John's former supervisors at the University of Minnesota, often remarked, "The half life of a well placed criticism is about twenty years, while the half life of a solid compliment is about twenty minutes." In this case, the compliments are intended to suggest that the therapist has the skills and knowledge that are needed to recognize when problems emerge and to effectively respond to them.

When a positive difference is noted in the client, we invite the therapist to stop the tape, and we ask:

- How did you do that?
- What did you do that might have influenced this change?

These questions are also declarations that the therapist is making a difference, that therapy does work, and the therapist's efforts can be generalized across situations and clients.

Other "techniques" that may be used during the supervisory sessions are versions of the scaling question and the miracle question. In fact, we have made a practice of asking the scaling question at the conclusion of nearly every supervisory session.

- On a scale of 1 to 10, where 1 is that was the worst session you ever had and 10 is that was the best session you could ever possibly have, where would you rate that session?
- What would have been different if the session were a _____?
- How will you do that in the future?

After a brief conversation about these responses, we take a consultation/think break and construct feedback that we come back and present to the therapist. This feedback parallels solution-focused therapy. It includes compliments, bridging statements, and tasks, all communicated in the therapist's language and from his or her frame of reference.

CASE ILLUSTRATION 1:
BEGINNING THE RELATIONSHIP

In an initial supervision meeting, a young therapist was asked what he hoped to achieve/what he expected from supervision–particularly with regard to videotaping and reviewing tapes of his sessions. This therapist was rather new to the profession (he was in his first week of clinical experience), and this was his first experience with clinical supervision and videotaping. Typical of many beginning therapists (and some experienced therapists), he presented himself with seemingly low self-confidence as a therapist, as experiencing a great deal of anxiety/nervousness, and a fair amount of self-doubt and self-deprecation. He explained that he was rather anxious about seeing clients for the first time and the idea of taping his sessions seemed to make matters worse. He expressed a lot of self-consciousness about the process of videotaping and reviewing those tapes with a supervisor–seemingly becoming more and more anxious as he described how self-critical he gets upon seeing and hearing himself on tape. The following conversation took place:

Supervisor: As you become more confident and more experienced as a therapist over the next few weeks (communicating presupposition of positive change/development), what, do you suppose (using tentative language), will you notice about yourself (goal construction)?

Therapist: I don't know. I guess I'd like therapy to be like driving a car. I'd feel comfortable, and it would be automatic. It would feel natural and spontaneous.

Supervisor: Like driving a car? Yes, that would be good (validating the therapist's metaphor and affirmatively evaluating the therapist's goal of being comfortable, natural, and spontaneous).

Therapist: I would know what to say and when to say it, and my focus would be on the client more than on myself. I'm afraid that taping will create a heightened sense of self-consciousness and that I'll be more tuned in to the VCR and supervision than the client and therapy (the therapist is describing the great paradox of supervision and therapy–attempting to simultaneously attend to both).

Supervisor: I see (acknowledging the therapist's dilemma). If we were to review one of your tapes in supervision, and you were quite pleased with what you saw (notice emphasis of evaluation is on the therapist, not the supervisor), what would you notice–what would you see that would indicate to you that this was a good session, that you did a good job (returning to goal construction)?

Therapist: Well, first, I'd be about 40 years old (nervous laughter). Actually, I don't think . . . I don't expect it to be all that good yet.

Supervisor: O.K., but when it is 'all that good,' before you're 40, what will you notice (joining the therapist through use of his own words/language and continuing a presupposition of the goal being achieved)?

Therapist: Well, I'd see the interview going well, going smoothly. I'd look like I was feeling comfortable and, on the surface, things will be going well. Mostly, I'd be feeling comfortable and relaxed and spontaneous. There would be some purposeful structure to my interactions with the client. I might even see some client progression. I guess it will just take some time and practice.

Supervisor: Time and practice. Yes.

Therapist: Is one semester enough (laughter)?

Supervisor: (With laughter and using therapist's words for goal clarification/specification) I guess with time and practice, we'll find out. What will be signs that the interview is going well, going smoothly; that you were feeling comfortable, relaxed, and spontaneous?

Therapist:	There would be less hesitation and stumbling around. There wouldn't be long pauses while I was thinking of what is supposed to come next.
Supervisor:	Oh, I see. Let me think for a minute . . . (intentional and exaggerated lengthy pause) Tell me about other times or other social situations in your life where you feel more comfortable, confident, and spontaneous.
Therapist:	I usually do better in one to one interactions than in group settings. I feel a lot more comfortable in one to one interactions.
Supervisor:	That's great! One to one interactions like a lot of therapeutic relationships (complimenting the therapist's successes/exceptions and bridging these exceptions to the therapeutic relationship)! And so there's less hesitation and stumbling around, or at least you feel more comfortable with it in one to one interactions.
Therapist:	Yeah, I guess so. I've never thought of it like that. . . . Or maybe I hesitate and stumble around internally until I think of what I want to say.
Supervisor:	Oh, I see. So (indirectly complimenting through reframing), you do a good job of giving yourself permission to take pause and formulate what it is, precisely, that you want to say.
Therapist:	Yes.
Supervisor:	That's great! I noticed a moment ago, that you were pretty respectful and didn't seem to mind too much when I took a long pause to think and formulate what I wanted to say to you (using parallel process to reinforce this revelation). Do you recall?
Therapist:	Yes, it didn't bother me at all.
Supervisor:	And you didn't think I looked stupid or not confident or inexperienced, like I was just stumbling around (again, using the therapist's language)?
Therapist:	No. Actually, just the opposite. I was interested and more attentive to what you were going to say.

Notice how this conversation helps this beginning therapist to formulate what he would most like to change/gain through his participation in supervision. By identifying and clarifying what the therapist wants, the supervisor is able to begin to encourage a sense of competence with the therapist through an exploration of his past successes and strengths. Please notice also how the therapist's language evolves to a much more confident and competent level of self-perception as the interaction proceeds. One might infer that his perceived self-efficacy is already on the rise.

CASE ILLUSTRATION 2:
CONSTRUCTING CONFIDENCE AND COMPETENCE

In this case, the therapist presents for supervision with a videotaped session that she is convinced is terrible. She has requested that the supervisor help her review all of the things she did wrong during the session. John's grandmother used to say, "It's a mighty ill wind that doesn't blow some good." Just as we believe that client problems cannot *always* be present, we believe a therapist would have to work pretty hard to conduct a session in which there wasn't some good. Accordingly, we search for the successes during supervision in an attempt to construct a sense of competence within the therapist, constructing a 'success identity' which is stronger than the 'failure identity' being presented.

Therapist: After watching a portion of a videotaped session, the therapist pauses the tape and exclaims, "I suck!"

Supervisor: You suck!?! I'm not sure what you mean. What would you like to have done differently?

Therapist: Everything.

Supervisor: That's a lot. What do you suppose the client would say about your abilities?

Therapist: I don't know.

Supervisor: Well, let's slow down and try to figure this one out. When you say, "I suck" what do you really mean? (Clarifying language and making the conversation more meaningful)

Therapist: I mean I suck! I'm just not very pleased with how that session went.

Supervisor: Compared to what? (Looking for exceptions)

Therapist: Compared to other sessions I have done. I wasn't connecting. I wasn't listening. She (the client) wasn't answering my questions.

Supervisor: You suppose those two things might be related? You said compared to other sessions you have done. What do you mean? Sometimes you do a better job?

Therapist: Big time.

Supervisor: What is different about those times when you are doing a better job? (Moving the conversation from one that is failure focused toward a more useful conversation of successful exceptions)

Therapist: Well, I actually relax and listen once in awhile.

Supervisor: Really?!? How do you manage that?

Therapist: I know what you're doing.

Supervisor: Good, then you know that I really do want to know how it is that sometimes you actually do relax and listen.

Therapist	I tell myself to calm down, to slow down. I pay more attention to the client and what she is saying than myself and the team.
Supervisor:	What else is different?
Therapist:	I'm somehow not worried about silence and what the client is thinking about me.
Supervisor:	Really! Seems to me that there might have been some of those times even during this session. Is that possible?
Therapist:	I suppose. Later in the session.
Supervisor:	Interesting. How did you get back on track?
Therapist:	I don't know.
Supervisor:	Perhaps it would be useful for us to advance the tape and find out how you did that.

The therapist is then asked to advance the tape to the "better" portions, and these successful exception times become the focus of supervision–particularly the transitional aspects from "This sucks!" to "This isn't so bad." At the end of this same conversation/supervision meeting:

Therapist:	I guess that session wasn't as bad as I thought.
Supervisor:	Yeah. I don't know what you were thinking. Let's try this. On a scale of 0 to 10, where 0 equals, "That really sucked! It was the worst session imaginable!" and 10 equals, "That was an awesome session! She must have thought you were Milton Erikson!" Where would you put yourself on that scale?
Therapist:	Probably about a 4.
Supervisor:	A 4? I thought you said this wasn't that bad. Where would the client put you on that same scale?
Therapist:	I don't know. Maybe a 5 or a 6.
Supervisor:	A 6. That's more like it. So, a 6 means it didn't suck. When you meet with her again, and she sees you at a 6 1/2 or a 7 on that scale, what will you be doing differently?
Therapist:	Well, for one thing, I'll be more relaxed.

From here, the conversation continues with the therapist providing more examples of a "better" session, and the supervisor asking, "How would you do that?" and "What else?" Notice how a focus on successful exceptions rather than the evident problem areas helps the therapist avoid viewing herself as a failure. It is important to recognize (particularly as we discuss the issues of hierarchy and our role as evaluators later in this article) that the supervisor is not arguing that there weren't any problems with the session, he is merely choosing to "co-evaluate" (with the therapist) the successful exceptions. The concluding scaling question helps her conclude the supervision hour on a positive note with specific examples of things she can do differently with this client *and* other clients to influence more successful outcomes.

CASE ILLUSTRATION 3:
WHEN THERAPY DOESN'T SEEM TO BE WORKING

The previous case illustrations have been of our work with beginning therapists. A common challenge of supervision, even with the most experienced therapists, involves the perception of being stuck–at an impasse where therapy does not seem to be as productive or useful as one might expect or desire. Our experience is that most therapists are more critical of themselves than their clients–that therapists often see their work as ineffective and a waste of time, while clients view that same work as useful, supportive, and encouraging. The following case illustration involves a supervisory conversation (no videotape) in which an experienced and skilled therapist describes his work as ineffective. The client (a family) agrees with the therapist's assessment of the situation.

Therapist: I'd like some help with this family I've been seeing.
Supervisor: O.K. What do you want help with?
Therapist: Well, I'm getting frustrated. We don't seem to be getting any-where.
Supervisor: What about the family? Are they frustrated, too?
Therapist: Yeah, I think so.
Supervisor: You *think* so. How do you know? (Clarifying/confirming the therapist's perception that the family is also frustrated–obtaining three-way consensus)
Therapist: Well, for one thing, we've talked about it and we're definitely on the same page with being frustrated.

(If the therapist is only guessing about the frustration, we would scale it here. On a scale of 0 to 10, where would you rate your frustration level? Where would the family rate it? Etc. If the therapist is unsure, we encourage him or her to have that conversation with the client. Often, the therapist is inaccurate; the client/family is not as frustrated as the therapist thinks.)

Supervisor: That's interesting. I'm surprised they keep coming back. (It makes little sense for clients to continue with therapy that is frustrating and unproductive.)
Therapist: No kidding (laughter). It makes you wonder.

Supervisor: What do you suppose keeps them coming back?
Therapist: I don't know. I think maybe they keep hoping that I'll have some answers–that something will change.
Supervisor: What would they say keeps them coming back?

(As in earlier illustrations, the supervisor is using the client's frame of reference to keep the focus on the therapist. These are easy cases to focus on the client and *blame* them rather than focusing on what the therapist needs to do differently.)

Therapist: I think they'd say the same thing.
Supervisor: What else?
Therapist: I don't know. Maybe they'd say it helps to just come in and vent–get things off their chest in front of a referee.
Supervisor: So they might argue that you are doing your job a little bit. Let's get back to this frustrated thing. On a scale of 0 to 10, with 1 being extremely frustrated and 10 being not frustrated at all, where are you on the scale right now?
Therapist: About a 3.
Supervisor: And the family? (Therapists who know about our approach to supervision can often *predict* our next question(s). Consequently, we use a lot of short hand with them in order to best utilize the supervisory hour.)
Therapist: The same.
Supervisor: O.K. Suppose you and the family were just a little less frustrated–perhaps a 4 on that scale. What kind of things would they see you doing differently?
Therapist: I don't know. . . . That's a good question. . . . I guess they wouldn't notice my frustration as much. They'd probably see me as being a little more patient. I don't know. I guess I'd spend more time helping them see the things that are going well in their lives–the things and times that their relationship is going well. I don't know.
Supervisor: Sounds like you do know. (Agreeing/corroborating the therapist's perceptions and co-constructing a more positive perceived self-efficacy) What else would they see you doing differently?
Therapist: I guess maybe I've fallen into the frustration too much and have maybe tried to control the situation too much.
Supervisor: I'm not sure what you mean. What would they see you doing instead?

Therapist: I think I may have joined with mom's exasperation a bit, and I've gotten on the kid's case a little bit. Man he's frustrating.

Supervisor: Sounds like an adolescent. (Normalizing) But assuming mom has already tried that tactic several times without success . . . most do, I guess neither of us are surprised it didn't work for you either. What do you think they'd like to see you do instead?

Therapist: I guess some of the things I was talking about earlier. Looking at what is working and going well.

Supervisor: You're sure these exceptions exist?

Therapist: Oh, definitely! They've got a lot of things going for them. They are playful, mom is an incredible survivor, she's got some good ideas about chore lists with rewards and consequences. Basic parenting and behavioral mod stuff. He plays soccer and she goes to most of his games. He is choosing to stay with her as opposed to his father and his grandparents.

Supervisor: You're starting to sound a little less frustrated. Do you know what you need to do differently?

Therapist: Yes.

Supervisor: Do you want to do the next session in front of the team? (Economically, it is not feasible to work with the treatment team all of the time. We do find, however, that it is easy to get *lazy* when working alone. Bringing cases back in front of the team often fixes this problem.)

Therapist: It might not be a bad idea.

Supervisor: Good. Sounds like an interesting case to watch. What else do you want to talk about?

CASE ILLUSTRATION 4: BEING DIRECT

Clearly, therapists are required to have some knowledge base to meet credentialing standards, if not to be competent: ethics, basic skills, psychopathology, multicultural counseling, systems theory, theories and techniques, assessment, etc. We assume (require) that therapists entering their clinical experience have acquired these basic skills and knowledge. We also look for evidence of this base before working with experienced therapists. Naturally, our professions (psychiatry, psychology, counseling, marriage and family therapy, social work, etc.) are broad and ever expanding, so it is impossible for therapists to know everything. Likewise, it is impossible for supervisors to know everything.

When therapists ask their supervisors questions about skills and/or knowledge, the supervisor has to be careful to not feed into the perception that he or she *does* know everything. At times, in the interests of efficiency and simply responding to the therapist's request, the supervisor may choose to answer those questions directly. We find this process similar to what many of us do when clients ask us specific questions. At other times, the supervisor will encourage the therapist to research and find that information independently. There will also be times when the supervisor will *invite* the therapist to seek out specific information about a content area.

Consider the following example that occurred during a live supervision session. During the session, the supervisor and treatment team noticed that the client might be going into withdrawal from alcohol. The client had a known history of alcoholism, health, and heart problems and was sweating profusely and trembling. Unfortunately, the therapist didn't seem to notice and/or be concerned, so the supervisor interrupted the session with a phone call.

Therapist:	(To client upon hearing the phone ring) Excuse me, I think the team would like to ask us something. (Answering the phone) Hello?
Supervisor:	Yes, It looks like the client is rather uncomfortable–sweating and shaking quite a bit. Is this accurate? Do you notice this?
Therapist:	Yes.
Supervisor:	Is it possible that he is going into withdrawal?
Therapist:	I don't know.
Supervisor:	Can you find out?
Therapist:	How do I do that?

We try to keep phone calls and interruptions to live sessions to a minimum. When we do interrupt, however, we try to be brief and succinct so as not to be more disruptive to the therapeutic process than necessary. In this situation, it did not seem appropriate to launch into a lecture about chemical dependency and withdrawal symptoms. Accordingly, the supervisor merely scripted questions for the therapist to ask and directed her, step by step, what to do. The client was ultimately admitted to the hospital for a medical detox. In situations that are too complicated and/or the therapist is having difficulty implementing or following directives from the phone, the supervisor can simply walk into the room (we typically tell the therapist over the phone that we are coming into the session and knock at the door first), introduce him or herself, and join the conversation.

The following is an excerpt from the supervision session immediately following the above scenario.

Therapist:	I guess I blew that one. Thanks for bailing me out!
Supervisor:	I wouldn't say you blew it. I'm glad I could be useful. You did a good job of following my suggestions. You don't seem to have a lot of experience with clients who drink too much.
Therapist:	Yeah, nothing like that! That's the first alcoholic I've seen.
Supervisor:	What is your understanding . . . ? How much do you know about this thing we call chemical dependency, withdrawal symptoms, detox?
Therapist:	(Somewhat defensively and scared) Apparently not much.
Supervisor:	That's all right. (In a supportive and reassuring fashion) I wouldn't necessarily expect you to, yet. Do you suppose it might be helpful to brush up on that a bit? (Tentatively inviting further study on the topic)
Therapist:	(Laughing) Obviously.
Supervisor:	O.K. How are you going to do that?
Therapist:	Do you have any references or articles I could read?
Supervisor:	I do, but I think it might be more useful for you to research this one independently. Or maybe you could talk to your academic advisor about resources that might be helpful.
Therapist:	O.K.
Supervisor:	And, then, maybe we can talk about this next time we meet. Would this be O.K.?
Therapist:	Yes. Sure.
Supervisor:	Good, then let's talk about the parts of the session that went well (not wanting to belabor the point).

Notice that the supervisor has respectfully and nonpunitively accomplished two things: he has corroborated the therapist's advisor, and he has directed the therapist to increase her knowledge of this topic. At times we have also assigned papers and annotated bibliographies for therapists to write, but this is largely an issue of the supervisor's personal style and relationship/history with the therapist.

ENHANCING SUCCESS THROUGH FORMAL EVALUATIONS

Many of you reading this article may be surprised to see us discussing the role of evaluation as constructive supervision. You may also be surprised to know we also talk about the issue of hierarchy. While it was perhaps not obvious, hierarchy and evaluation are necessary components of the job description and case illustrations presented. Many constructivist supervisors portray hierarchy and evaluation as inconsistent with, if not directly opposed to, the purposes and philosophies of their supervisory efforts. Accordingly, they make artificial attempts to minimize and/or deny their hierarchical position. Some make similarly negative assessments about the concept of evaluation by emphasizing how evaluation is inherently critical, negatively judgmental, and focused on finding deficiencies in those they are supervising.

This is where our approach is distinctive. We believe these well-intentioned arguments are frequently taken too far. Ironically, the argument for minimizing and/or denying hierarchy can paradoxically amplify that hierarchy and *implies* that the supervisor actually *does* have privileged knowledge about how therapy should be conducted. By artificially focusing on the reduction of hierarchy and evaluation, a supervisor can create unnecessary diversions that focus supervisors' attention away from doing their jobs as supervisors. To suggest that supervisors should pay attention to *not* being hierarchical and *not* being evaluative is to unnecessarily complicate matters. No doubt, there are supervisors who can meet all of these conditions, be we are quite sure that we cannot. We just want to do our jobs as supervisors and we have found that hierarchy and evaluation are necessary aspects (perhaps even welcome) of these jobs.

Let's begin with hierarchy. While we do not set out to have hierarchical relationships with the therapists we supervise, the relationships still involve varying degrees of hierarchy, some more than others. Clearly, the most basic hierarchical aspect of our supervisory relationships is that we ask more questions of therapists than they ask of us. Supervisors sometimes overlook this source of power, but we are rather certain that therapists being supervised do not. Beyond the obvious, there are at least two other sources for hierarchy in Success Enhancing Supervision that should be noted. The first happens when we observe problems or mistakes that we feel must be addressed if the therapist is to develop as a clinician. Therapists are another source for hierarchy in Success Enhancing Supervision. Sometimes therapists (like clients in therapy) ask their supervisors to provide expert observations and suggestions about some issues. We have likely been selected and sought out by the therapists we supervise because of this expertise. Supervisors who are unresponsive to these requests risk alienating the therapists that they supervise, appearing aloof, and paradoxically amplifying the hierarchy (I know something you don't know, and I'm not going to tell you). We do not know how to enhance the success of therapists who are put off by our refusal to respond to their heartfelt and legitimate requests just because we fear that it will introduce hierarchy (hierarchy that naturally exists) into our relationship.

This brings us to evaluation in Success Enhancing Supervision. We are proud to say that we are aggressively evaluative in our supervisory relationships. We could not do Success Enhancing Supervision without evaluating. Indeed, we learned the importance of evaluation as children in school. Think about the times when the teacher told you that you did a good job with your spelling, arithmetic or some other assignment. Children know that *good job* is an evaluation. Unfortunately, adults sometimes forget what they knew as children, even though they are surrounded by evidence of what they once knew. Consider, for example, "What a meal, you are such a good cook," "I don't know how you always come up with such good ideas," and "I love you."

These are examples of what we call affirmative evaluations, although we also use other names (such as compliments) to refer to them. Affirmative evaluations abound in Success Enhancing Supervision. They are fundamental and important. One reason why we stress affirmative evaluations is because they help us to create supportive social contexts for the occasional times when we feel the need to point out and discuss therapists' mistakes. Again, we have learned from our childhood experiences in school. Think about how you interpreted criticism from teachers who had previously demonstrated that you had ability, were a good person, and/or had done a good job. We remember that we took these teachers' criticisms seriously and we assumed that the criticisms were intended to help us, not harm us. It was only when we got older that we learned that this is called constructive criticism. Evaluation takes many forms; it is not always destructive and often it can be quite constructive.

With these ideas about hierarchy and evaluation in mind, we have developed evaluation forms that are largely consistent and compatible with our work (see Appendix A). Many supervisors are now familiar with the concept of 360 degree ratings and evaluations that are used in many organizational and corporate settings today. Their purpose is to allow the *employee* to evaluate himself along with his supervisors/managers, co-workers/peers, and reports. We use a similar approach. The therapist uses these forms to evaluate herself along with her supervisor and her clients. We invite other supervisors to copy and use these forms at will.

In using the forms, the supervisor and therapist should construct a response to the following item: "The following is a brief statement of *Therapist's Name* goals for his/her development as a therapist during this evaluation period. Please read the statement carefully and respond to the questions that follow:" This can be done immediately before the evaluation, but we recommend completing it during the initial/goal-setting stages of the supervisory relationship. The supervisor and therapist co-construct an edited version immediately prior to the evaluation, recognizing that goals in supervision (like therapy) are fluid. Obviously, the therapist's name is edited into the document and it is distributed to all of the parties from whom the supervisor and therapist are interested in receiving feedback. Once the feedback is received, the supervisor and therapist can go over the feedback together. This form can also be readily adapted for a similar evaluation of the supervisor depending on the circumstances and requirements of various training programs.

ENDING REMARKS

The parallels, philosophies, and methods between solution-focused therapy and Success Enhancing Supervision are readily evident. We continually strive to co-construct fluid goals for supervision, focus on exceptions to poor or problem therapy, emphasize specific things the therapists can do differently or instead, attend to the therapist's *and* the client's frame of reference, employ scaling questions, and amplify successful or good therapy. Finally, maintaining an appropriate focus on the therapist, rather than the client, allows for greater development and generalization of therapist skills and competencies. This, along with our acknowledgement of hierarchy and aggressive use of evaluation discriminates Success Enhancing Supervision from others.

If Bandura's (1977, 1986) theory of perceived self-efficacy applies to therapists–as we believe it does–a critical, negatively evaluating, all knowing, and negatively judging supervisor is incompatible with the development of confident and competent therapists. This constructive approach, regardless of the methods used by the therapist, will foster greater perceived self-efficacy and, accordingly, greater confidence and competence amongst therapists we supervise.

REFERENCES

Anderson, H., & Goolishian, H. (1992). The client is the expert: A not-knowing approach to therapy. In S. McNamee & K. J. Gergen (Eds.), *Therapy as a social construction* (pp. 25-39). Newbury Park, CA: Sage Publications.

Bandura, A. (1977). *Social learning theory.* Englewood Cliffs, NJ: Prentice Hall.

Bandura, A. (1986). *Social foundations of thought and action.* Englewood Cliffs, NJ: Prentice Hall.

Berg, I. K., & DeJong, P. (1996). Solution-building conversations: Co-constructing a sense of competence with clients. *Families in Society: The Journal of Contemporary Human Services, 77,* 376-391.

Berg, I. K., & Miller, S. D. (1992). *Working with the problem drinker: A solution-focused approach.* New York: Norton.

Bush, J. V., Powell, N. J., & Herzberg, G. (1993). Career self-efficacy in occupational therapy practice. *American Journal of Occupational Therapy, 47* (10), 927-933.

Cherniss, C. (1989). Burnout in new professionals: A long-term follow-up study. *Journal of Health and Human Resource Administration, 12* (1), 11-24.

DeJong, P., & Berg, I. K. (1998). *Interviewing for solutions*. New York: Brooks/Cole.

de Shazer, S. (1982). *Patterns of brief family therapy*. New York: Guilford Press.

de Shazer, S. (1985). *Keys to solution in brief therapy*. New York: Norton.

de Shazer, S. (1988). *Clues: Investigating solutions in brief therapy*. New York: Norton.

de Shazer, S. (1991). *Putting difference to work*. New York: Norton.

de Shazer, S. (1994). *Words were originally magic*. New York: Norton.

Duval, S., & Wicklund, R. A. (1972). *A theory of objective self awareness*. New York: Academic Press.

Goolishian, H., & Anderson, H. (1992). An essay on changing theory and changing ethics: Some historical and post structural views. *American Family Therapy Association Newsletter, 46,* 6-10.

Hale, K. K., & Stoltenberg, C. D. (1988). The effects of self-awareness and evaluation apprehension on counselor trainee anxiety. *The Clinical Supervisor, 6* (1), 49-70.

Hoyt, M. (Ed.). (1994). *Constructive therapies* (Vol. 1). New York: Guilford Press.

Hoyt, M. (Ed.). (1996). *Constructive therapies* (Vol. 2). New York: Guilford Press.

Marek, L. I., Sandifer, D. M., Beach, A., & Coward, R. L. (1994). Supervision without the problem: A model of solution-focused supervision. *Journal of Family Psychotherapy, 5* (2), 57-64.

Miller, G., & de Shazer, S. (1998). Have you heard the latest rumor about . . . ? Solution-focused therapy as a rumor. *Family Process, 37,* 363-377.

Miller, G., & Briggs, J. R. (In press). Mixing techniques and models in therapy: Some practical consequences. *Therapie Familiale.*

O'Hanlon, B., & Weiner-Davis, M. (1989). *In search of solutions: A new direction in psychotherapy*. New York: W. W. Norton.

Stoltenberg, C. D., & Delworth, U. (1987). *Supervising counselors and therapists*. San Francisco: Jossey-Bass.

Thomas, F. N. (1996). Solution-focused supervision: The coaxing of expertise. In Miller, Hubble, & Duncan (Eds.), *Handbook of solution focused supervision* (pp. 127-151). San Francisco: Jossey-Bass.

Webster (1990). *Webster's New World Dictionary*. New York: Warner Books.

Wetchler, J. L. (1990). Solution focused supervision. *Family Therapy, 17,* 129-138.

APPENDIX A
Constructive Feedback Form

The following is a brief statement of Therapist's Name goals for his/her development as a therapist during this evaluation period. Please read the statement carefully and respond to the questions that follow:

_____
_____
_____
_____
_____

On a scale of 0 to 10, where 0 is not at all successful and 10 is completely successful, how successful was Therapist's Name in accomplishing these goals? _____
What would have you seen him/her doing differently if he/she were at the next higher point on that scale?

_____
_____
_____
_____
_____

On a scale of 0 to 10, where 0 is not at all helpful/useful and 10 is completely helpful/useful, how helpful/useful has Therapist's Name been in accomplishing your goals (his/her client's goals) for coming to therapy? _____ What would have you seen him/her doing differently if he/she were at the next higher point on that scale?

_____
_____
_____
_____

Of the things Therapist's Name did in therapy that you didn't like and/or didn't find useful/helpful, what would you like to see him/her do differently or instead?

_____
_____
_____
_____
_____

Sometimes, Therapist's Name was undoubtedly more helpful than others. What was different about the times he/she was more helpful?

_____
_____
_____
_____
_____
_____
_____

What goals, do you suppose, should <u>Therapist Name</u> be working on now?

_____

_____

_____

_____

_____

_____   _____
(Signature)   Date

_____   _____
Name   Relationship to Therapist

Solution-Focused Supervision: Returning the Focus to Client Goals

Jay D. Trenhaile

SUMMARY. This article discusses the use of solution-focused supervision questions and their perceived effect on a class of counseling practicum students. Rating scales have been used as a tool to evaluate therapist development since the 1960s. In this case study, questions were asked of student therapists from the perspective of the client. Student reports find that the questions were beneficial in helping direct future sessions toward client goals. *[Article copies available for a fee from The Haworth Document Delivery Service: 1-800-HAWORTH. E-mail address: <docdelivery@ haworthpress.com> Website: <http://www.HaworthPress.com> © 2005 by The Haworth Press, Inc. All rights reserved.]*

KEYWORDS. Solution-focused supervision, training therapists, client goals, counselor rating scales, therapist effectiveness, case studies, identification of goals, focus on the client

---

Jay D. Trenhaile is affiliated with South Dakota State University, Brookings, SD.

Address correspondence to: Jay Trenhaile, Box 507, Wenona Hall #318, SDSU, Brookings, SD 57007.

The author gives special thanks to Michael Houtkouper, Jayson Zeller, and other students who participated in responding to the structured questions.

[Haworth co-indexing entry note]: "Solution-Focused Supervision: Returning the Focus to Client Goals." Trenhaile, Jay D. Co-published simultaneously in *Journal of Family Psychotherapy* (The Haworth Press, Inc.) Vol. 16, No. 1/2, 2005, pp. 223-228; and: *Education and Training in Solution-Focused Brief Therapy* (ed: Thorana S. Nelson) The Haworth Press, Inc., 2005, pp. 223-228. Single or multiple copies of this article are available for a fee from The Haworth Document Delivery Service [1-800-HAWORTH, 9:00 a.m. - 5:00 p.m. (EST). E-mail address: docdelivery@haworthpress.com].

Available online at http://www.haworthpress.com/web/JFP
© 2005 by The Haworth Press, Inc. All rights reserved.
Digital Object Identifier: 10.1300/J085v16n01_46

The solution-focused approach has gathered intrigue and interest over recent years due in part to the effectiveness of the approach and the increased need for brief therapy. This support seems apparent throughout the helping professions as noted by the increase in publications throughout the major helping profession associations' journals. This includes special journal issues focused solely on the approach. In addition, there also has been support for solution-focused supervision as indicated in at least three publications (Juhnke, 1996; Presbury, Echterling, & McKee, 1999; Thomas, 1996). A major benefit of solution-focused supervision as described by Presbury et al. (1999) is "Focusing on solutions emphasizes collaboration in the supervisory relationship, encourages supervisees to become curious about their own potentials, illuminates the possibilities for continued professional development, and highlights the importance of discovery in the supervision experience" (p. 148).

Presbury et al. (1999) believe that through solution-focused supervision, students are able to see their potential as therapists and decrease the time needed on development from the self-efficacy perspective. Other researchers such as Cresci (1995) believe that support has been noted for a more collegial supervision model instead of hierarchical, while Thomas (1996) agrees that supervision and evaluation should be more cooperative with an increased focus on well-defined therapist and supervisor goals. Because interviews within the solution-focused approach are organized around development of client goals and solutions based on exceptions, it seems logical that any solution-focused supervision would be a positive, strength-based experience for the student. According to Presbury and colleagues, supervisors should model successful strategies and interventions, which lead to a decrease in discussion and identification of ineffective ideas.

One common tool in helping therapists improve through examination of their skill development has been the use of rating scales. These rating scales have been a consistent part of counseling skill supervision for quite some time dating back to the late 1960s-early 1970s (Benshoff & Thomas, 1992; Fong, Borders, Ethington, & Pitts, 1997; Fuqua, Newman, Scott, & Gade, 1986; Myrick & Kelly, 1971). One of the most widely used tools has been the Counselor Evaluation Rating Scale (CERS) developed by Myrick and Kelly. The initial purpose of the instrument was to evaluate effectiveness of student counselors in supervised experiences including practicum and internships. In addition to using the CERS as a template to measure student counselor effectiveness, Myrick and Kelly also supported use of the CERS as a self-rating tool for counselors-in-training.

There appears to be a variety of researchers, including Bozarth and Grace (1970) and Fuqua, Johnson, Newman, Anderson, and Gade (1984) who have found that ratings of counselor performance can vary considerably, depending on the source of the rating (i.e., peer, client, supervisor, counselor). However, there is support for self-assessment of counselor-in-training skill development (Benshoff & Thomas, 1992; Bradley, 1989). In addition, activities that help the counselor attend to the critical factors needed for effective counseling is invaluable. Clearly, self-evaluation will not replace effective supervision; however, it can be a useful tool in the development of counseling skills.

Because a major tenet of the solution-focused approach is that "clients are the experts about their own lives" (DeJong & Berg, 2001, p. 20), it would seem logical that a component of supervision should be to help the student therapist focus on client goals. Since clients provide information about what will be different in their lives when the problem is solved and these disclosures are taken at face value, student therapists must be able to recognize and use this critical information. DeJong and Berg also place a significant emphasis on recognizing client strengths from a discussion of exceptions to current problems. Thus, the emphasis is placed on the client and the therapist is not viewed as the expert for assessing and intervening on client problems, which enhances the need for therapists to focus on the client. By increasing the focus on clients' frames of references, client resistance also ceases to be a concern (de Shazer, 1984).

This case study was designed to review student beliefs regarding the usefulness of the client-focused questions. It was believed that through strength-based structured questions, students would become more focused on client goals and needs.

CASE STUDY

In the fall of 2002, I was teaching a counseling practicum course and wanted to encourage students to start self-reflection on the content and focus of therapy sessions they were facilitating. A solution-focused worksheet was developed to help the student counselors analyze their performance of counseling sessions for which they were seeking supervision. This worksheet focused on four different questions:

1. On a scale from 1 to 10, with 1 being the "pits" and 10 being pretty darn good, how would you rate your work?
2. What would have made the session increase by a point or two?
3. What worked well during the session and when did you do it?
4. What do you need to do more of in the future?

After initiating the use of this worksheet, I became concerned that the worksheet focused strictly on the counselor and allowed for no discussion on the role of the client and more specifically, what the client's goals were for therapy. Around the time of the start of this class, I attended a presentation by Steve de Shazer and Harvey Ratner at the European Brief Therapy Association that encouraged supervision of sessions from the client's perspective (de Shazer & Ratner, 2002). Shortly after, I adjusted the initial questions and asked the following questions during supervision:

1. On a scale from 1 to 10, with 1 being the "pits" and 10 being pretty darn good, what would your client say about the session?
2. What would the client say would have made the session increase by a point or two?
3. What was the client doing when things were going the best during the session?
4. What would the client say you need to do more of?

These questions were asked after some initial discussion of the case and the student therapists had rated their performances in sessions. While answering these questions, students processed the questions thoroughly and were thoughtful in their responses. I believe the questions were effective in helping the student therapists recognize that therapy is for the client, not what the therapist believes is most important. An example of one response from a student included:

1. On a scale from 1 to 10, with 1 being the "pits" and 10 being pretty darn good, what would your client say about the session?

   Student Response: *An 8 because they want to come back for another session.*

2. What would the client say would have made the session increase by a point or two?

   Student Response: *Asking if there were other issues that they wanted to discuss.*

3. What was the client doing when things were going the best during the session?

   Student Response: *When she was hearing the progress she had made during the sessions, which I was doing to compliment her.*

4. What would the client say you need to do more of?

   Student Response: *Be sure I am addressing what she wants, such as asking if there are other issues going on.*

Some of the initial comments from the students who received supervision through use of this format were focused on the usual concerns of participating in practicum experience such as "I was so nervous during the initial sessions that I couldn't focus on the client at all, I just wanted to look effective." Consequently, some believed that the use of these client-centered questions became more helpful as their skills as a counselor developed. In addition, students articulated that the questions helped them focus on client goals by forcing the student therapists to "put yourself in their shoes." Furthermore, students found the structured questions were effective in providing direction for future therapy because client goals seemed to be clearer. Finally, there was consensus that the implementation of the questions did encourage students to keep their individual biases outside of the counseling session.

CONCLUSION

Clearly, there is a need to effectively research ways to enhance treatment of the client as the expert and focus therapist energies on what the client wants differently. The use of structured, client-based questions seems to help reinforce the need for therapists to treat the client as the expert.

REFERENCES

Benshoff, J. M., & Thomas, W. P. (1992). A new look at the Counselor Evaluation Rating Scale. *Counselor Education and Supervision, 32,* 12-22.

Bozarth, J. D., & Grace, D. P. (1970). Objective ratings and client perceptions of therapeutic conditions with university counseling center clients. *Journal of Clinical Psychology, 27,* 117-118.

Bradley, L. J. (1989). *Counselor supervision: Principles, process, practice* (2nd ed.). Accelerated Development: Muncie, Indiana.

Cresci, M. M. (1995). How does supervision work? Facilitating the supervisee's learning. *Psychoanalysis and Psychotherapy, 13,* 50-58.

DeJong, P., & Berg, I. K. (2001). *Interviewing for solutions* (2nd ed.). Pacific Grove, CA: Brooks/Cole.

de Shazer, S. (1984). The death of resistance. *Family Process, 23,* 79-93.

de Shazer, S., & Ratner, H. (September, 2002). *"I've tried that!" Supervising the solution-focused practitioner.* Presentation at the European Brief Therapy Association, Cardiff, Wales.

Fong, M. L., Borders, L. D., Ethington, C. A., & Pitts, J. H. (1997). Becoming a counselor: A longitudinal study of student cognitive development. *Counselor Education and Supervision, 37,* 100-114.

Fuqua, D. R., Newman, J. L., Scott, T. B., & Gade, E. M. (1986). Variability across sources of performance ratings: Further evidence. *Journal of Counseling Psychology, 33*(3), 353-356.

Fuqua, D. R., Johnson, A. W., Newman, J. L. Anderson, A. W., & Gade, E. M. (1984). Variability across sources of performance ratings: Further evidence. *Journal of Counseling Psychology, 31*, 249-252.

Juhnke, G. A. (1996). Solution-focused supervision: Promoting supervisee skills and confidence through successful solutions. *Counselor Education and Supervision, 36*, 48-57.

Myrick, R. D., & Kelly, F. D., Jr. (1971). A scale for evaluating practicum students in counseling and supervision. *Counselor Education and Supervision, 28*, 71-79.

Presbury, J., Echterling, L. G., & McKee, J. E. (1999). Supervision for inner vision: Solution-focused strategies. *Counselor Education and Supervision, 39*, 146-155.

Thomas, F. N. (1996). Solution-focused supervision: The coaxing of expertise. In S. D. Miller, M. A. Hubble, & B. L. Duncan (Eds.). *Handbook of solution-focused therapy* (pp.128-151). San Francisco: Jossey-Bass.

The Listen and Describe Approach to Training in Solution-Focused Brief Therapy

Dan Gallagher

SUMMARY. This training exercise introduces trainees to the basic notions of solution-focused therapy. Exercises teach trainees the art of observation and description without explanation, essential for good solution-focused therapy. *[Article copies available for a fee from The Haworth Document Delivery Service: 1-800-HAWORTH. E-mail address: <docdelivery@haworthpress.com> Website: <http://www.HaworthPress. com> © 2005 by The Haworth Press, Inc. All rights reserved.]*

KEYWORDS. Solution focus, training

This article describes a way of leading solution-focused brief therapy workshops based on client teaching and therapist questions. I use exercises that create conversation strategies with workshop participants that resemble ways a solution-focused brief therapist and client work together in a session. By doing workshops this way I find that it is easier to keep the focus on what the client is

Dan Gallagher is affiliated with the Center for Solutions, Walden, NY.
Address correspondence to: Dan Gallagher, 29 Halcyon Rd., Millbrook, NY 12545.

[Haworth co-indexing entry note]: "The Listen and Describe Approach to Training in Solution-Focused Brief Therapy." Gallagher, Dan. Co-published simultaneously in *Journal of Family Psychotherapy* (The Haworth Press, Inc.) Vol. 16, No. 1/2, 2005, pp. 229-252; and: *Education and Training in Solution-Focused Brief Therapy* (ed: Thorana S. Nelson) The Haworth Press, Inc., 2005, pp. 229-252. Single or multiple copies of this article are available for a fee from The Haworth Document Delivery Service [1-800-HAWORTH, 9:00 a.m. - 5:00 p.m. (EST). E-mail address: docdelivery@haworthpress.com].

Available online at http://www.haworthpress.com/web/JFP
© 2005 by The Haworth Press, Inc. All rights reserved.
Digital Object Identifier: 10.1300/J085v16n01_47

doing that is telling the therapist, and therefore workshop participants, what is useful and not so useful in a session. Some examples of other exercises that also reinforce the aim of the workshop are included.

The *Listen and Describe* approach was first offered at a workshop I conducted for drug and alcohol professionals at Center for Solutions[1] in 2002. The approach was born and bred in the contexts of numerous workshops I have facilitated and attended over the past 20 years. Several variations of *Listen and Describe* have been used in workshops, presentations, and classes since. Please note that this article is not intended as a substitute for the kind of live training offered, for example, at Center for Solutions. We still need training contexts for therapists, live work with clients, and skilled experienced facilitators, working together, to practice what a document like this can only describe. What I am trying to provide here is simply a flavor of what happens in this approach to training.

Workshop participants, for the purposes of this article, range from people totally unfamiliar with SFBT ideas and practice, to those who are skilled in the approach. I am interested in finding useful ways to help workshop participants develop their skills, talking plainly and clearly with clients in language based on what the client says her or his wishes are for their life after the problem is gone. As I do when I meet with clients, I use language with workshop participants that enhances and promotes utilizing the *client's* ideas about building and maintaining a satisfactory solution of their own, in the context of the client's own life. Part of my job is to find ways to listen for how the participants are using language differently, in the course of a workshop, by the ways they listen to and talk with and about a client.

Listen and Describe is a simple approach to solution-focused brief practice in workshops. It involves workshop participants' listening to and noticing what clients and therapists are saying and doing in live and videotaped therapy sessions, accomplishing four tasks at various intervals:

1. Notice what the client is doing/saying that tells you that the conversation between client and therapist is useful for the client.
2. Notice what the client is teaching the therapist about what questions are most useful for the client.
3. Notice what you are learning from the client about useful SFBT ideas.
4. Suppose the client has joined us for this workshop. On a scale from 0 to 10, with 10 being total agreement and 0 being the client can't make heads or tails about what we are talking about, where would the client put this conversation so far? Where would persons in the client's life (best friend, family members, co-workers, etc.) put things on the scale if they were present?

The tasks are discussed by the workshop group as a whole. Lists are compiled under four columns outlining the tasks described above. As the workshop continues, the list grows and can be used for reference and to bring the focus of discussions back to what the client and therapist are doing that is useful for the client. I am finding that these four tasks help participants stay practice-focused instead of getting sidetracked with content issues with the client and/or with each other. For example, I have heard solution-focused presenters asking workshop participants similar questions based on their own perceptions and concerns instead of the client's. One result is a discussion between participants and leader with the client erased from the context or frame.

Once I introduce the exercise to the participants, I begin with a variation of Steve de Shazer's *Inside and Outside*[2] exercise, which goes like this:

> Groups of 6 are set-up with one person role-playing a client and one person serving as an observer. The other 4 are to role-play being one therapist. This they do by taking turns asking one question each after the first question. Each subsequent question must be related, in some way, to the previous response/answer. The observer's task is to keep track of how the therapist's questions are related to the previous response/answer. Furthermore, they are to watch for differences between Part 1 and Part 2. (Part 2 can either be explained now or at the end of Part 1.)

Part 1: The first question–which is the traditional SFBT first question–to the client is: "What needs to happen here–in our work together–so that you know that coming here has been worth it to you?"

Each of the 4 questioners gets 2 or 3 turns to ask questions, depending on how much time is allotted.

Part 2: "Now all of you–except for the observer–need to pretend that round one did not happen. With the same observer and client try this substitute first question: 'What needs to happen here–in our work together–so that your best friend knows that your coming here has been worth it to you, not a waste of time for you?'"

Again, each of the 4 questioners gets 2 or 3 turns to ask questions.

DISCUSSION

Taking each group in turn:

1. Begin by asking the observer from one of the groups to compare round 1 with round 2, beginning with anything he/she observed and then to talk

about how the therapist's questions were related to the client's responses/answers.
2. Next, ask the client to make comparisons between rounds 1 and 2. Focus on how the client helped the therapist to ask useful questions.
3. Ask the people playing the therapist what they learned from the exercise. Then ask for a comparison (if it does not happen spontaneously). Focus on how the client helped them ask useful questions.
4. Then the next group, then the next, and the next, etc. The first question in Parts 1 and 2 can be reversed.

The *Inside and Outside* exercise provides a natural transition into *Listen and Describe*. After participants answer the discussion questions, the workshop facilitator can begin asking what they learned from the exercise that are useful SFBT ideas and begin listing them. Some ideas participants have come up with are "Visualizing change that your best friend will see puts it in their real lives." "By taking what the client said and building the next question on it, the client knows you care." "Helping the therapist ask helpful questions made me feel like this was softer and a little more personal." "Thinking about my own life instead of the therapy made all the difference." "I think that the second question she was asking, what your best friend would notice, requires being more specific, because in the first, the client was more vague and throwing jargon around about the right thing to do." These ideas go on the list.

Then I tell the participants that I am going to show them a tape. *Their job is to listen and describe solution-focused ideas they learn from it.* The tape I use here is a particularly useful one, because it is full of solution-focused ideas in practice, followed by a brief interview between the client and a colleague from behind the one-way mirror. This transcript of a videotaped session with a client is simply an example of how I use tapes. You may have videotapes of your own you would like to use while trying out this approach. And, of course, the approach can be adapted for use with live interviews as well.

FIRST MEETING VIDEOTAPE[3]

Amanda said that she came to see a therapist because her counselor in an outpatient drug program thought it would be a good idea. She said the counselor was worried about Amanda hitting a wall and injuring her right hand when she was feeling angry. The counselor, who considered herself "not trained to deal with that," sent Amanda over to see us.

Dan:	· Do you agree with her sending you over here?
Amanda:	I don't know what the difference is between there and here. I mean, there is basically substance abuse.
Dan:	It was their idea anyway?
Amanda:	She said they're not able to handle . . . I mean, I've never hit a counselor. I just go home and if I'm mad or even if I bowl bad I hit the wall. That's how I hurt my hand.
Dan:	How is that helpful for you?
Amanda:	It just releases . . . when I'm mad, rather than yelling or hitting them, I'll hit the wall.
Dan:	So that's useful?
Amanda:	It is to me. It's my way to release my anger and my frustration.
Dan:	How else is it useful for you?
Amanda:	That's about it. It hasn't helped my hand any (holds hand up). My hand doesn't straighten up all the way.
Dan:	What other ways is it better than doing something else?
Amanda:	I've been doing that since I stopped using drugs and alcohol.
Dan:	Is that right?!
Amanda:	Yeah, because before when I was mad, I'd go to the bar and drink and drink and drink and I'd go do coke and it would make me feel better.
Dan:	And what other ways do you deal with it–a little bit better or successfully?
Amanda:	That's basically the only way I deal with anything now. I get mad and I just go upstairs and shut myself in my room.
Dan:	O.K. You do that too. And that helps? Some?
Amanda:	Some. It's just so I don't blow up at anybody or–I just go up to my room and I turn on the TV and I'll probably fall asleep.

Listen and Describe: How is the therapist building his questions on the client's answers? How is he managing to gently direct the client toward solution talk? How is he inquiring about how hitting the wall is useful/helpful for her? What do her answers teach us about that? How is he beginning to set a context for talking that is based on what the client finds helpful and useful in terms of what she came to see the therapist for? How is what therapist and client are doing in the session helpful to workshop leader and participants in building a context for *their* continuing to talk about what they are finding helpful and useful about what they are doing? What would the client agree with if she were here? Summarize the participants' answers on the list. The tape continues:

Dan:	All right. So, given that, what do you suppose we could talk about today–that in the time we have together you could leave here saying, "I'm glad I talked to that guy"?
Amanda:	(laughing) I don't know. There's nothing really. I don't see anything really wrong. It's just since I've stopped using and what not.
Dan:	So, what are you doing right?
Amanda:	(laughs) I don't know. I'm not working. I'm just sitting at home. I go to counseling once a week and that's it.
Dan:	And that's working?
Amanda:	Her and I disagree. Once I went out and had a couple of drinks. But to me the main problem was the cocaine. So I had a couple of drinks and my mother calls up two months later and tells Joan that I had a drink. So, why'd you wait two months to call her?
Dan:	Wait a minute! You had a couple of drinks and you didn't go off the deep end or do anything else?
Amanda:	Nope. I just had a couple of drinks and the people I was with weren't ready to leave so I walked home.
Dan:	How'd you do that?
Amanda:	Because I knew if I got really drunk I'd be in trouble. But it was just this guy's going away party so I had a couple drinks and walked home.
Dan:	So, how do you suppose we can help?

Listen and Describe: The therapist is keeping his focus (and therefore the workshop participants' focus) on what the client wants and how she will know when we have done something worthwhile for her. Pause here, use the Listen and Describe exercise and write participants' ideas on the list.

Amanda:	(laughs) I honestly don't know. I don't know. The only thing I know is that I'm just getting angry, and I'm getting angrier easier. Getting more agitated, more angry, and I go off at the littlest things. That's something I've noticed.
Dan:	And then, how do you keep going? How do you . . .
Amanda:	Then I just beat the hell out of a wall and then go back to what I was doing.
Dan:	You keep going?
Amanda:	Yeah.
Dan:	O.K. What are some of the other things you're doing that are good for you?
Amanda:	Well, I'm bowling.

Dan:	You are? With that hand?
Amanda:	Yeah.
Dan:	O.K.
Amanda:	Because when I'm mad I hit the wall because I bowl bad. But when I bowl 279 I'm not hitting the wall.
Dan:	279! You mean you can bowl 279?!
Amanda:	Yeah. I bowled a couple. One ball short of 300.
Dan:	My God!
Amanda:	But I used to work there, so–that's where all my problems started–with the drugs.
Dan:	You're a good bowler?
Amanda:	I try to be. I just bowled this morning. That's the only thing that I do that I enjoy. And in the beginning they wanted to take that away–because there was a bar there. And I used to work there and a lot of the problems came with employees and people who hung out down there. So, you know, one night, you know, I'll go back and I'll try to bowl. You know, something to do. And I'm using my hand more and more.
Dan:	So, you go in there today and bowled and bowled . . .
Amanda:	And I left after I bowled.
Dan:	What's different?
Amanda:	(laughing) I was hoping you could tell me. I don't know; it's just that I know I don't need it.
Dan:	That's amazing! You know that!
Amanda:	Yeah. But I don't know. I know I can just go in and bowl. Even lately. Wednesday night was my night. Wednesday night I'd go in an hour early before bowling and sit in the bar. I could do a shot a frame for the last game. I could do 10 shots a night and still bowl.
Dan:	So, what's different now?
Amanda:	Now I just don't. Now I just go past the bar, get a bottle of water or soda and that's it. But rather than, if I threw a bad ball, rather than I'm going to go do a shot, I go home and hit the wall.
Dan:	O.K. And that's better.
Amanda:	My hand doesn't agree, but . . .
Dan:	. . . compared to before . . .
Amanda:	Yeah.

Listen and Describe: This is another good place to pause and ask workshop participants to identify solution-building talk between client and therapist. Continue adding to the list: "You kept the discussion positive." "You didn't let her talk about her problems." "I would have wanted to know more about her hurting her hand, her relationship with her mother, her social life, and her still drinking, but you didn't." "You even saw her problems as useful in some way." At this point it seems easier for participants to talk about what the therapist is doing than what the client is doing/saying that tells the therapist and us what we are doing that is helpful for her–how good a job we are doing learning from her. The idea of client as teacher in this way may be quite new to some participants. Continuing to ask participants to describe how the conversation in the consulting room is helpful for the client, what the client is teaching us about what questions are useful for her, and what we are learning from the client that might lead to useful SFBT ideas, much as the therapist is doing with the client, is crucial to keeping the frame active. By eliciting these answers from the participants, as the therapist did with Amanda, the facilitator can keep the conversation focused on what the client and therapist are doing that is useful and helpful for her. *Learning is happening in relation to the client and to solution-building practice.* A participant will often provide a useful segue back to the tape, as when a person commented that we still didn't have much idea about what Amanda wants from our meeting today.

Dan:	O.K. Do you mind if I ask you a really weird question?
Amanda:	O.K. I'll try it.
Dan:	Just suppose, tonight (pause) you finish whatever you were going to do for the day, you're home and you go to bed. (pause) And you go to sleep. (pause) And while you're sleeping, (pause) a miracle happens (pause). And the miracle is that the problem that brought you here today is gone, (pause) just like that. (pause) (she giggles) But you don't know it because you're asleep. (pause) How are you going to know in the morning when you wake up that the problem that brought you to see me is solved? What will be the first small thing that will tell you?
Amanda:	Probably when I walk down, if my mother and I got in a fight or not. Usually when I first get up we argue a lot. So if everything works out O.K., then . . .
Dan:	O.K., so what will be happening instead?
Amanda:	We'll get along. We get along, it's just, I blow up because of nothing, so if she makes a little comment to me and I don't blow up . . .
Dan:	O.K. So you get up and go down, and . . . what will be different?
Amanda:	My mother and I won't argue.
Dan:	Paint me a picture.

Amanda:	Usually it's over my dog. My dog, 5:30 in the morning, gets up every morning. So I get mad because everybody else in my family's up but I have to get up to let the dog out. Simple little things like that. So, I get up and I start yelling and cursing and drag the dog outside.
Dan:	What will be different when the miracle is happening?
Amanda:	Usually my mother says let your dog out, let your dog out, so if I just get up and let her out without arguing or me blowing up because the dog wants to get up at 5:30 in the morning because she wants to go to the bathroom . . .
Dan:	When's the last time you did that?
Amanda:	This morning.
Dan:	This morning? You got up and did it?
Amanda:	I just did what I did and went back to bed.
Dan:	What difference did that make for you?
Amanda:	Not a lot. I mean, it was nice not to argue the first thing in the morning.
Dan:	How about everyone else? What difference did you notice?
Amanda:	Basically nothing because I don't talk to my brothers that much.
Dan:	So you did that this morning!
Amanda:	Yeah. Something different.
Dan:	Is that something you'd like to do more?
Amanda:	Not argue? Not blow up as easily?
Dan:	And get up and do what you did this morning?
Amanda:	Yeah, if I can stay up all day. I'd like to get some sleep. I can stay up. I'm up until late because when I lay down it's hard for me to go to sleep. It's 3:30 or 4 o'clock in the morning and I'm up still. And then I go to bed and at 5:30 the dog wants out. I just got to bed. I've got to go to bed in the afternoon and then I go out at night.
Dan:	So, would getting a good night's sleep be something important?
Amanda:	Yeah.
Dan:	What do you think the chances are that you can do that?
Amanda:	I haven't been sleeping right since I started work. I used to work nights.
Dan:	So this would be a big change for you?
Amanda:	And then I stopped work at the end of October. Then I went to the hospital for a week and that was the best sleep I got. They got me up in the morning and I was up at 7:30 and they wouldn't let me go back to bed until it was bedtime.
Dan:	And you did that? You slept all night?

Amanda:	Yeah. Then I came home and back to the same routine–up all night, even though I'm not working.
Dan:	How did you manage to do it in the hospital?
Amanda:	It was a routine that I had to get up and I had to go to group and I had to have lunch and had to go to group afterwards.
Dan:	And you did it.
Amanda:	Yeah.
Dan:	And when it was time to go to sleep, you did.
Amanda:	Because I was up all day so I was tired. I wasn't used to being up at 7:30.
Dan:	Oh, O.K. So your present job has different hours?
Amanda:	I'm not working right now. They told me not to go back to work at the bowling alley. So now I have a couple phone calls in to friends trying to get something in line. I've been out of work since the end of October. I owe my mother so much money, I'm supposed to be paying her rent and the phone bill. I owe 500 some dollars because my best friend who was there through it all lives in Jersey. So, when I have a bad day, I can talk 3 hours on the phone with her.
Dan:	You talk to her. And that's helpful?
Amanda:	It's helpful until my mother and I argue about the phone bill.
Dan:	Yeah. Mothers are going to do that all right.
Amanda:	Because I have no money to pay her.
Dan:	So, what else will be different?
Amanda:	I should get up and be motivated to do something. Usually I get up, let the dog out, argue and come back to bed. Get up in the afternoon, go out and play with my nephew for a little while– that's about the most energy I have–play ball with him a couple times, and then I just lay on the couch.
Dan:	Yeah. Now, is that something you want to do?
Amanda:	No, that's just the way it is. I usually go from the bed to the couch.
Dan:	So, that morning after the miracle, what would you be doing?
Amanda:	I'd actually do something. I'd be playing more with him or doing something around the house. The other day I got motivated and I almost cleaned my room.
Dan:	How would doing some of those things make things different with your mom?
Amanda:	Because that's what we argue about–that I do nothing. I don't have a job, I don't do anything. I exist.
Dan:	So what would you do instead of arguing?

Amanda:	Usually, if I get really mad I hit the wall or I go upstairs to my room.
Dan:	I mean . . . a miracle.
Amanda:	A miracle would happen?
Dan:	Yeah.
Amanda:	I could probably do it. I'd probably start.
Dan:	You could?
Amanda:	I can do it now. If I really wanted to I guess I really could. But I have no motivation. I don't want to do anything right now. I just want to exist.
Dan:	O.K.
Amanda:	I mean, that's how it is right now.
Dan:	How will you know it's time for that to start happening?
Amanda:	I don't know. I guess when I get sick and tired of doing nothing. When I'm fed up with just doing nothing.

Listen and Describe: What does Amanda want to do after our meeting together? Although a few participants may want to talk more about what's wrong and getting Amanda to stop, others indicate that they are learning from Amanda that she is concerned about what she and her mother think she should be doing more. Some also think that Amanda may getting ready to do more now that she sees herself already taking useful action. I add their answers to the list of solution-focused ideas.

Now that we have a good idea of what the client wants today, how she wants her life to be when things are "better," it is time to ask her to fill that picture with more and more details of what "better" looks like. The therapist's job is to help the client hear how she is describing making things better already that she can do more, based on the responses she has given so far. Workshop participants are asked to continue to *listen and describe*. Let's listen:

Dan:	How close are you to–let's say you have a scale of 0 to 10, where 10 is as close to getting tired of doing nothing as you can get before you do something . . .
Amanda:	I'm about a 3.
Dan:	About a 3. How come 3 and not 0?
Amanda:	Because every once in a while I'll do stuff. Like when I first got home from the hospital rehab I just sat there. I didn't get out of bed some days. I didn't even take a shower. At least I'll get up, I'll take a shower. I make sure every day I have some time with my nephew.
Dan:	That's important to you?

Amanda: Yeah.

Dan: What do you suppose things will look like when you're at a 4? What will you be doing? Or what would your mom see you doing? The dog, what would the dog see?

Amanda: The dog's going to be an outside dog. I don't know.

Dan: Your mom, where would she put you on that scale?

Amanda: She'd probably put pretty much the same, about a 3.

Dan: You would agree about that?

Amanda: I think so. It would be about the only thing we'd agree on.

Dan: If she was talking this way, what would she see you doing that she would think, hmm, she's at a 4 today?

Amanda: Just doing more stuff around the house or even looking–doing more to find a job than just making phone calls.

Dan: What would be the first thing she'd see?

Amanda: Me in a better mood. (laughs)

Dan: Is that a 4 or is that a 10?

Amanda: It can be a 4.

Dan: O.K. Another one of these scales, where 10 is things are going well, things are going the best they possibly can for you at the moment and 0 is the way things were when you called for the appointment, where are you today?

Amanda: I'd say about a 2.

Dan: That's a lot! What's the highest you've been on that scale recently?

Amanda: I've been about a 5 or 6.

Dan: What was happening then?

Amanda: It's when my ex-boyfriend and I were trying to get back together. And we had some good times.

Dan: Things were better when you were with him?

Amanda: We were just trying to work things out and I don't think it's going to work and . . .

Dan: O.K. And when you were doing that you were up around 5?

Amanda: Yeah. And my best friend from Jersey and I argued just recently, so, before we argued, before she started dating my baby brother, everything was better.

Dan: What? Nobody dates your baby brother?

Amanda: She's married. She got married in June. She got separated in October. And now she's dating my 20-year-old brother. That's a subject that we deal with a lot.

Dan: Because you're friends?

Amanda:	Yeah. But I will go out if she goes out, like if she wants me and Andy, my ex-boyfriend, kind of, whatever, to go out with her and my brother, I told her that's not going to happen.
Dan:	And you're still friends?
Amanda:	Yeah. We've been through a lot.
Dan:	Friends mean a lot to you?
Amanda:	Yeah. Pretty much.
Dan:	O.K. Let me ask you another one of those scales, 0 to 10. 10 is you're willing to do just about anything that's legal, within your code of ethics, to get going with these things, and 0 is you don't give a damn, where are things at?
Amanda:	I'd say a 4.
Dan:	A 4!
Amanda:	Because right now I'm really getting sick and tired of just doing nothing. I've made phone calls and that's an improvement. When I first got home and when I first started therapy I wasn't going to do anything. I was just going to sit there and let mom pay the bills, let my brother pay for all my bowling, my other brother.
Dan:	And how did you decide it was a good time to make those calls?
Amanda:	I just got sick of doing nothing. I was sick of doing nothing and sick of my mother yelling, "do something."
Dan:	O.K. One more. You might have one for me in a minute. Ten is you're really confident that you're going to do these things, that you're going to get on with things the way you want to and 0 is not a chance, where are you at?
Amanda:	My thing is, if it happens, it happens. I don't know where that pretty much puts me but . . .
Dan:	Well, where would you put yourself?
Amanda:	Probably a 3. If it happens, if I get a job, where I'm looking, I don't know. But if I don't, oh well.
Dan:	So, how can we help?
Amanda:	I was hoping you could tell me. I don't know. I don't know. Joan is making a big thing about me hitting the walls. My concern is finding an orthopedic that takes Medicaid. There isn't one around here. I can make one an hour away, but it's like a 2 1/2 month wait. But then I don't want to have to wait 2 1/2 months, so . . .
Dan:	How come that's important to you?
Amanda:	Because it's my bowling hand. It may sound stupid but that's my bowling hand. It doesn't bother me that that's the hand I

	write with and the hand I do everything else with, but I want to
	keep on bowling. That's the only thing I feel that I enjoy.
Dan:	Well, O.K. I think I've done it. I think I've run out of questions.

It is my custom to take a short, 10-minute break before returning to meet with the client briefly before ending the meeting. You might want to try this yourself before reading on. With workshop participants, I stop the tape and confer with them as colleagues behind the mirror. During this pause, I avoid thinking/talking about so-called problem-dynamics and why I did some things and not others. Instead, I direct my thinking (or the discussion when there are colleagues behind a mirror) toward evidence and clues the client gave me/us about what would be helpful compliments and what might be a useful suggestion for the client to help her continue to gather evidence for "better" after this meeting.

Dan:	Well, I've got to tell you, we're impressed!
Amanda:	Why?
Dan:	Well, you've come a long way! You've taken some big steps (nods yes). And you're not using coke, you didn't go off the deep end with those drinks, you're thinking seriously about things, very seriously (nods yes). I know it's not easy, but you're listening to people, you're weighing all the ideas, opinions, advice that's coming at you, some preaching and all that kind of stuff (nods yes) at a time when you want to give yourself all the time you need to get on with your life–it's not easy to do that when everybody around you wants you to do more (nodding yes), even your dog.
Amanda:	5:30 in the morning!
Dan:	Yeah.
Amanda:	He's got some nerve.
Dan:	Yeah. On the other hand, we can understand how your counselor is concerned. You've made great progress. You're not taking it out on people. You're hitting the wall. I guess the counselor is concerned about that, too. And, even more–well, first of all, I think you have a great sense of humor . . .
Amanda:	(laughs) I try. I try.
Dan:	And you have a heck of a lot of energy.
Amanda:	A lot of energy, if I could get my butt up and . . . a lot of energy.
Dan:	You're full of energy. And we can see that somebody like you, full of energy, can get tired of just hanging around, too. It's like you're bugging yourself some, too.

Amanda:	Yeah.
Dan:	And we can see how the hospital was helpful to you because of the routine. And it makes a lot of sense to us that your getting a job would help you get that routine going again.
Amanda:	Yeah. It would get me up in the morning.
Dan:	So, a couple of ideas, a couple of suggestions. Somebody behind the mirror had this kind of off the wall idea. What do you suppose would happen if you just started hitting the wall with your other hand?
Amanda:	I never tried that.
Dan:	And I wanted to ask, do you think you want to come back?
Amanda:	If it's going to help. I just figure that I was drinking since I was 14, and I started doing cocaine at 22, my body just has to get back to–I just thought it was normal. I just thought it would take time just to . . .
Dan:	So if we can be helpful helping you do that . . .
Amanda:	As long as it's not a group. I'm not good in group.
Dan:	O.K. It's up to you. It's not something that we can decide (nods O.K.). I'll keep asking. We agree with you. And I know that instead of kind of buckling in a way and changing everything right away, we have a suggestion for you.
Amanda:	I'm sitting down, go ahead.
Dan:	How about noticing the times when you're thinking about the things you want to do: I've got to get a job, I've got to do this, I've got to do that, and keeping track of what's different when you're doing that, whatever it is that tells you that that's useful, and when you come back, we can talk about that.
Amanda:	Do you want me to keep a journal, or . . .
Dan:	I don't know. Do you think that would be useful?
Amanda:	Should I document whenever I feel like doing something like getting a job?
Dan:	Yeah. However you would do that. What's different about those times? So, when do you think you'd want to come back?
Amanda:	My days are free, as long as my mother's car is free.
Dan:	What do you think would impress your counselor?
Amanda:	Two weeks.

'ASK THE CLIENT' EXERCISE

After this tape segment and a brief discussion about what to add to the Listen and Describe list, the facilitator asked participants these questions:

- I'm trying to figure out, was there anything that happened in that interview that you didn't expect, or that you expected might happen that didn't happen?
- Anything that was helpful?
- That was helpful? Can you say something more about that?
- Did anything happen that was particularly useful or not so helpful? Could you give us some feedback on this?
- Anything that could have happened differently that could have been more helpful?

Some participant answers were:

> I don't think I really expected her to be so happy and like so excited. She was able to get into it and really enjoy you and what she was talking about and really felt great being there.

> I thought some of your questions were really interesting. As far as some of your responses to things, in comparison to traditionally a therapy session would go. A couple of times she said things I think a traditional therapist would have been like, "Oh, do you want to talk about that more?" or they would have attached some kind of label to it or whatever. For example, when you came back and reported what the other people had said, "Have you ever thought of punching the wall with the other hand?" I think that's brilliant. But normally I think, therapists wouldn't say that. They'd say things like, "You have to control your anger," so that kind of stuff I thought was really cool.

> I think just the way you used scales was really important. And whatever her answer was, you helped her identify wherever she was, it was better than zero. And particularly when you said you're at three and at least that's not a zero but what would four look like? And you helped her draw a picture about that. You helped her visualize. I thought that was very important.

> You didn't say anything about the problem.

As you may have noticed, most of the answers still had to do with what the therapist did. They came as therapists to learn something from another therapist. They were talking about what the therapist was doing that they thought was useful and helpful for the client instead of what they thought was wrong with her, although there was still some use of problem-focused language, too. I wanted to bring them closer to describing how the client is helping me do my job. I'm not sure they were listening much for that yet. I can overtly direct them toward that or I can slowly and gently continue pointing in that direction by the questions I ask and what I choose to do more of (and how I choose).

The last question before we returned to the tape was, "In your opinion, who would have been the best person to ask for the answers to these questions I just asked you? The participants answered unanimously: "Amanda." Then we return to the tape. Amanda and I are deciding on what would be a good date and time to meet again, a colleague from behind the mirror enters the room and asks Amanda's permission to ask a few more questions. The interviewer in this segment is Insoo Kim Berg.

Dan:	This is Insoo.
Amanda:	Hi.
Dan:	Insoo wants to ask you a couple of questions.
Amanda:	O.K.
Insoo:	Do you have a couple minutes to spare?
Amanda:	Yeah.
Insoo:	I just wanted to ask you–I know this is all new for you, but it's not group.
Amanda:	Yeah. I don't like group.
Insoo:	We're sort of trying to figure out, was there anything you didn't expect that happened here or that you expected would happen that didn't happen?
Amanda:	I didn't even know exactly why I was coming. I mean my counselor at substance abuse just told me to come and talk to him. I didn't really know what to expect, honestly.
Insoo:	Well, O.K. So that's even better then because you didn't have any preconceived notions about this.
Amanda:	No.
Insoo:	Anything happen here that was particularly useful, not so useful, helpful, not so helpful?
Amanda:	Oh, he was great. He was great! I really liked that man.
Insoo:	Really?
Amanda:	Yeah.
Insoo:	I think his humor matched your humor.
Amanda:	Oh yeah, I have a sense of humor once in a while.
Insoo:	Both of you have it.
Amanda:	Right. What he was talking about really made sense.
Insoo:	It made sense to you?
Amanda:	Yep.

Insoo:	Anything else that struck you was helpful, not as helpful, or could have been more helpful?
Amanda:	Just putting things in perspective.
Insoo:	That was helpful?
Amanda:	Yeah.
Insoo:	Can you say some more about that? Perspective. What kind of perspective?
Amanda:	Like what I wanted to do. Basically he made me think about it a lot. He made me think about waiting for a job that I called about and getting up in the morning instead of sleeping all day.
Insoo:	O.K., O.K., O.K. Anything else?
Amanda:	No. That's it.
Insoo:	Anything that could have happened differently to be more helpful?
Amanda:	I don't know. It was good.
Insoo:	It was good. Really! I guess I'll have to tell him that!
Amanda:	(laughs) I really liked him. He was good. I was coming to a strange place, but . . .
Insoo:	So he put you at ease.
Amanda:	Yeah.
Insoo:	Obviously he didn't make you do something you didn't want to do.
Amanda:	No.
Insoo:	Yeah. That was helpful to you.
Amanda:	Yeah.
Insoo:	O.K.

Suggestion for the Reader: Compare the answers the workshop participants gave to the questions I asked them at the end of the tape session with the answers the client gave when Insoo asked her similar questions. How were their comments related to the client's responses? How were Dan's questions related to the client's responses? How did the client help Dan ask useful questions? How did the client help Insoo ask useful questions?

I think the discussion that followed was summarized best when a participant commented, "I'm seeing what you're saying, with solution-focused and your putting some of the ownership on the client, that it's very possible that the therapist could stay excited about their field, and hopeful and energetic and healthy rather than burned out or desperate, because it's a tough service to be in, to think that we're going to cure and change and get all the answers. It's exhausting." I was still seen as "putting some of the ownership on the client," but that made sense to the participant in terms of the language she was using when she came to the workshop. Perhaps now there was more room and some useful techniques for listening to the client as teacher.

By now we have quite a list of solution-focused ideas. I want to keep promoting the inductive learning we have been practicing in the workshop so far. Keep it simple. Listen to what the client is teaching. Listen to how the therapist responds to the client in ways that promote his or her learning from the client, thereby reflecting and amplifying the client's teaching so the client's strengths, resources, abilities, and what the client wants become the main topic of discussion. Perhaps this will increase the odds that the client will continue thinking this way in her own life more outside the consulting room.

The workshop continues with the tape of the second meeting with Amanda two weeks later. She decides that things are better enough. She was doing more outside the bowling alley including going fishing with friends. She has qualified for a statewide bowling tournament. She scaled her progress at an 8. She was arguing with her mother less, had a good job prospect. Her counselor told her she had successfully completed the rehab program. She was not complaining about having no energy. She talked about what she was doing instead of what she was not doing. She was confident enough that she could maintain her progress (6) that she wasn't sure if she needed to come back to see me. We decided that she could call for another appointment if she wanted to.

Following this, the workshop continues with more discussion among participants. I continue listening for how their use of language changes as they listen to learn more from clients.

Participant:	So, you didn't stretch it out to an hour?
Dan:	Amanda didn't seem to think we needed to.
Participant:	It's funny, but I have felt that way. There have been times that by the second session so many things have totally improved. And you can tell, they're wondering why they should come back. And I'm thinking, how am I going to get her back because they're not cured yet–because I've decided they're not cured yet.
Participant:	Letting the client determine when it's done rather than it being the therapist's agenda.
Dan:	Any other solution-building ideas?

One participant described a case example:

> Something I was thinking about is that people are changing all the time. I've been working with this lady who has a drinking problem. When I asked the question, "How will you know that our time together has been

useful," she said, "I will not have had a relapse for 10 weeks." That sort of set up an expectation that she wouldn't have a relapse. And I said, "well O.K. We can work with that." And she proceeded the next week to have a relapse. She brought that in. And then we had the opportunity to talk about what she did differently in this relapse, and that led to her actually noticing what she did differently, and the whole thing just exploded from there, and she came back the next week and she was noticing everything right and left, all these tiny things. And I was asking her, "How the hell did you do this?" She's kind of disappeared for the past month and I was thinking that was a problem and a dilemma, but . . . And then we continued by email, and another thing came up, that she used to see relapses as "monumental failures," but that was contradicting what she was doing.

Another part of it was that her husband had a long history of going out to dinner and drinking wine and not being aware of how much she drank and she would end up collapsing in a corner somewhere and waking up the next morning saying, "What happened?" Her husband was really down on her for that. For 20 years, everyone was telling her she was alcoholic. And in her first relapse, her husband just went ballistic. He came in the next week and he really did care about her. He just had this history of looking at it in a certain way. "I was concerned when she stopped coming. Then I was surprised how well it went."

The participant said that the client went on to do well after she started looking at how she succeeded in getting back on track from relapses. Here was an instructive workshop participant giving an example of an instructive client!

MIRACLE QUESTION EXERCISE[4]

It was time to have the participants return to practice role playing client-therapist again. This time, after a colleague demonstrated the miracle question, with all the pauses, I asked them to break into groups of two. One person was to ask the miracle question, just as it was demonstrated, and the other person was the client. After finishing and returning as a group to discuss it, they would switch roles and do it again. Once again we met as a group to answer certain questions. This time my questions had to do with learning from the participants who were role-playing clients.

Dan: *Clients, what parts of that question made the most contact with you? What parts made you feel like responding the most?*

Client: Actually, it was the concreteness of it. I could follow along with what she was saying, "when you left here today," it kind of drew

	me in to the details. And it made me think about the details in the morning. It helped me focus on details.
Dan:	*What parts helped you do that?*
Client:	Well, you left here and you went about the business of the day, you know, you went home, you had dinner. She didn't use that much detail. You can use as much as you want, but it helped you focus in on, "Oh, you can notice that." And after you wake up, there can be things you can notice.
Dan:	*What else?*
Client:	I think just having this fantasy about how things would be. It's exciting to think about having everything the way I wanted it!
Dan:	*What part of the question made that connection for you?*
Client:	I'd be driving back home. And I also pictured, O.K. I'll go to sleep tonight. And it was just that waking up. Oh, yeah, and you didn't know that a miracle occurred. Things were just different. For some reason that just struck me. Oh yeah, I'm not planning this. This just happened. And I'll know it.
Dan:	*That connected?*
Client:	Yeah, like I'm not planning it. Yeah, it's funny. When we were first talking about it earlier, I was thinking, "Now, what's the purpose of that part of it?" When we did it, it just hit me.
Client:	Yeah. I thought it was going to be easy, but it wasn't. One of the things that stood out was just the reality of like a visualization of that or sensing that that could happen and that you wake up in the morning and imagine and feel what that might be like. Just those initial first steps. When she said specifically what was that first thing, and then I could make a concrete statement about something. I said, "Well there'll be a little smile." And just the thinking practice of that helped it become more real.
Client:	Making it more specific, to get concrete responses.
Dan:	*Was there anything else that comes to mind about that question that makes contact with you?*
Client:	It was when she said, even though I've heard the question before, I was surprised by the way that she said it. It was like, ". . . and the problem's gone." And it gives you total freedom. "O.K. The problem's gone?"
Client:	Elation almost.
Client:	It was just the tone of her voice. It just rose and it was hopeful.
Client:	I was the therapist in it, but it's also somehow being told you were sleeping and you didn't know this has happened also emphasizes it; you don't have to find out what the steps are. So you don't have to look at what the obstacles are. You can jump right

over them past all the obstacles. "What is it like?" It's intriguing.

Dan: *So, what parts of the question made contact with you?*

Client: I thought that the most important part was, "and you didn't know it was happening, when you wake up, how would you know?" I don't know why.

Client: Yeah. I just imagined opening my eyes and being a different person and how refreshing that could be for someone who was having trouble.

Dan: *So, how does that connect?*

Client: Wonderful. It works.

Client: I also found, more than leading, building a picture together so that the picture gets clearer and clearer about what I would be doing, what they would be doing in their life that would actually be different. How would that look? What would actually be happening?

Client: Yeah. I would agree with that. It's just that vision of what it's going to look like so that you have a goal and you know what you need to do to get there.

Dan: *So, how important do you think it is to ask a lot of questions about that picture? To get as many details of that as you can?*

Client: It seems that there's a lot that can continue with the miracle question.

As I listened, I heard the workshop participants catching on to how clients can be helpful in surprising ways when we meet with them, when we ask them useful questions. By this point, they are usually very engrossed in the practice of solution-building.

And so we continue with the questions with more practice, case discussions based on what the client would say, and more *Listen and Describe* work along the way. Maybe the best way to conclude this article is to let a workshop participant do it. At the end of another workshop using *Listen and Describe*, I gave the participants a transcript of the meeting with Amanda and asked them to read it over and write me about what they were learning from her. One person[5] wrote:

Considering that Amanda didn't see "anything really wrong," and was there only because someone else thought she should come, she did pretty good work in getting ideas about "actually do[ing] something." Having started the process of thinking differently about herself, her activities she actually begins to "do" between sessions. No doubt about the part the therapist plays in this conversation: the kinds of questions he asks help her also begin to see herself in a new light. From the start, there is a respectful acknowledgement of the value of the client's opinion: "do you agree with [the referring counselor]." The therapist goes very SLOWLY, repeating the basic (useful) questions such as, "how is that helpful," "so that's useful," "how else is it useful," and so on until the client begins to notice what she is doing right, what is useful and what is not. The focus on "process" seems particularly evident in the therapist's adherence to those questions. Asking repeatedly, "so how can we help" seems to not only put the onus for determining the course of the conversation on the client, but also tells them that they are in charge and their ideas are valued.

The content of the conversation is negotiated by the therapist's selectively focusing on information that can lead to desired outcome and ignoring those that will lead to "problem talk." This process allows Amanda to bring out what she clearly sees as her accomplishments. (I was very impressed with her story that "they" wanted to bar her from going into the bowling alley to bowl and was curious to how she succeeded in convincing them otherwise.) As she notices her accomplishments and begins to clarify her miracle, I liked the sensitive pacing the therapist is using, thus negotiating reality (?) Amanda says she has no motivation to do anything now, and soon the conversation is about action she already started taking.

All the details brought out in the conversation are reinforced in the feedback, acknowledging and complimenting on her accomplishment. The inclusion of the counselor's concern is framed in a way that fits with what Amanda also wants (not to keep hitting the wall). The easy, conversational, friendly, and humorous tone continues in the feedback as in session. Clearly, not only has this conversation been useful to Amanda as seen in the 2nd meeting. She puts it nicely herself: "just putting things in perspective" was helpful.

In the second meeting, it's striking to hear the answer to "what's better" in its original form ("otherwise things are just about the same") and to follow the development of the "process" conversation to elicit all the various aspects of "what's different." (I have the same experience with clients' original "nothing" and how they discover the changes as we speak.) Even more striking is how the client discovers the significance of the changes they have already started making through the simple process questions, the variants of "how does it make a difference," scaling, etc.

As I was reading, I thought at one point, "WOW, all this in 2 weeks!" And then I realized how this case could have gone on and on–with a different therapist–to talk about all kinds of other "issues" the client mentions. This therapist chooses to ignore them and congratulating Amanda on all her accomplishments, he takes her word for things being "good enough."

Of course, she can always come back.

One more thought re: the ongoing conversations about having to establish a relationship with the client in order to help clients make changes. It certainly looks like a nice relationship between Amanda and Dan.

I hope this is somewhat useful.

To summarize, what I have been learning from clients, workshop participants, and my own association with BFTC and solution-focused brief therapy ideas over the past 20 years is that the job of teaching belongs as much to each client I meet with as it does to me. From that, I am learning that my job is to help the client do her or his job by asking the kinds of questions that elicit answers that point the client and me in a positive, useful direction the client wants to go. The client helps me do my job by giving me answers that point me in that direction. In this way, it's what the client says and does that teaches the interviewer what to do more of and what to ignore. Similarly in workshops, it's how the participants respond to my persistent invitations to solution-talk that teaches me what to do more of and what to ignore. Of course, there is nothing like participating in a workshop with others so you can have direct experience with clients' teaching in "live" and videotaped sessions and dialogue with fellow learners as we *Listen and Describe* together.

NOTES

1. Center for Solutions, Inc. 175 South Montgomery Street, Walden, New York, U.S.A.

2. Steve de Shazer. Inside and Outside Exercise, this volume.

3. Transcript of Amanda session: © Dan Gallagher 2003.

4. Idea for the Miracle Question Exercise attributed to Insoo Kim Berg and Yvonne Dolan via personal communication with Michael Hjerth and Peter de Jong. EBTA Conference. Dublin, Ireland. September 2001.

5. Haya Caspi. Personal Communication. 2003.

Creating a Different Reality: Expanding Points of View

Jennifer Andrews

SUMMARY. Solution-focused therapy presents a different paradigm for mental health professionals, and it is not always easy for trainees to make the switch from a problem-oriented, deficit focus to a solution-building strengths focus. This article presents an exercise that uses a TV show episode to help trainees make a paradigm shift. *[Article copies available for a fee from The Haworth Document Delivery Service: 1-800-HAWORTH. E-mail address: <docdelivery@haworthpress.com> Website: <http://www.HaworthPress.com> © 2005 by The Haworth Press, Inc. All rights reserved.]*

KEYWORDS. Postmodern therapy training, multiple realities, family therapy training, video-assisted training

For more than twenty years, I have met the task of introducing MFT students who have been moving along in a track where they have been steeped in modernist ideas and philosophy to their first experience of more contemporary

Jennifer Andrews is affiliated with Loma Linda University, Loma Linda, CA.
Address correspondence to: Jennifer Andrews, 10650 Kinnard Ave. #109, Los Angeles, CA 90024.

[Haworth co-indexing entry note]: "Creating a Different Reality: Expanding Points of View." Andrews, Jennifer. Co-published simultaneously in *Journal of Family Psychotherapy* (The Haworth Press, Inc.) Vol. 16, No. 1/2, 2005, pp. 253-255; and: *Education and Training in Solution-Focused Brief Therapy* (ed: Thorana S. Nelson) The Haworth Press, Inc., 2005, pp. 253-255. Single or multiple copies of this article are available for a fee from The Haworth Document Delivery Service [1-800-HAWORTH, 9:00 a.m. - 5:00 p.m. (EST). E-mail address: docdelivery@haworthpress.com].

Available online at http://www.haworthpress.com/web/JFP
© 2005 by The Haworth Press, Inc. All rights reserved.
Digital Object Identifier: 10.1300/J085v16n01_48

ideas. I used to call these ideas *postmodern* but finally stopped using that term because it immediately created an "us and them" situation where I was the "us" and they were the "them." At that point it would take weeks of lecture, videotape demonstrations, experiential exercises, etc., just to get back to ground zero where I could introduce an idea and not have to defend it. Given that these students have just completed a course including structural family therapy and then Bowen work where they constructed elaborate genograms accompanied by a final paper that explained how they became who they are now, it was not helpful to them for me to say that there is no core self and that all reality is relational.

Reaching into my experiential training from a lifetime or two ago, I decided that I needed to become creative and start the class with an exercise in which the students would experience a certain reality. I also wanted them to discuss what they were experiencing and to have a scribe write all of their ideas on the black/whiteboard. Next I would give a brief lecture, which would guide them to repeat the task but have a different experience. This would also be discussed and written. Then the students needed to work out the differences so that I wasn't the target for their upset. More words from me would follow the experience. So I devised the following experiment: I needed a short piece of videotape that would demonstrate something differentially describable. Many of the family shows on television are ideal for this purpose. They each have about three themes and they alternate scenes every two to three minutes. Some shows are more useful than others. I find that *Judging Amy*, *Hack*, *Providence*, *Family Law*, and *The Guardian* are useful. *The Sopranos*, *Sex and the City*, and *Six Feet Under* would be useful, but some of their language can be offensive. The evening that I was looking for a clip was a Friday and *Providence* was on. From the first six minutes of the show, I created my clip that the class would see. There were three scenes in six minutes. My ultimate goal for the class was to introduce them to the idea that you can get further with compliments and strengths than with problem talk and to have them start to recognize strengths and resources.

The following Tuesday evening, I was introduced to a class of thirty-two first-year students with whom I had not worked before. I settled on the idea that I would show the short piece of tape with the single direction, "You will get into groups of about 10 and discuss what you have seen." There were three groups, with each one responsible for the description of only one scene. After watching the entire clip, I let them meet and talk for about 10 minutes and each group elected a reporter. A scribe recorded everything on the whiteboard and because they had all seen the entire clip, I solicited additional comments from all groups in case something was missed. The entire group agreed that what was on the board met everyone's perceptions.

The most difficult part of this task was to find a piece of tape that would be short and easily describable in two different ways. In the recording of the show *Providence*, there is one sister who is a doctor and she is telling the family that she has a patient who is accused of Munchausen's [syndrome] by Proxy. The father is a veterinarian and there is an unmarried sister who is a single parent with a toddler. In six minutes, there are three scenes. TV shows are better for this than movies, because the writing is tight and incredibly brief. The first scene is at breakfast and, of course, the class did not remark on the relationships, the conversations, the respect between the characters, the loving bond between the single-parent mom and her baby. The second scene was in the hospital with the accused mother and her 11-year-old daughter. This was perfect! All the class saw was a "manipulative woman" and a suspicious doctor. The third scene was with the doctor and her mentor. Again, all the class saw was pathology-based. Putting it in writing on the board helps because it reifies their current belief system.

After that, I lectured about the format of solution-focused therapy and the need to attempt to notice things that we can legitimately compliment. We needed to look for and comment upon strengths, resources, or anything that was laudable and I invited them to re-look at the six minutes of tape and have the whole group comment upon what they saw. This time the class saw relationships, caring, sharing, respect, non-hierarchical communications, family planning, and on and on in the first scene. In the second scene, they noticed that the mother was sitting next to the bed of the child holding her hand. They saw that she seemed really concerned and really appreciative of the doctor's non-pathologizing of her connection to the child. The third scene became one where the consulting doctor was attempting to mentor the young doctor and she had a strong conviction to follow her intuition and do further investigation. The "believing is seeing" statement became reified and the class had a very different and exciting experience.

I have repeated this experiment with three classes and have experienced similar outcomes each time. The mutability of reality is a non-issue now. I no longer have to defend the philosophical ideas of contemporary family therapy and these situations are isomorphic to what we see in therapy. When we label a problem, we have a problem. When we recognize strengths, resources, and positive motives, we generate these things. This is an exercise that really assists students to become at least binocular and frequently polyocular in their perceptions.

For me, this relational process is a better fit than a lecture on constructivism, social constructionism, or related postmodern ideas and practices. In the first three hours of the course, they allow themselves to stretch and incorporate difficult new ideas that are not connected to anything they have previously learned. And because this always has an effect on me, it truly is a collaborative learning experience.

Teaching Practice via Success Stories

Peter DeJong

SUMMARY. This article presents a way of helping social work practice trainees learn solution-oriented ways of relating with their practice setting agencies. The author describes a process whereby students learn basic principles by applying them to the difficulties they face in their practice settings that often are more problem-focused. By sharing success stories with each other, trainees learn more about the process of solution-focused therapy and ways to work within their practice sites. *[Article copies available for a fee from The Haworth Document Delivery Service: 1-800-HAWORTH. E-mail address: <docdelivery@haworthpress.com> Website: <http://www.HaworthPress.com> © 2005 by The Haworth Press, Inc. All rights reserved.]*

KEYWORDS. Internships, practice successes, solution-focused therapy in agency, teaching solution-focused therapy

I teach practice courses and supervise internships of social work students in an accredited, undergraduate social work program. In this sequence of courses, students first take a course in solution-focused (SF) interviewing skills taught via a lab format in which students practice interviewing in small

Peter DeJong is affiliated with Calvin College, Grand Rapids, MI.

Address correspondence to: Peter DeJong, Sociology and Social Work, Calvin College, 3201 Burton SE, Grand Rapids, MI 49546.

[Haworth co-indexing entry note]: "Teaching Practice via Success Stories." DeJong, Peter. Co-published simultaneously in *Journal of Family Psychotherapy* (The Haworth Press, Inc.) Vol. 16, No. 1/2, 2005, pp. 257-262; and: *Education and Training in Solution-Focused Brief Therapy* (ed: Thorana S. Nelson) The Haworth Press, Inc., 2005, pp. 257-262. Single or multiple copies of this article are available for a fee from The Haworth Document Delivery Service [1-800-HAWORTH, 9:00 a.m. - 5:00 p.m. (EST). E-mail address: docdelivery@haworthpress.com].

Available online at http://www.haworthpress.com/web/JFP
Digital Object Identifier: 10.1300/J085v16n01_49

groups of six with two experienced lab instructors. The interviewing practice revolves around scenarios taken from the internship experiences of graduating students. The second course is one in individual and family practice and is taken concurrent with senior internships. A common concern I hear from students in this course has been that the agencies in which they are placed, while often believing they are strengths-based in their practice, use little of the SF outlook and skills the students worked on in their interviewing course. Students say they receive little reinforcement or additional training in SF practice and, being so new to it, find themselves getting caught up in agency practice models of problem assessment and service referral while paying little attention to co-constructing what their clients might want different and exploring related strengths and resources.

After spending class time exploring with students what they do about this situation and what else they might want to do, it occurred to me that students' concrete success stories of how they incorporated SF practice into internship experiences was the content of most interest and value to the class. Consequently, I have now instituted devoting the initial minutes of our Friday morning class in the individual and family practice course to students' sharing "Practice Success Stories." During this time students can share any practice success experience, no matter how small or large, they have experienced with the clients or agency personnel they have encountered in their internships. At first, students shared stories of general case outcome such as a case in which a mother, whose children had been removed from her care and placed in foster, regained custody of her children. I and other students would then ask for details about how the success happened. Eventually, we were asking presenters, "who had said what to whom" and the success stories started to be reported in more of a dialogical or an, "I said . . . ; she said . . ." format. I now ask students to write up these success stories in return for additional points toward their final course grade. And, because so much of practice involves dialogue, I tell them that I prefer that the stories incorporate segments of the dialogue between the participants. Here are several examples of the stories in my file:

BE "NOT KNOWING"

I am placed at a residential center for teens who are pregnant and homeless. Nearly all my clients are African American or belong to other racial minority groups and I am white. I have really struggled to find a way to connect with them but their experiences seem so different from what I grew up with. Last week my supervisor was on vacation and she handed me her caseload for the week. I was told to meet with her clients two at a time and see how they were doing that week and try to be helpful if I could. By the third pair, I was really getting discouraged because no matter what I said, they said, "I don't know" or they just shrugged their shoulders and looked at the floor. About the time I was ready to give up, I remembered about trying to be not-knowing. I thought about how to do it and then I said, "You know, I am just learning how to be a social worker and I want to be the best social worker I can be. Do you have any advice for me?" Well, the floodgates just opened and they had lots to say. In fact, the first thing they said was, "You can forget about telling us about parenting like everyone else around here." So I said, "What can I do instead?" That got them thinking and we were off and on our way then.

COMPLIMENTING "PERSONAL STRENGTHS"

My internship is at a substance abuse center that has a residential program for women and their children. I was doing an assessment. Usually the assessor is the case manager but since I am the intern, I get to do some too. This is often the first time that the client has seen the case manager and has lots of questions and concerns. The assessment usually takes an hour and a half. Jenn was an 18-year-old girl who has a history of an alcohol and crack cocaine dependency. She was also having problems with the legal system because her two children were taken away. This was her first time in the treatment program. During the assessment, Jenn kept telling me that her fiancé was telling her that she couldn't do it, that she would relapse, and not be able to last in treatment. As she was telling me this, I could notice a change in her posture. She began to slump over and the tone of her voice changed and she became more depressed. She was obviously suffering from low self-esteem and self-worth because she could not separate her fiancé's opinion of her from reality. I knew that I had to change the tone of the interview by turning something into a personal strength of hers. So I asked, "Do you see any bars on the windows?" Puzzled at the direction of the question, she answered, "No." "That is right," I said, "This is not a jail or prison, you are choosing to be here. So already you have begun to prove your boyfriend wrong just by being here, so that is a strength." "You are right," she responded, "I am doing it, I could leave anytime but I am not!" After this, Jenn's posture changed, she started to look me in the eye, not slouch as much and was able to be proud of herself for *choosing* to remain in treatment.

UNPACKING "JUST ONE BOX"

My client is a 43-year-old woman with diagnoses of PTSD and major re-current depression with severe psychosis. I called her last week to sched-ule her annual home visit (our agency does home visits to renew paperwork and 6-month home visits to update assessments), and this was purely a business call, but she ended up crying as she often does be-cause she is so troubled. The thing that seemed to be most upsetting to her was that she had just moved and she was overwhelmed by the task of unpacking all of her boxes. (The paperwork says she is also claustropho-bic, paranoid, and cannot stand silence or darkness, but that is all sort of peripheral in this situation.) So she's crying and she says to me, "Jane, I just don't know if I can go on sometimes." So I wait a second and say, "Okay, let me ask you this–are there times that things are better–when you DO feel like you can go on?" And she totally worked with this and over the course of a few minutes, she identified that things were better (1) during the day, (2) when people were around her, (3) when she gets outside to take a walk, and (4) when she is able to accomplish some-thing. So I did the whole summarizing/repeating bit and found out why these times are better and what she can do to recreate these times. It happened to be a gorgeous week last week, so that helped with the get-ting outside part. She also told me a little bit later in the conversation that she wanted to start unpacking, but she was overwhelmed by the huge task. I asked her if she was looking at the boxes right now and she said she was, then added that she was looking at a specific box full of dishes. So I asked her what it would take to start unpacking, and she said if she could just do one box that would help. So I asked her if she thought she could unpack just that one box she was looking at and she said she thought she could. So I encouraged her to take just that one box and start unpacking it and ignore the other boxes for now and if she started to feel overwhelmed to go outside and take a walk around the block, which she thought she could do. And then (and I didn't even have to say anything–this was so great) she said: "And maybe when I see you next week, I'll have unpacked some of these boxes and I won't feel so overwhelmed anymore." So I told her it sounded like a great plan and we would talk about it at the home visit when I saw her.

I went to the home visit yesterday and it could not have gone better. She was very proud to tell me (before I even prompted her) that she had unpacked several boxes (a feat for which I gave her a healthy dose of praise) and she had gone outside several times in the past week and that had helped her considerably. And she also told me (which made me think someone must be paying her to be the model solution-focused client) that after she and I talked last week, she really thought about what I'd said and started unpacking the box of dishes and really did feel like she'd accomplished something. So, anyway, it was very rewarding–as much for me as it was for her 😊.

ASKING FOR EXCEPTIONS

Eleven-year-old Suzie lives with her guardian Auntie. Suzie attends an alternative school for children with serious behavioral issues. The children work on a grading system whereby their behavior and school performance is rated. The scale has 36 possible points with 9 areas, each worth 4 points. This day, Suzie earned 28. Up to this point (during an interview on a home visit), the primary clinician and Auntie were involved in problem talk. The clinician made many attempts to pull Auntie into problem-solving activity, but Auntie kept trash talking and would not praise Suzie for any improvement she had made. Suzie slumped in her chair and kept her hand in front of her face and would respond to the clinician with inaudible grunts. When it was my turn to address the client the conversation went like this:

C: Suzie, today you scored a 28 out of 36, right?
S: M-hmm.
C: Has there been a day when you scored different than 28?
S: Yeah. Yesterday
C: Wow, yesterday. What did you score yesterday?
S: 18
C: 18! Wow! And today you score 28?
S: Yeah. 28
C: That's an improvement of 10 points!! That's great! How did you do that? (Suzie is visibly brightening, takes her hand away from her face, and gives a sort of smile.)
S: I don't know.
C: You must've done something different to get such a higher score from one day to the next. What can you think of that you did differently that made today so much better than yesterday?
S: I did my work.
C: Instead of goofing off? OK, what else?
S: I didn't pester the girl next to me.
C: OK, you kept your hands to yourself. What else?
S: I drank my orange juice instead of flicking it at the girl next to me.

C: Good. Good. What else?

S: Nutt'in.

C: OK, What do you think it would take to get a 30 tomorrow?

S: I don't know.

C: Think. Remember the thing that made it better from yesterday to today?

S: I guess I could do my work again.

C: Good. Do you think you can do that?

S: Yeah.

C: Great! What else can you do to get a 30?

S: Not pester the girl next to me.

C: Great! So what score do you want to get tomorrow?

S: 36! (Smiling)

C: That would be great, but maybe you should shoot for a 30 and keep shooting a little higher each day.

S: Yeah.

The primary clinician then turned to Auntie and asked her how she felt about Suzie's chances of getting 30 the next day. Auntie ignored the question and jumped right back into problem talk.

Students clearly enjoy telling and listening to each other's practice success stories. They have suggested that I keep a file of them and share the file with students who come after them. I agree with the wisdom of the suggestion. As I listen to students share their successes and observe the reactions and follow-up questions of other students, I know that students are using these Friday morning opportunities to teach one another creative and effective practice.

Solution-Focused Practice Teaching in Social Work

John Wheeler
Yvonne Greaves

SUMMARY. A social work practice teacher and social work student met to explore their mutual experience of solution-focused supervision. The practice teacher reflects upon the theoretical inspirations that shaped his practice, whilst the student reflects on her experience of being on the receiving end. The exploration follows the course of the place-ment from beginning to end, drawing on particular examples of solu-tion-focused supervision and other theoretical approaches including adult learning theory and narrative practice to illustrate their impact on both parties. The account adds weight to the importance of ensuring that techniques are sensitively attuned to the emotional climate and timing. *[Article copies available for a fee from The Haworth Document Delivery Ser-vice: 1-800-HAWORTH. E-mail address: <docdelivery@haworthpress.com> Website: <http://www.HaworthPress.com> © 2005 by The Haworth Press, Inc. All rights reserved.]*

John Wheeler is a social worker/family therapist with the Child and Mental Health Service, Gateshead, UK.

Yvonne Greaves is a Primary Mental Health Worker, Gateshead Health Trust, Gateshead, UK.

Address correspondence to: John Wheeler, 5 Runhead Gardens, Ryton, NE40 3HH, En-gland or Yvonne Greaves, 30 Ell-Dene Cresent, Felling, Gateshead, NE10 9UN, England.

[Haworth co-indexing entry note]: "Solution-Focused Practice Teaching in Social Work." Wheeler, John, and Yvonne Greaves. Co-published simultaneously in *Journal of Family Psychotherapy* (The Haworth Press, Inc.) Vol. 16, No. 1/2, 2005, pp. 263-276; and: *Education and Training in Solution-Focused Brief Therapy* (ed: Thorana S. Nelson) The Haworth Press, Inc., 2005, pp. 263-276. Single or multiple copies of this article are available for a fee from The Haworth Document Delivery Service [1-800-HAWORTH, 9:00 a.m. - 5:00 p.m. (EST). E-mail address: docdelivery@haworthpress.com].

Available online at http://www.haworthpress.com/web/JFP
© 2005 by The Haworth Press, Inc. All rights reserved.
Digital Object Identifier: 10.1300/J085v16n01_50

KEYWORDS. Adult learning, social work training, solution-focused supervision, beginnings, endings

INTRODUCTION

Practice placements play a key role in helping social work students in the UK to synthesise their learning and practice. This is often the last opportunity to read, reflect, and discuss at length before entering the busy environment of the workplace. In 18 years of being a social work practice teacher I have added to my supervisory practice anything that promised to contribute to the learning of students on placement. Impressed by the impact of Solution-Focused Brief Therapy (SFBT) on my work with clients, I quickly incorporated the approach into my supervision of students.

My practice setting is an outpatient Child and Adolescent Mental Health Service (CAMHS), an interesting and challenging setting for students who spend 80 days with us on their final placement. Initially, students are offered opportunities to see how others carry out the work of the agency, myself included. Students then take on a primary role in working with clients.

The following account has been created by myself, John, as practice teacher, and Yvonne, a student on placement. An account is given of the thinking behind the practices I drew on to promote Yvonne's learning and professional development. Links are made to various perspectives from adult learning and therapy that informed my thinking and that sit comfortably with a solution-focused approach. The account follows the process of the placement from beginning to end. At each stage, Yvonne reflects on her experience of being the recipient of the supervision. We often spoke together about the placement experience. The act of writing this account became a process of further discovery. Solution-focused thinking reminds me that as supervisor I can only be expert over the doing of my supervision. Expert knowledge of the impact of the supervision resides with the supervisee. It is hoped that the uniqueness of this account will be of interest beyond the boundaries of social work training, shedding light not only on the practice of solution-focused supervision, but, crucially, providing an account of the direct experience of being on the receiving end. The account has been written 18 months after the placement ended.

Yvonne: My route to training started after the birth of my children. I wanted to learn more about what children need and how they develop. I started out by setting up a parent and toddler group, and embarked on formal learning at college. As I became more aware of different life chances and influences that impact on children and families, I decided I wanted to contribute something, no matter how small, to the lives of children who experience disadvantage. I worked as a sponsored childminder, then as a Social Work Auxiliary in a Children and Families Team.

After several years as an unqualified worker I embarked on social work training. I completed my first year of social work training through self-funded, part-time study, drawing on my experience of practice within my workplace to produce evidence of competence for a portfolio. During the second year, I negotiated, with some trepidation, a placement in a CAMHS. I welcomed the opportunity to work within mental health, because I wanted to learn more about the roles of different disciplines within a multidisciplinary setting, and to develop skills in SFBT. I also, however, was acutely aware of the level of expertise and professionalism that existed in the team, and the challenges that this placement would present for me as student. I viewed the placement as a mixed blessing and hoped I would be up to the challenge.

STARTING WELL

John: The relationship between practice teacher and student is inevitably hierarchical. Whilst students have their own learning goals when they embark upon a placement, the learning path in the UK is substantially influenced by the Central Council for Education and Training in Social Work (CCETSW, recently reconfigured as the Social Care Council), the training body for social workers, and the decision to pass or fail resides with the practice teacher. Despite this, a solution-focused approach can both reduce the power differential and ensure that the learning experience is tailored to the student's needs and interests.

Kolb (1984) argued that adults vary in their approach to learning. Some like to act and then reflect upon action; some like to read before acting; and so on. This relates well to a solution-focused assumption that students know best how to do their own learning. It also serves as a reminder that I too have a preferred approach to learning, which can influence how I organise placements and supervision. At the beginning of the placement I profile my own learning style via a learning styles questionnaire (Honey & Mumford, 1992: a development of Kolb's [1976] original Learning Style Inventory) and invite the student to profile theirs. Together we look at similarities and differences. With Yvonne it emerged that we both enjoyed reflecting on practice. I asked Yvonne what she thought we should look out for in our discussions, given this mutual tendency. Yvonne saw that we might enjoy reflection so much that we could forget other responsibilities such as planning and making decisions. It was thus agreed that either of us could move on from reflection if something else needed attention. A variety of self-scoring Learning Styles Questionnaires are easily accessed via the Internet (for example, http://www..northern. ac.uk/online_learning/key_skills/essay_writing/Learning_to_learn/ls_ questionnaire.htm).

In the UK, students have to satisfy six areas of competency and five values requirements (CCETSW, 1996). A solution-focused approach generates questions that ensure that the student is not simply producing something to satisfy a government body, but also is orienting themselves to their own professional development. For example, I can ask, "How will you know you are forming and developing working relationships with services users?" (Competency 1.1). "How will they be able tell?" "What might I notice?" "Who else in this agency might notice?" "What might they say to me?" Without such a discussion, a student is left just to hope that the practice teacher shares their criteria of what counts as evidence. I also use a cardex system for recording evidence of competencies and values, explaining that the cards can be written on by either of us, and will be the basis for the final report. Once this process is underway, the student is taking an active role in her own assessment.

Supervision sessions also lend themselves to a solution-focused construction. I invite students to share the responsibility for defining the content of the supervision from the outset, to reduce the hierarchy and personalise the supervision around their interests and concerns. Much as a therapist might notice increased assertiveness in a client, I also pay attention to how much students contributed to the supervision agenda. Early on, Yvonne presented me with a complete agenda for supervision. Most students build up gradually. When I commented on the degree of confidence Yvonne was demonstrating, we then had a fruitful discussion on what this step represented to Yvonne in the shaping of her future professional identity.

Yvonne: John's approach to the learning style questionnaire turned out to be empowering and supportive. Initially, I felt intimidated by the questionnaire. I felt anxious about exposing too much of myself too soon, and I was wary of criticism. I did not want John to form hasty or wrong impressions about me based on a questionnaire. Past experiences of using this type of questionnaire had left me feeling labelled as having a particular learning style: not necessarily the most valued one. John's sensitivity and his interest in hearing all of what I had to say reassured me that the questionnaire could be used in a value-free, non-threatening way. I discovered the questionnaire could be used as a working tool, that my learning style is not static and will change depending on context and experience.

John's use of competency cards also was a familiar approach. However, it took me some time to feel confident about writing on the cards. I felt I first needed to discover what John's expectations were of me as a student and how this "fitted" with the competencies laid down by CCETSW. I felt wary of putting pen to paper, apprehensive about whether I would be able to prove myself and pass the placement. When John recognised my efforts and commented on my abilities, I felt reassured and looked forward to discovering and demonstrating further abilities as the placement progressed. So, even though I wrote in pencil, I did contribute evidence to the cards.

Once I felt my voice and opinions were valued and respected, I soon felt comfortable enough to contribute to the supervision agenda. I think this particular sign of confidence initially startled John. During my previous year in training, I had to be self-motivated and take responsibility for agenda-setting in supervision, because no one else was familiar with what was expected from a portfolio route. I became used to setting my own goals, based on what I needed from supervision. I also wanted to use the time productively to maximise my development and make the most of the opportunity for reflection. Through discussing this in detail, I came to know more about my ability to take such steps both now and in the future.

SUPERVISOR POSITION

John: The position taken by a practice teacher is a substantial determinant of the supervisory relationship and the position consequently adopted by the student.

Thomas (2000) proposes that supervisors tend to adopt one of three positions. The "guru" imparts expert knowledge on practice and supervisees seek to copy. The "gatekeeper" arbitrates over whether supervisees will belong to the community of practitioners. The "guide" collaborates with the student to foster learning, which will elicit their unique version of practice. Yvonne did see me as an experienced practitioner and potential guru: prior to the placement I had given a presentation as an external lecturer to her student group. My responsibility to pass or fail did give me the duties of a gatekeeper. Nonetheless I hoped that I could be more of a guide, with Yvonne coming to know more about her unique way of doing social work, both then and into the future. As Thomas points out, a guide can be a person who knows a way but leaves the traveller free to work out their own path, stepping in only to prevent serious harm. Solution-focused supervision relates well to the position of guide and helped me avoid slipping unnecessarily into being a guru or gatekeeper.

When I see families with students, we usually take a break before finishing to share thoughts and ensure the meeting ends usefully for the family. Early in the placement, the interview would be led by myself, which potentially places me in the position of guru in the eyes of a student. The break offers me an opportunity to set aside my expert knowledge and invite students to say what their thoughts and impressions are. When I asked Yvonne, "What are your thoughts?" she may have feared my judging her reply as a gatekeeper. "You think what! Well you'll never pass this placement if that's all you can say!" The solution-focused approach reminds me that whatever a student says in such a situation is the best they can come up with in that moment and a clue to me of their particular talents. Yvonne's response was very much to the point and told me that she had not only followed the interview well, but also had been processing the information given by the family and working out how she might have worked with them herself. Had I not asked, I might not have known that all this had happened.

Later in the placement, we reached a point in supervision where Yvonne had seen a family for one meeting and was unsure what to do next. As guru, I could have said what I would do if I were working with the family. From the position of guide I asked, "What were you thinking you might do?" Yvonne's ideas were less confidently articulated than mine might have been. Nonetheless, her own ideas were a clue to what the next step in the work might be. When I asked Yvonne to elaborate, the ideas grew into more distinct plans for practice. White (1999) has described these tentative thoughts as "invisible presences": hunches about how to practice, which, over time, become more confidently articulated and developed. In solution-focused supervision, I look out for such "presences," seeing the placement as an important opportunity for students to discover their particular version of practice.

Yvonne: Prior to my placement and following my experience of John as an external lecturer to my student group, I did see John as a potential guru. My initial thoughts were that I'd never be able to emulate him. I was a little frightened of demonstrating the required competencies to John, given his wealth of knowledge and experience. However, I soon realized that John could both acknowledge my apprehensions and relate to me as a creative individual and expert in knowing about my own abilities.

Feelings of insecurity at times led me to tap into the guru in John, so I could draw on his experience and seek to copy in the hope that this would ensure the gatekeeper in John would be pleased with me and award me a pass. I had never considered that there was such a thing as a guide. I expected direction rather than guidance. John's approach invited me to explore a very different route to learning. At first I was hesitant and a little cautious of my guide. I doubted myself and became a little preoccupied with wanting to please the gatekeeper. However, John encouraged me to look at and own aspects of my practice that mattered to me. This gave me an opportunity to discuss, reflect and develop my own thoughts and to be creative within my own practice style.

When I observed John working with families I became engrossed in the situations that families found themselves in. However, as well as observing, I also began assessing and formulating my own thinking. After the initial shock of being asked by John for my thoughts during a break, I felt surprised and pleased with myself when John confirmed that my thinking was on a useful path. This encouraged me to respond to further questions. As the placement progressed, I gradually felt able to explore our respective views during case discussions and enrich my understanding of my own possibilities as a practitioner.

Solution-focused supervision equipped me with a solution-focused approach to both my practice and my own learning. This not only helped me to pass the placement, but also made me more enthusiastic about being a social worker. This has subsequently been carried forward and adapted within my current post-qualifying practice and has remained with me as a valued and treasured part of the supervision experience. Since qualifying, I have noticed I use solution-focused questions to self-supervise. I ask myself scaling questions to measure change and increase awareness of my abilities. When feeling under pressure, I ask myself coping questions and think about exceptions. This clarifies the limits of a problem and helps me to consider the strategies I already know that will help me to proceed.

CENTRES OF EXCELLENCE

John: Schon (1991) argues that whilst universities have become the centres of excellence for the professions, once in the world of practice, professionals often feel ill-equipped to cope with the actual situations they find themselves in. Schon coined the phrase "knowledge-in-action" to describe the practical learning that comes about when the professional generates responses that are specific to the work they engage in. I look upon the interactions between students and clients as alternative centres of excellence. These centres of excellence are a rich topic for solution-focused questions such as, "How did you do that?" "How did you know that might help?" "How does that connect to what you've read?" "Which social work value were you demonstrating?"

On one occasion when I asked Yvonne what had pleased her about a first session with a teenager and parent who were new to the service, Yvonne spoke of her success in engaging the teenager in conversation, the teenager having started off with his back turned to her. When I asked Yvonne to explain how she had achieved this she gave a detailed account of a critical piece of interaction. In response to a question from Yvonne, the mother had named some of her son's qualities. Yvonne expressed admiration for these qualities and then said to the boy in a teasing tone, "I can see that smile of yours spreading round the sides of your face." This comment broke the ice; the boy turned round and joined in. When I asked Yvonne how she knew this might work, she took stock of her experience of working with teenagers and being a parent. Together we reflected that the success of this comment laid not so much in what she had said, but the manner in which she said it. Yvonne recalled that she had hoped to become a social worker, in particular, to help teenagers who ran into difficulty. This meant that she had also gone out of her way to watch how others engage reluctant teenagers. We consequently discovered a rich heritage to this ability.

On another occasion I observed Yvonne presenting her assessment of a family in a multi-professional meeting with family members present. Yvonne's voice started to disappear, but she then took action and successfully completed the presentation. We discussed this after the meeting. Problem-focused supervision might have led me to ask why she'd lost her voice. Using a solution-focused approach, I asked how she'd got her voice back. This resulted in Yvonne recalling the deep breath and self-coaching she had used to increase her confidence. When I asked Yvonne to describe her self-coaching, she explained how she had reminded herself that she had prepared the presentation thoroughly, had her notes on her lap, and so could use these as a prompt to keep her focused.

Yvonne: At the beginning of the placement I wondered whether I had sufficient knowledge and experience to address the needs of the people I was working with. Initially, I found John's questions hard work, especially when trying to recall where and when I had read something influential. This stimulated my ability to reflect and prompted me to take this reflection further. John often encouraged me to think about experiences I was drawing on, where my ideas had come from and how I had developed them. I eventually found this challenge rewarding. I particularly enjoyed reading more about solution-focused practice. It was fascinating to reflect on what had happened in interviews, recognising and identifying the solution-focused elements I had used, and finding I was able to explain how and why I had incorporated this into my practice. When I looked back on successful work with clients, it was encouraging to see how my own practice was changing and progressing.

I came to recognise that I pay particular attention to minor details in conversations and body language, especially with teenagers. I have often wondered how involved the young person has been within the referral process and what influence this may have on the worker's attempts to build an effective working relationship. I search for signs of responsiveness and ask questions about all aspects of young people's lives. This often reduces the young person's sense of threat, allowing them to have some sense of control over the interaction. From the detail I shared with John, I was able to explore and utilise strengths from past experience and use this knowledge to further improve my work with clients.

I had previously been unsure of my ability to address multi-professional meetings on behalf of clients. I was afraid I would not be heard or would not say enough to get their story across. Discovering how I had regained my voice in the meeting put me in touch with the steps I had already taken to prepare the presentation. Since qualifying, I have addressed many more professional meetings. I am now more comfortable with my limitations in terms of experience and knowledge and recognise that more experience will further develop my abilities. Following one such meeting, I received feedback from the independent chairperson, complimenting me on how well I had presented information. I also heard from my line manager, who had noticed how much the family had contributed to the meeting, too. Looking back, I realised I had used solution-focused thinking to prepare all of us for the meeting–the family and myself.

OPPORTUNITIES

John: Miller, Duncan, and Hubble's (1997) summary of therapy outcome research makes surprising reading for therapists. Miller and colleagues report that only 15% of progress is attributable to therapist technique, 15% being due to the hopefulness of the client, 30% being down to relationship factors such as respect and a sense of alliance and 40% being due to factors extraneous to the therapy. As a practice teacher, I find these proportions relate well to my experience of supervision, too.

Solution-focused techniques clearly were of use. On one occasion, Yvonne was about to attend a school meeting, hoping to represent the interests of a young person she was working with and concerned that others in the meeting did not view him favorably. I asked Yvonne where her confidence was on a scale of nought to ten, ten being the highest. Yvonne said four, this being because she had prepared well. On her return from the meeting, Yvonne was fuming and when I asked her to scale how well she had done, she didn't even answer. After a more detailed look at what had happened, Yvonne recalled the extent to which she had voiced her views and avoided unnecessary argument in the meeting. She then was able to rate her effort on behalf of the young person at six out of ten, eventually recalling that the parents had specifically thanked her for her efforts.

A solution-focused approach to supervision often generates hope and helps to generate a purposeful relationship between supervisee and supervisor. The approach also relates particularly well to Miller et al.'s largest category: extraneous factors. Placements seldom go fully to plan and often the most unexpected events have provided the greatest scope for learning. On another occasion, we prepared well for a first meeting Yvonne was to have with a refugee family whilst I was away on leave. An interpreter had been booked. The interview fitted in with the work plan of fitters who were renewing our carpets at the time. We saw nothing to worry about. On the day of the appointment, the fitters were ahead of schedule and already lifting our carpet. Another room had to be found. When the family arrived, there was no interpreter. A telephone call clarified that he had a different time in his diary and was unavailable. Yvonne was left with little choice but to carry on with the meeting using an older child in the family to translate. Our next supervision could have focused on the awfulness of the situation Yvonne found herself in. Instead, we made use of lots of "how did you?" questions. This focused our discussion on Yvonne's abilities in managing resources, dealing constructively and effectively with outside agencies (the interpreter definitely had the right time for the next meeting), and staying calm and client-focused despite the confusions of the day. "How did you know to?" questions also reminded Yvonne of her preparatory reading. One particular article, for example, had outlined the risks of using older children in families as interpreters. So, although Yvonne did use an older daughter to interpret, she knew how to minimize harmful consequences.

Yvonne: A solution-focused approach to supervision offered a sense of equality within the supervisory relationship. This helped to reduce my initial defensiveness and created mutual respect, which enabled me to further expand on my learning and professional development. John's manner of questioning was respectful, empowering, and yet demanding.

John's use of the scaling question prior to the school meeting did help to bolster my confidence. My initial response was, "I don't know." I needed time to think. I then entered into a mixture of thoughts and feelings. My initial thoughts about naming a number on the scale were that I would be placed in a position of total exposure as to my own opinion about how I rated my ability within the professional arena I was entering, suspecting that my number was actually quite low. I wondered what John's thoughts would be. I felt defensive and considered rating myself as much higher on the scale, but I knew it would not be John I would be misleading, it would be myself. John remained silent, leaving me time to work through my thoughts. One part of me welcomed the thinking time John allowed, the other part hoped he might say something to end the silence and what I recognised was my turn to reply. Seeing myself as being at a four, a lot then depended on John's response. John offered the reassurance I needed by helping me to recognise that the four corresponded to detailed discussions with the young person and his parents, written preparation, and supervision. On my return from the meeting, I couldn't say much to John because of my anger over the potential impact of the meeting upon the young person. John again asked me a scaling question. This time he appeared to sense how angry I was and did not push for a reply. John allowed me enough space to give an account of the meeting at my own pace. This reduced my feelings of frustration and increased my sense of achievement. John complimented me on how well I had coped, how I had managed to think about the dynamics of the meeting and how I had found some ways to influence the process of the meeting to the benefit of the young person. John's questions enabled me to reflect on how I had contributed to the meeting, and what the family may have noticed about the part I played. This helped me to remember their thanks as we came away from the school. As a bonus, I have learned from firsthand experience the power of scaling questions.

Prior to John's leave and my first meeting with the refugee family, I found shared planning during supervision to be an empowering experience. The confidence and respect demonstrated through John in his trust and faith in my ability to work in a competent and confident manner affirmed me as a valued worker and team member. I felt able to rise to any of the potential challenges before me. I looked forward to bringing John up to date when he returned. I remember trying to wait to give John time and space to settle back into work before discussing what had happened. One part of me was keen to share how I had been able to manage in his absence, the other eager for confirmation of the practice abilities which had emerged. Solution-focused questions gave me the opportunity I needed to talk about how much evidence this experience had produced for the competency cards, in particular, "working in an organisation as an effective and accountable practitioner whilst contributing to the planning, monitoring and control of resources." The questions also enabled me to look at how I had incorporated newly gained theoretical knowledge into my practice and gained valuable insights into family dynamics and broader systems.

ENDING WELL

John: Social work placements finally come to an end. Fredman and Dalal (1998) suggest that the end of a therapeutic relationship can be experienced as loss, cure, relief, transition, or metamorphosis. There is often a sense of loss when placements end. A question such as, "What was good about this experience?" can help to acknowledge this in a constructive manner. Whilst the concept of cure does not relate so well to solution-focused supervision, there was some sense of relief when we finished. Practice teachers often have to fit supervision into busy lives. Students speak of an enormous sense of relief when the end of the placement and often the end of a demanding course arrives. Questions such as, "What will you do with the spare time?" can invite constructive speculation about the immediate future. Notions of transition and metamorphosis relate particularly well to a solution-focused position. Whilst the student's formal training has come to an end, their professional development and learning will continue.

Placements usually end with a final meeting with the college tutor. The competency cards provided an excellent opportunity to look at the evidence that justified my decision that Yvonne should pass. Such a meeting can take on the quality of a rite of passage as the student moves from being a trainee to a qualified worker. Whilst this may have helped to consolidate Yvonne's learning to an extent, I did wonder if there was something else Yvonne could specifically take into her future. During the course of the placement, Yvonne had metamorphosed into a professional, but this change is sometimes difficult to hold onto once people are immersed in the world of practice.

Yvonne had shown an interest in White's (1995) use of certificates, giving them to children who had worked hard to change their behaviour. Even though the college would ultimately award Yvonne their own certificate relating to their definition of social work, we decided to create a certificate that would celebrate the extent to which Yvonne had become the social worker she had planned to be. The certificate was based on the following questions. "Yvonne's qualities as a social worker are . . ." "The people who know of these qualities are . . ." "These are the people who have inspired Yvonne in her practice . . ." The final statement started, "These are the people who have encouraged and supported Yvonne in her plan to become a social worker . . ." This turned into a moving exploration as Yvonne recalled those who had provided her initial inspiration and others who had helped at key points along the way. We had previously recalled the saying that it takes a village to raise a child. Creating this certificate led us to realise how many people it takes to make a social worker. Social constructionist thinking suggests that our identities are substantially shaped and constructed by the key people in our lives. I hoped that this explicit naming of those who had believed in her potential would help Yvonne hold onto the qualities these people had noticed in her.

Yvonne: The discussion on endings was a fairly intense piece of learning on my part. At first I paid particular attention to exploring endings with families, rethinking my own position as the strengths of my clients came to the fore. I also noticed the same potential with regard to my professional development. In supervision, we worked together to address how I might be moving on. I did feel a sense of loss as I ended working relationships with families and children, John, other team members, and the ending of my time as a student. I thoroughly enjoyed my placement experience. However, I did feel a sense of relief in knowing I would be released from my obligations to my employer who had paid my fees and the university who had arranged my placement. Most of all I was relieved to know I had met social work competencies and passed the course.

John provided me with an opportunity to say goodbye to a jointly created mutual respect which evolved during the placement. It was very beneficial to take time to reflect on areas of practice and experiences that had been particularly useful and important to me and helpful for future practice. I gained a sense of validation with regard to formal learning, working knowledge, and experiences, which in turn empowered me to realise good-enough qualities did exist and were strengths on which I could build.

My initial response to John's question about spare time was to welcome what I hoped would be an opportunity to spend time with my family, but I soon realised that I wanted to be more than a taxi driver for my teenage children. My thoughts quickly returned to further developing my working practice, and for the first time throughout formal learning, a feeling of excitement emerged. I realised I had reached a point where I felt a sense of control and confidence in what my next step might look like and how I would be able to cope with and manage this next stage.

When John invited feedback from my college tutor during our final meeting, I become enveloped in an embarrassment that was mixed with self-pride and a sense of achievement. I realised how uncomfortable clients can be when hearing positive feedback about themselves. When John asked me to explain the evidence I had recorded on the competency cards, the ensuing discussion highlighted how much my practice and confidence had developed whilst on placement.

I did receive my certificate from university to confirm a successful pass and attended a graduation ceremony along with fellow students to celebrate the end of our course. However, the certificate I received from John holds a uniqueness of its own. I have on many occasions turned to this to remind myself of qualities I hoped for as a social worker. During demanding times I recall my reasons for wanting to be a social worker in the first place. Through the creation of the certificate I also realised the importance of key people in my personal and professional life and know that whenever I enter any professional arena, I take at least twelve people who know of my talents and twelve who inspire me. If I need to debrief, I know whom to ring and always have support readily at hand. Endings for me symbolise the beginning of a whole new process in terms of my future life experiences, education, training, and self-development as Yvonne the social worker.

CONCLUSIONS

John: Shappee (2001) reported that supervisees supervised by solution-focused supervisors appreciated working in collaboration with the supervisor, grew in confidence, learnt to self-supervise, and found the emphasis on their abilities to be much more useful than prior experiences of supervision that had been focused on their weaknesses. Our experience confirms the same benefits.

Yvonne: Two years ago I would have found it impossible to imagine myself on placement in such a setting. Through solution-focused supervision, I not only found the ability to practice effectively, I also unexpectedly gained the ability to self-supervise after the placement had finished. As a qualified worker I am now able to ask myself my own solution-focused questions, which inspire my thinking, enhance my creativity, and, most importantly, help me to identify achievable goals and actions I can take, one small but confident step at a time. Practice as a qualified worker is challenging, but with the benefits of solution-focused supervision, I am able to turn my "impossibles" into possibles and foresee a future in which my practice will continue to grow and develop way beyond the time I spent on placement with John.

REFERENCES

CCETSW (1996). *Assuring quality in the diploma in social work.* London: HMSO.

Fredman, G., & Dalal, C. (1998). Ending discourses: Implications for relationships and action in therapy. *Human Systems: The Journal of Systemic Consultation and Management, 9,* 1-13.

Honey, P., & Mumford, A. (1992). *The manual of learning styles.* Maidenhead: Peter Honey.

Kolb, D. A. (1976). *Learning style inventory: Technical manual.* Boston, MA: McBer and Company.

Kolb, D. A. (1984). *Experiential learning: Experience as the source of learning and development.* New Jersey: Prentice Hall.

Miller, S. D., Duncan, B. L. & Hubble, M. A. (1997). *Escape from Babel.* New York: Norton.

Schon, D. A. (1991). *The reflective practitioner: How professionals think in action.* Aldershot: Avebury.

Shappee, K. (2001). *The Experience of solution-focused Supervision.* Presentation at the Annual Conference of the European Brief Therapy Association. Dublin.

Thomas, F. N. (2000). Mutual admiration: Fortifying your competency-based supervision experience. *RATKES: Journal of the Finnish Association for the Advancement of Solution and Resource Oriented Therapy and Methods, 2,* 30-39.

White, M. (1995). *Re-authoring lives: Interviews and essays.* Adelaide, Australia: Dulwich Centre Publications.

White, M. (1999). *Narrative practice.* London: Workshop.

Thoughts from a Solution-Focused Supervisor

Teri Pichot

SUMMARY. The author shares her experiences helping substance abuse counselors move from an expert, problem focus to a collaborative, respect-based way of working with what is often seen as a "difficult" population. *[Article copies available for a fee from The Haworth Document Delivery Service: 1-800-HAWORTH. E-mail address: <docdelivery@haworthpress. com> Website: <http://www.HaworthPress.com> © 2005 by The Haworth Press, Inc. All rights reserved.]*

KEYWORDS. Solution-focused therapy, solution-focused supervision, supervisee

Graduate school is oftentimes filled with professional challenges and accountability. Professors and Field Placement Advisors frequently insist upon a purpose for every intervention and every decision. Everything is questioned and examined. This is just accepted as part of the learning environment. Students are learning to become the "experts," from whom scared and troubled

---

Teri Pichot is affiliated with the Jefferson County Department of Health and Environment, Substance Abuse Counseling Program, Lakewood, CO.

Address correspondence to: Teri Pichot, 260 S. Kipling Street, Lakewood, CO 80226.

[Haworth co-indexing entry note]: "Thoughts from a Solution-Focused Supervisor." Pichot, Teri. Co-published simultaneously in *Journal of Family Psychotherapy* (The Haworth Press, Inc.) Vol. 16, No. 1/2, 2005, pp. 277-279; and: *Education and Training in Solution-Focused Brief Therapy* (ed: Thorana S. Nelson) The Haworth Press, Inc., 2005, pp. 277-279. Single or multiple copies of this article are available for a fee from The Haworth Document Delivery Service [1-800-HAWORTH, 9:00 a.m. - 5:00 p.m. (EST). E-mail address: docdelivery@haworthpress.com].

Available online at http://www.haworthpress.com/web/JFP
© 2005 by The Haworth Press, Inc. All rights reserved.
Digital Object Identifier: 10.1300/J085v16n01_51

clients will seek answers and guidance. As new graduates move out of the University setting and into the "real world," reality soon sets in. Therapists many times lack the ideal level of clinical supervision, and clinical decisions at times are made in isolation without the protection of regular consultation. I have heard new graduates express fear as they leave the protected world of graduate school. They are well aware of how much they don't know, and how much this lack of knowing what is best for others places them in a difficult predicament as clients look to them to be the "expert." However, as the years go by this becomes the norm; the new professionals forget the luxury of constant professional exploration, looking to others rather than to themselves to be the "expert," and the insistence of purposefulness in every decision. Their awareness of how much they don't know seems to fade with time. They become the "experts."

My first experience as a clinical supervisor in a substance abuse agency was with a group of experienced therapists who thoroughly believed they were the "experts." They made clinical decisions and counseled clients from a personal as well as a professional stance. They often shared their own personal experience in an effort to create a therapeutic alliance with the clients, thereby enticing the clients to follow in their own footsteps. In addition, each team member believed in different theoretical constructs and frequently told me that they were "following my gut" when I asked for the purpose behind their interventions. There was a lack of professional unity on the team, aside from the belief that they were "experts" in the field of addiction. They were not significantly different from other clinical teams I had encountered.

As a solution-focused therapist, and now a supervisor, I was perplexed. How could I take this group of therapists and assist them in truly hearing their clients while respecting the uniqueness of each therapist? These therapists were not customers to changing their philosophy or approach. In fact, they were rather apprehensive of having a new supervisor at all. I decided that I would do what I knew best: question and listen.

One of my most memorable experiences during this time was while I was reviewing a videotape of a therapy group with one of the therapists. I watched as she presented the classic lecture of the dysfunctional family roles. She did an excellent job explaining each role, how these roles present themselves in the family system, and the ongoing damage they do to the client as well as to the system as a whole. It was textbook. As the lecture portion of the group concluded, I continued to watch the group unfold on the videotape. I then saw an African-American client calmly, yet firmly cross his arms across his chest in a defensive posture and state, "That's not my damn family!" The tape ended. I turned to my newly acquired supervisee and asked, "Wow! How did you handle that?" She shifted her weight uncomfortably in the chair, looked downward and said, "He's in denial. I still have some work to do with him." She then refocused on the lecture portion of the videotape, asking what I thought of her work. After complimenting her work giving the lecture and noting the accuracy with which she presented the content, I gently returned to the client's question. "So what would that client tell me his family is like?" She had no idea. After half an hour of exploring the group from the clients' perspective, she left the supervision session thinking. She had become curious. She had always viewed herself as the expert, the one who imparts knowledge to clients. I had challenged this thinking, inviting her to instead glean knowledge from her clients. A crack in her expert-based stance was made that day.

Solution-focused supervisors have dual roles. On one hand, they must make administrative decisions and enforce the direction of the agency. On the other hand, they model the curiosity and teachability of the solution-focused approach. Solution-focused therapists traditionally do not have a stake in the outcome of their clients' decisions, thereby making it much easier to remain objective. However, this is not true in solution-focused supervision. The supervisor is liable for the supervisee's decisions, and must balance this responsibility within the approach. In addition, the supervisor oftentimes serves as the teacher for this approach since it is infrequently taught in formal educational settings. This requires that the supervisor have the ability not only to model the approach, but to gently point out when the approach is being used inconsistently with its basic tenets.

When solution-focused supervision is effectively integrated within all aspects of an agency, it oftentimes creates a learning environment that was only previously thought to exist in a formal teaching setting. Learning becomes the goal: learning from the clients, from each other, and from the supervisor. (Even the supervisor is learning from the clients and the team.) Everything is explored and clinical decisions have the heightened expectation of purposefulness. Mistakes are viewed as opportunities for learning. Consultation is highly valued, and "not knowing" and the resulting curiosity and energy for exploration are seen as signs of success. The value system shifts.

As the years have passed and I have now been with this team of therapists for over seven years, I am struck by the emotionally energizing nature of using this approach as a supervisor. It reminds me of how much I don't know, thereby leaving me with a sense of wonderment, curiosity, and appreciation of change. This resulting energy is often seen as unusual for someone in my position. In an attempt to explain this energy and resultant innovation, my own supervisor recently wrote on my performance evaluation that I am "easily bored." What she doesn't know is that boredom for me would be a sign that I had become complacent. It would lead to my forgetting how much I don't know, thereby putting me at the greatest risk of all for a supervisor or therapist: being an "expert."

Index

Page numbers in *italic* designate figures; page numbers followed by the letter "t" designate tables.

BOOK ORDER FORM!

Order a copy of this book with this form or online at:
http://www.HaworthPress.com/store/product.asp?sku=5610

Education and Training
in Solution-Focused Brief Therapy

____ in softbound at $24.95 ISBN-13: 978-0-7890-2928-7 / ISBN-10: 0-7890-2928-6.
____ in hardbound at $39.95 ISBN-13: 978-0-7890-2927-0 / ISBN-10: 0-7890-2927-8.

COST OF BOOKS _____

POSTAGE & HANDLING _____
US: $4.00 for first book & $1.50
for each additional book
Outside US: $5.00 for first book
& $2.00 for each additional book.

SUBTOTAL _____

In Canada: add 7% GST. _____

STATE TAX _____
CA, IL, IN, MN, NJ, NY, OH, PA & SD residents
please add appropriate local sales tax.

FINAL TOTAL _____
If paying in Canadian funds, convert
using the current exchange rate,
UNESCO coupons welcome.

❑ **BILL ME LATER:**
Bill-me option is good on US/Canada/
Mexico orders only; not good to jobbers,
wholesalers, or subscription agencies.

❑ **Signature** _____

❑ **Payment Enclosed: $** _____

❑ **PLEASE CHARGE TO MY CREDIT CARD:**
❑ Visa ❑ MasterCard ❑ AmEx ❑ Discover
❑ Diner's Club ❑ Eurocard ❑ JCB

Account # _____

Exp Date _____

Signature _____
(Prices in US dollars and subject to change without notice.)

PLEASE PRINT ALL INFORMATION OR ATTACH YOUR BUSINESS CARD

Name		
Address		
City	State/Province	Zip/Postal Code
Country		
Tel	Fax	
E-Mail		

May we use your e-mail address for confirmations and other types of information? ❑ Yes ❑ No We appreciate receiving
your e-mail address. Haworth would like to e-mail special discount offers to you, as a preferred customer.
We will never share, rent, or exchange your e-mail address. We regard such actions as an invasion of your privacy.

Order from your **local bookstore** or directly from
The Haworth Press, Inc. 10 Alice Street, Binghamton, New York 13904-1580 • USA
Call our toll-free number (1-800-429-6784) / Outside US/Canada: (607) 722-5857
Fax: 1-800-895-0582 / Outside US/Canada: (607) 771-0012
E-mail your order to us: orders@HaworthPress.com

For orders outside US and Canada, you may wish to order through your local
sales representative, distributor, or bookseller.
For information, see http://HaworthPress.com/distributors

(Discounts are available for individual orders in US and Canada only, not booksellers/distributors.)

Please photocopy this form for your personal use.
www.HaworthPress.com

The Haworth Press Inc.

BOF05